Primo Levi

NEW DIRECTIONS IN EUROPEAN WRITING

....

Editor: John Flower, Professor of French, University of Exeter.

As the twentieth century draws to a close we are witnessing profound and significant changes across the new Europe. The past is being reassessed; the millennium is awaited with interest. Some, pessimistically, have predicted the death of literature; others see important developments within national literature and in movements cutting across frontiers. This enterprising series focuses on these developments through the study either of individual writers or of groups or movements. There are no definitive statements. By definition they are introductory and set out to assess and explore the full spectrum of modern European writing on the threshold of a new age.

ISBN 1350-9217

Previously published titles in the Series:

Allyson Fiddler
Rewriting Reality: An Introduction to Elfriede Jelinek

C. Davies
Contemporary Feminist Fiction in Spain: The Work of Montserrat Roig and Rosa Montero

Chris Perriam
Desire and Dissent: An Introduction to Luis Antonio de Villena

NEW DIRECTIONS IN EUROPEAN WRITING

Primo Levi

Bridges of Knowledge

Mirna Cicioni

BERG
Oxford • Washington, D.C.

First published in 1995 by
Berg Publishers Limited
Editorial offices:
150 Cowley Road, Oxford, OX4 1JJ, UK
13590 Park Center Road, Herndon, VA 22071, USA

Library of Congress Cataloguing-in-Publication Data

A catalogue record for this book is available from the Library of
Congress.

British Library Cataloguing-in-Publication Data

A catalogue record for this book is available from the British Library.

ISBN 1 85973 058 2 (Cloth)
       1 85973 063 9 (Paper)

Printed in the United Kingdom by WBC Bookbinders, Bridgend,
Mid Glamorgan.

To my son Daniel,
with friendship and hope.

Contents

Acknowledgements

I would like to thank La Trobe University for awarding me a Central Starter Research Grant, which helped me research this book while I was on an Outside Studies Programme in 1993.

This book would never have been written without the help of many people in Turin. First and foremost, Alberto Cavaglion and Paola Valabrega shared their time, memories and photocopies with me, allowed me to read their work, and gave me invaluable insights into the culture of Turinese Jews. Annapia di Aichelburg, of the press office of the Einaudi publishing house, granted me access to the huge collection of press cuttings on Levi and gave me permission to print his photograph. Some valuable material was provided by Paolo Momigliano, the Director of the Istituto Storico della Resistenza in Valle d'Aosta, Cesare Manganelli of the Istituto per la Storia della Resistenza e della Società Contemporanea in Alessandria, and Luigi Spriano, the councillor in charge of Cultural Affairs in San Salvatore Monferrato. Giuseppe Grassano and Daniele Jalla discussed their work on Levi with me and gave me many literary and historical leads. Paola Accati (the general manager of SICME-SIVA-SCET), Francesco Ciafaloni, Guido Davico Bonino, Bianca Guidetti Serra, Felice Malgaroli, Ferruccio Maruffi, Lorenzo Mondo, Silvio Ortona and Renato Portesi were willing to talk to me about their friendship with Levi and their memories of different aspects of his life. Fiorella Levi, with her sister Daniela, her mother Carmela and her family, offered constant friendship and kept sending me precious material. The Portesi and Visintin families provided encouragement and support.

I am also indebted to my colleagues and friends in Melbourne, too many to mention here. Special thanks are due to Steve Wright for important perspectives on the Italian left-wing movements in the 1970s, Tom Behan and Martin Lloyd for their comments on parts of the first draft, and Marisa Stirpe and Consuelo Di Leo for their help with the production of the manuscript. John Gatt-Rutter and Verina Jones provided extremely helpful comments on the whole of the first draft. Morgen Witzel gave generous assistance and advice in editing the book. Valerie Burley of the La Trobe University Assistance with English Unit solved hundreds of lexical doubts and scores of syntactic ones, cajoled and bullied me into transforming my complex Italianate sentences into concise English sentences and paragraphs, and contributed invaluable feedback, different perspectives, insights, understanding and humour.

Finally, I would like to thank my parents, who helped in their own special way.

Preface

> I always thought that [building] bridges is the best job there is ... because roads go over bridges, and without roads we'd still be like savages. In short, bridges are like the opposite of borders, and borders are where wars start.
>
> Primo Levi, *La chiave a stella (The Wrench)*

On the evening of 12 March 1992, almost five years after Primo Levi's death, one thousand people participated in a torch-lit march in Rome. They were marching against the resurgence of racism and anti-Semitism, specifically as a response to a demonstration by young neo-Nazi skinheads who called themselves *naziskins*. On their banners was the number 174517: the number which was tattooed on Levi's arm in Auschwitz in 1944 and which is engraved on his tombstone immediately after his name.[1]

On 25 April 1994, two hundred thousand Italians assembled in Milan. They wanted to celebrate the forty-ninth anniversary of the liberation of Italy from Fascism and Nazism and to reaffirm the values of anti-Fascism to a newly-elected right-wing coalition government which, for the first time since the Second World War, included members of a neo-Fascist party. One of their banners read '174517: lest we forget'.[2]

These episodes have a dual significance. On the one hand they reveal that Levi's writings on the Holocaust[3] have become symbols of the struggle of reason against anti-Semitic and racist ideologies, now and in the future. On the other hand they are indicative of the central problem in any critical evaluation of Levi's work: both inside and outside Italy, it has been read predominantly in terms of Holocaust testimony. Despite the fact that he is probably the contemporary Italian writer who has received the most literary awards[4] and has been most widely translated,[5] serious critical responses to his work as a whole have developed only after his death in 1987.

It is true that, as Levi himself admitted repeatedly,[6] without his experience of deportation he probably would not have become a writer, and that this experience is central to both his life and work. His writings on the Nazi death camps are internationally recognised as among the most powerful and profound testimonies to have come out of the extermination of European Jewry. They have also inspired other artists such as the musician Sergio Liberovici, who composed the concerto *Ivrit* in Levi's memory,[7] and the painters David Rankin[8] and Larry Rivers.[9] However, the primary feature of the entire body of Levi's work is the emphasis on conscious participation in history, based on different kinds of knowledge: historical, cultural, scientific, and technical. In this 'interaction with diverse and divergent contexts and value systems' (Cannon 1992: 42), what characterises Levi's writing is his constant passionate attempt to understand, clarify and explain in order to build bridges between different cultures: Jewish and Gentile, scientific and literary, technical and intellectual, Piedmontese and international.

> Anyone who is on the margins of a group, or in fact is isolated ... can leave whenever he wants to and can get a better view of the landscape. My own fate, helped by my choices, has kept me at a distance from groups. I have been too much of a chemist, and a chemist for too long, to consider myself a genuine man of letters; yet I have been too distracted by the landscapes around me, varied, tragic or strange as they were, to feel a chemist in every fibre. ... I often set foot on the bridges which link (or should link) scientific culture with literary culture, stepping over a crevasse which has always struck me as absurd. (Preface to *L'altrui mestiere* (*Other People's Trades*): III, 585–6.)

Internationally, Levi's writings have become central texts not only for anyone reflecting on the Holocaust, but also for anyone interested in secular European Jewish culture and literary representations of the intellectual and moral lessons of science and of the ethics of work. His morality is 'an old-fashioned compound of reason, tolerance, trust in language, trust in silence, containment of anger, liberalism, cool Sephardi Jewishness, scepticism, good humour, wit and natural philosophy' (Rudolf 1990: 4).

This book aims to provide a general introduction to Primo Levi for English-speaking readers. I have attempted to situate Levi in some of the contexts of Italian culture and society from the 1920s to the 1980s: the integration of middle-class Italian Jews before the anti-Semitic laws of 1938, the beginnings of the anti-Fascist

Resistance, cultural life during the 'economic miracle' of the 1960s and the political conflicts of the 1970s, discussions of 'Jewish identity' in Italy in the 1980s, especially in the light of the controversial policies of Israeli governments, and the recent arguments about European 'historical revisionism'. Biographical details on Levi's life are, however, sketchy because of the understandable reticence of his family, who will not release his correspondence or be contacted by researchers.

I have also endeavoured to explore some of the tensions in Levi's works.[10] He fully shares the notion, central in Jewish culture, of the importance of memory and communication, yet all his writings on the Holocaust are pervaded by the consciousness that any memory of it is entrusted to those who, like himself, did not fathom its full depths. He repeatedly states that what happened cannot be fully comprehended; yet he asks questions relentlessly and rejects facile judgements, in the hope that even a partial understanding might help future generations prevent a recurrence.

Levi's reflections on 'Jewish identity' show a tension between 'integration' and 'difference'. As a middle-class Jew almost completely assimilated into Italian society, in 1938 he was forced to rethink the notion of 'integration' by the shock of the anti-Semitic laws. His contacts with representatives of diverse Jewish cultures, in Auschwitz and later, also caused him to wonder whether it is possible to postulate one 'Jewish identity', and to come to the conclusion that the 'centre of gravity' of world Jewry is to be found in the Diaspora communities.

Levi's representations of science oscillate between a view consistent with positivist philosophy and reflections on the problems posed by its social context. He saw science as an individual testing-ground and a source of progress, yet he was conscious that it can never be divorced from politics and economics, and that the world – and science itself – are becoming increasingly more complex and less comprehensible.

Although most of Levi's works have been translated into English, the passages I quote are my own translations from the original Italian. The page numbers refer to the three-volume collected works in Italian (*Opere*) published by Einaudi, which includes all of Levi's original writings.

Notes to Preface

1. See the report in *La Repubblica* of 13 March 1992, p. 1 of the Rome supplement.
2. See the report in *Il manifesto* of 26 April 1994, p. 5 of the supplement on the demonstration.
3. The word 'Holocaust', created towards the end of the 1950s (Traverso 1991: 88), is problematic. Many Italian intellectuals reject it because it associates genocide with ancient religious rituals and implies that the extermination of Jews has some, however hidden, religious meaning (see Bravo and Jalla 1986: 27; Meghnagi 1987: 19; Traverso 1991: 88–9). It is used in this work because it is the most widely used and understood term in English, and has been used in many works in English by Jewish scholars such as Langer (1975), Ezrahi (1980), Rosenfeld (1980) and Hartman (1994).
   Primo Levi found it 'philologically wrong' (see his 1986 radio interview with M. Spadi, reprinted in *L'Unità*, 7 November 1992, p. 2) and used instead 'Auschwitz' or the German word *Lager* (concentration camp), which has become part of the Italian vocabulary.
4. He received the Strega Prize – the most prestigious of Italian literary awards – in 1979 for *La chiave a stella* (*The Wrench*). He won the Campiello Prize twice, for *La tregua* (*The Truce*) in 1963, and for *Se non ora, quando?* (*If Not Now, When?*) in 1982. *Se non ora, quando?* was also awarded the Viareggio Prize in 1982. Levi also won the Bagutta Prize in 1967, for *Storie naturali*, and the Prato Prize in 1975, for *Il sistema periodico* (*The Periodic Table*). In November 1987, seven months after his death, the Accademia Nazionale dei Lincei awarded him the Antonio Feltrinelli Prize, which some have called 'the Italian Nobel Prize'.
5. Levi's books have been translated into seventeen languages in eighteen countries.
6. See, as an example, the afterword to *Se questo è un uomo* (*If This Is a Man*): 'If I had not lived my season in Auschwitz, I probably would never have written anything ... It was the experience of the camp that compelled me to write.' (I: 211)
7. See Benedetto (1987).
8. Rankin, an Australian, was inspired by Levi's last book, *I sommersi e i salvati* (*The Drowned and the Saved*), in 1988 (see

Carbines 1988).

9. Rivers, an American who had never met Levi, painted three large pictures of him which were donated to *La Stampa* by Giovanni Agnelli in 1989. See the report in *La Stampa* of 13 April 1989, p. 8.

10. For a comprehensive, lucid overview of these tensions see Cases (1987). See also Rosato's review of the first volume of Levi's collected works.

1

The First Elements

*A*t the time of Primo Levi's birth (31 July 1919) most Italians, Jews and Gentiles alike, would have agreed that in their country there was neither a 'Jewish problem' nor significant explicit anti-Semitism.

Piedmont, the region of Levi's birth, had – like the rest of Northern Italy – several small Jewish communities. Most of their members were of Southern French origin, and had come to Piedmont following a wave of successive expulsions from France in the fourteenth century. Others had come from Spain and Portugal around the turn of the sixteenth century, after they had been forced to choose between death, exile and conversion to Catholicism by the law of 31 March 1492, proclaimed by the Catholic sovereigns Ferdinand and Isabella. The Jews introduced silk technology to Piedmont and for the most part lived uneventfully, although they were confined within their ghettoes, subject to limitations on their activities and forced to endure sporadic manifestations of anti-Semitism.[1]

The community in Turin, the capital of Piedmont and Levi's birthplace, included a ghetto which had been established in 1679 but remained relatively small until after 1848. In that year Charles Albert, King of Piedmont and Sardinia, became the first among the rulers of the many states into which Italy was then divided to proclaim the emancipation of the Jews, repealing all restrictions on their choice of residence or employment. This emancipation, combined with the industrialisation of Piedmont in the last three decades of the nineteenth century, led to a swift process of urbanisation: by the 1920s, 4,000 of the 5,000 Piedmontese Jews were living in Turin, forming one of the largest of Italy's twenty-six Jewish communities (Stille 1991a: 24).

Italian Jews achieved emancipation in 1859–60 as the various other states joined the Kingdom of Piedmont and were unified into the Kingdom of Italy; in 1870, Rome's ghetto was opened after the Pope withdrew into the Vatican City and Rome was proclaimed the national capital. The logical consequence was the development of a sense of profound loyalty on the part of Jews to the newly-unified Italian nation and a desire to become fully integrated into its political, cultural and economic life (see Hughes 1983: 11–20; Allegra 1984: 34–6). Integration was facilitated by the high degree of Jewish literacy: less than 10 per cent of the Jewish population in the immediate post-unification period was illiterate, at a time when national illiteracy was close to 80 per cent. Therefore, although they were a very small proportion of the Italian population (approximately 1 in 1,000 at the turn of the century), Jews held prominent positions in politics,[2] the armed forces,[3] law, business and, above all, cultural life[4] (see Zuccotti 1987: 15–18; Di Castro 1992; Milano 1992: 382–91).

Integration, in Italy as in other Western European countries, also involved attendance at state schools, which exposed young Jews to a diversity of cultural stimuli, and active participation in local social and civic life. This, along with a widespread interest in abstract and experimental sciences, led to a swift secularisation of Jewish culture and a progressive relinquishing of strict religious observance: knowledge of Hebrew, and consequently knowledge of the Torah and the Talmud, declined rapidly in the years following emancipation.[5] The specificity of the integration of each Jewish community is demonstrated by their linguistic usage. Italian Jews did not have a Jewish language such as Yiddish, which was used in many countries of Eastern Europe, but communicated instead in standard Italian when writing and in the regional and local dialects, to which they added a number of phonologically and morphologically integrated Hebrew expressions, when speaking.

Integration, however, did not mean total assimilation. Religious traditions were maintained through the celebration of the main high holidays (the Jewish New Year, the Day of Atonement, Passover) and through the ceremonies connected with the rites of passage (circumcisions, *bar mitzvahs*, marriages and funerals). Until the First World War, Jews also tended to marry other Jews, often from their own region. The best summary of Italian Jewish identity at the time of the rise of Fascism can be found in an often-quoted statement made in 1924 at a Zionist conference in Leghorn by Nello Rosselli, who was to become one of the leading Italian anti-Fascists and was later murdered, on Mussolini's orders, by French Fascist assassins in 1937:

> I am a Jew who does not go to the synagogue on Saturdays, who does not know Hebrew, who does not observe any religious practice. Yet ... I call myself a Jew and value my Jewishness because ... the monotheistic conscience is indestructible in me ... because I have a very real awareness of my own personal responsibility ... because I regard with Jewish firmness the duties of our lives on earth, and with Jewish serenity the mystery of what lies beyond the grave – because I love all men as in Israel it was commanded ... and I have therefore that view of society which, it seems to me, descends from our best tradition.[6]

The Turin community reflected Rosselli's synthesis in that it was secular rather than observant, interested in the sciences rather than the humanities, influenced by positivism, and mainly middle-class, well integrated into the city's industrial and business life (see Cavaglion 1989b: 551–5 and Cavaglion 1991). As Primo Levi himself summed it up in 1984, when – as the most famous Turinese Jew – he was asked to write the preface to a collection of essays entitled *Ebrei a Torino (Jews in Turin)*, 'the integration of Italian Jews is a peculiar phenomenon ... however, a possibly even more peculiar phenomenon is the equilibrium of the Turin and Piedmontese Jews, who easily integrated without giving up their identity' (Levi 1984c: 13).

The attitudes of Italian Jews towards politics reflected the general attitudes of the Italian people as a whole. Before the rise of Fascism, Jews were members of or sympathised with all political parties, although the majority of politically active Jews tended to support the left (two, Giuseppe Emanuele Modigliani and Claudio Treves, were prominent Socialist deputies). However, at least five Jews were among the 119 Italians who founded the *Fasci di combattimento*, Mussolini's first national organisation. Some Jewish industrialists, like their Gentile counterparts, backed and financed the Fascist movement between 1920 and 1922; over 200 Jews took part in the March on Rome, and a number of Jews held important positions in the Fascist governments of the 1920s and 1930s (see De Felice 1977: 88–93 and Zuccotti 1987: 23–7).

Levi's own background fully exemplifies the integration of his people. An ancestor, after whom he was named, had been one of Garibaldi's followers in 1860 and subsequently edited a periodical entitled *La Riforma*. Through complex kinship ties, Levi's family was connected with the communities of many Piedmontese towns and villages. The story 'Argon', which opens Levi's masterpiece *Il sistema periodico* (*the Periodic Table*), is a succession of homely portraits of members of this extended kinship network:[7] 'wise, tobacco-smelling patriarchs and women who ruled their households, who would yet define themselves, in Piedmontese dialect, as "the People of Israel"' (I: 431). They are, with gentle irony, compared to the gases known as 'noble, inert, and rare':

> Not all of them were materially inert, for that was not granted to them. On the contrary they were, or had to be, quite active; but inert they undoubtedly were in their innermost selves, inclined to disinterested speculation, witty conversation, elegant, subtle, and gratuitous discussion. It can hardly be by chance that the events attributed to them, varied as they were, share a static quality, an attitude of dignified abstention, of deliberate (or accepted) relegation to the margins of the great river of life (I: 430).

The text firmly situates their Jewish identity in family events and traditions rather than history or religion. It outlines their gradual merging, both individual and collective, into Piedmontese society through anecdotes about their family life, business deals and relationships with Gentiles. At the centre of each anecdote is a dialect phrase containing a borrowing from Hebrew. The biblical context, adaptation and/or semantic pejoration of the Hebrew word are described: language becomes the symbol of integration.

> Uncle Gabriele was a rabbi.... Old and nearly blind, he was returning from Verzuolo to Saluzzo on foot, under a blazing sun. He saw a carriage coming, stopped it and asked for a lift. A bit later, while speaking with the driver, he gradually realised that this was a hearse, carrying the corpse of a Christian woman to the cemetery: an abominable thing, since, as it is written in Ezekiel 44: 25, a rabbi who touches a dead person ... is contaminated and impure for seven days. He jumped up and shouted (in dialect): 'I have been travelling with a *pegartà*, a dead woman! Driver, stop!' (I: 433).

In Levi's discourse, the language of his ancestors has two other important roles. One is its 'dissembling, secret function, that of an underground jargon'. The other is that it bridges their experience of the sacred and the profane:

> wonderful comic strength, which springs from the contrast between the texture of their speech, namely the rugged, sober, and laconic Piedmontese dialect . . . and the Hebrew interpolations, snatched from the language of the fathers, sacred and solemn . . . .. But this contrast reflects another, the essential one of Diaspora Jews, scattered among the Gentiles . . . trapped in tension between their divine calling and the daily misery of exile (I: 434–5).

Levi quotes many instances of biblical words being used incongruously. *Kiním*, lice, the third of the ten plagues of Egypt, was used in the Turin rag trade to mean 'polka dots', as in *'na vesta a kiním*, a polka-dot dress. *Fé sefòkh*, to throw up, came from the Hebrew root *shafòkh*, to spread, as used in Psalm 79. *Tiré un ruàkh*, to break wind, came from the Hebrew *ruàkh*, breath, as used in Genesis 1:2, and Levi adds that in this example 'it is possible to identify the biblical intimacy of the Chosen People with its Maker' (I: 436–8).

The chapter ends with sketches of Levi's paternal grandmother, his father and Levi himself as a child, represented as shy and bookish ('top of the class', as his father informed his grandmother). His maternal grandfather was a cloth merchant, whose shop – which Levi described engagingly in the 1984 essay 'Il fondaco del nonno' (Grandfather's Store)[8] – was in Turin's central street, Via Roma. His paternal grandfather, an engineering graduate, country landowner and failed banker, had lived in a country town and taken his own life. Both Levi's parents also had degrees in engineering, but only his father, Cesare, practised his profession.

Levi's reminiscences of his father are scattered through his work. The cumulative image that emerges is that of a much-travelled, worldly man whose faith in the printed word had replaced religious faith. In *La ricerca delle radici (A Search for Roots)*, Levi says that his father 'used to read books "when he was at home, when he walked by the way, when he went to bed and when he rose" (*Deuteronomy* 6:7)' (p.viii); the quotation directly refers to, and recontextualises in a secular statement of belief, the orders to love and praise God contained in *Shema Israel*, the most common of Jewish prayers. Cesare Levi both belonged to the Turin positivist circles and attended seances, 'not because he believed in spirits, but to understand what was really going on' (Levi and Regge 1984: 17), and he encouraged his young son's scientific interests by buying him a microscope, a projector and books popularising current scientific theories.[9] Levi's mother, Ester Luzzati, was almost twenty years younger than her husband and is only a fleeting presence in her son's writings. Since, according to those who knew him well, Levi was extremely close to her, it can only be left to speculation whether this reticence is due to innate reserve or to the fact that the models available in his formative years were based on public male achievements more than the private sphere of feelings and emotions.

Levi's childhood and adolescence were uneventful. In comparison with the early recollections of other Italian Jewish writers (such as Vittorio Segre, Gaia Servadio or Natalia Ginzburg), he says very little about the relationships or conflicts within his family and focuses almost exclusively on his own autobiographical persona. This construct, developed in the first three stories in *Il sistema periodico* and other stories written later,[10] is of a 'self' whose main characteristics remain basically unaltered in Levi's representation of himself as an adult. It is that of an introverted adolescent, short and slightly built, more enterprising and assertive when observing nature than when relating to other young people. In a description of his time at school – the prestigious *liceo classico* [11] D'Azeglio – he says: 'I was accepted because I was good at Latin and allowed others to copy during class tests, envied because I owned a microscope, but suspected of being a dissident because, in spite of my efforts, my vocabulary was not sufficiently coarse' ('Un lungo duello' (A Long Duel), III: 802). Another recurring trait of Levi's young narrated self is his yearning for girls who are not his intellectual equals, do not reciprocate his longing, and with whom he feels self-conscious and tongue-tied: 'I believed myself doomed to an everlasting male loneliness, forever denied a woman's smile, which I nevertheless needed as much as air' ('Zinco' (Zinc), I: 439).

The social definition of Levi's youthful persona is predominantly in terms of its intellectual aspirations, limitations and choices. In 'Idrogeno' (Hydrogen), the second story in *Il sistema periodico*, Levi represents his decision at the age of sixteen to become a chemist through a biblical reference, implicitly rejecting its religious components while affirming its cultural significance:

> For me chemistry represented an indefinite cloud of future powers, which enveloped my own future in black swirls torn by fiery flashes, like the cloud which had hidden Mount Sinai. Like Moses, I expected that from that cloud would come my law, order within me, around me, and in the world (I: 448).

That all order, law and certainty were expected to come from science is particularly significant considering that the year of this commitment was 1935, the time when the Fascist regime achieved its greatest mass consensus and anti-Fascist activities in Italy were at their lowest point. This was particularly noticeable in Turin: a few months earlier, in November 1934, some Turin members of *Giustizia e Libertà*[12] had been arrested after two of them, Sion Segre and Mario Levi,[13] were stopped as they were crossing the Swiss-Italian border carrying anti-Fascist leaflets. Many of those arrested were Jews, a fact which was contemptuously pointed out by the Fascist papers. Nearly two hundred more Turin anti-Fascists, including most of the leaders of *Giustizia e Libertà*, were arrested in May 1935 and sentenced to long jail terms in 1936. By then most opponents of the regime were in jail, interned, or in exile.

By the mid-1930s, Italian culture had been to a large extent appropriated by the Fascist regime. Schools, especially after the dismissal or arrest of openly anti-Fascist teachers, were directly controlled by the Fascist School Association. In Turin, one of the teachers in Levi's own school, Augusto Monti, who had been a supporter of *Giustizia e Libertà* and until 1935 had exerted an indirect but powerful influence on all students, had been arrested. University lecturers were ordered in 1931 to swear an oath of loyalty to the regime; of approximately 1,200 only thirteen – four of whom were Jews – refused, and were required to retire. The few anti-Fascist periodicals which had been allowed to circulate had been closed down by 1935. The regime had a monopoly on radio and the cinema as well as the press.

The military conquest of Ethiopia (October 1935 – May 1936), preceded by a well-orchestrated media campaign, was enthusiastically backed by most of the population, which proudly acclaimed the proclamation of the Italian colonial empire in 1936. Even those Italians who were privately critical of the regime were forced to cooperate passively with it. Levi's own father, in spite of a deep distaste for its parades, had become a party member so as not to have problems with his business, and Levi had been a member of the *balilla* and the *avanguardisti*, the Fascist boys' and teenagers' organisations.[14] For the young men and women of Levi's generation the only alternative to identification with the dominant ideology was, therefore, a total rejection of politics in favour of other intellectual pursuits.

A third choice, that of individual distancing from Fascism, began to seem possible to Levi in 1937. In the Spanish Civil War, Italian volunteers – Fascist ones armed and trained by the government and fighting alongside Franco's troops, and anti-Fascist ones fighting with the International Brigades – faced one another. This foreshadowed future open confrontations between international fascism and international anti-Fascism. In June 1937, during his matriculation exams, Levi handed in a blank sheet instead of writing an essay on the Spanish Civil War, and consequently had to resit all subjects in September (see Toscani 1990: 22).[15] However, the following year, in order to avoid being drafted into the Italian Navy for two years, he chose the lesser evil of enrolling and participating in a cadet course conducted by the Fascist Militia. He enjoyed the physical exercise if not the politics, until he was expelled as a consequence of the anti-Semitic measures of November 1938 (Levi 1986d). Significantly he states in 'Zinco', which follows 'Idrogeno' in *Il sistema periodico* and is set in the early autumn of 1938, that his 'spiritual sustenance' in that period was Thomas Mann's *Magic Mountain*. What he found particularly relevant were the debates between the humanist Settembrini, who advocates personal commitment to science and democracy, and the Jesuit (ex-Jew) Naphta, who argues that all human efforts are pointless, and that humankind's only aim is absolute order, which coincides with death.

Until 1938, the Jewish identity of Levi's autobiographical persona had been – as he outlines in his preface to the 1965 edition of his second book, *La tregua (The Truce)* – 'a vague notion, not really a problem':

> it meant a quiet awareness of the very ancient history of my people,
> a sort of benevolent attitude of disbelief towards religion, a definite

tendency towards the world of books and abstract discussions. In everything else, I did not feel I was different from my Christian friends and fellow students, and I felt at ease in their company (1965: 5).

In 'Zinco' this evaluation is expanded in an ironic, self-deprecating tone: the identity of Levi's persona is presented as superficial, dismissive and – as shown by the negative relative clauses – defined merely as non-Gentile:

> until those very months being a Jew had not meant a great deal to me: within myself, and in my contacts with my Christian friends, I had always considered my background as an almost negligible, if peculiar fact: a small amusing anomaly, like having a crooked nose or freckles; a Jew is somebody who at Christmas does not have a tree, who should not eat salami but eats it anyway, who has learned a bit of Hebrew at thirteen and then has forgotten it (I: 460).

The evaluation, however, is belied by the context in which it is placed, the anti-Semitic campaign of 1938. In Levi's discourse, a first-year chemistry practical involving zinc, which when pure resists the attack of acids and when impure reacts with them, becomes at the same time a source of reflections and a metaphor for his changing sense of self:

> For the wheel to turn, for life to exist, impurities are necessary. . .. Dissension, diversity, the grain of salt and mustard, are necessary: Fascism does not want them, forbids them, and that's why you are not a Fascist; it wants everyone to be the same, and you are not. . . . I am the impurity which makes the zinc react, I am the grain of salt and mustard. Impurity, indeed: because in those very months *La Difesa della Razza* was beginning to appear, and a great deal was being said about purity, and I was beginning to be proud of being impure (I: 458–60).

La Difesa della Razza (Defence of Race), a fortnightly paper which first appeared in August 1938, was part of an anti-Semitic campaign initiated by the government at the time of the 1934 arrests and intensified from mid-1936 on, as part of the *rapprochement* between Mussolini's Italy and Hitler's Germany. The campaign was an obvious forerunner to the introduction of discriminatory laws to bring Italy into line with the anti-Semitic legislation passed in Germany after 1933. At the same time it had the subtler aim of strengthening the feeling of 'national unity' by directing the anxiety Italians felt about the future, especially after Hitler's annexation of Austria in March 1938, onto one recognisable 'other'.[16]

On 15 July 1938 the Italian papers published a 'Manifesto of Italian Racism', subdivided into ten chapters with such titles as 'The present population of Italy is of Aryan origin, and its civilization is Aryan', 'The time has come for Italians to openly declare that they are racists' and 'Jews do not belong to the Italian race'. On 29 July the Ministry of the Interior ordered the 26 Jewish Communities to hand in copies of their records and on 11 August a census of all Jews in Italy began, obviously to make it easier to implement the forthcoming anti-Semitic measures.[17]

These measures – better known as the 'racial laws' – began on 12 September, when Jews were forbidden to both study and teach in state and private schools. On 26 November textbooks written and edited by Jews were banned. On 17 November a comprehensive set of 'measures for the defence of the Italian race' became official. Mixed marriages were forbidden; Jews were expelled from the Fascist party and its organisations, barred from military service, not allowed to own or run businesses employing more than 100 people, and not allowed to own land worth more than 5,000 lire or houses worth more than 20,000 lire. They were excluded from all levels of public administration and from working as journalists and notaries public, and were forbidden to have 'Aryan' servants. Further measures, passed on 29 June 1939, ordered Jewish doctors, midwives, accountants and solicitors to practise their professions exclusively for Jewish clients. The only Jews to be exempted from discrimination were the families of Jews who had died or been decorated while fighting in World War I, Ethiopia or Spain, or of those Jews who had been early Fascists or who had 'acquired exceptional merit' to be defined on a case-by-case basis by a special committee of the Ministry of the Interior.

The laws were an instant catalyst for both Jews and Gentiles. The profound injustice of the discrimination led a number of hitherto non-political people, especially the young, to understand the real nature of Fascism and to move away from it. In the words of Bianca Guidetti Serra, a contemporary of Levi's and one of his closest long-time friends,

The discriminations they [the racial laws] brought about made me understand what Fascism was. From that time I knew I would always be against it. The bonds of friendship which I had already had with some young Jews and others who had anti-Fascist views became stronger and remained important through the years; Primo Levi was among those friends (Guidetti Serra 1991: 450).

For Jews, the shock of being declared 'other' and excluded from the full citizenship which had been theirs by right for over fifty years not only raised anxious questions about the future, but also led some of them to attempt to redefine themselves in terms of their difference rather than their integration. Some – Levi among them – began to develop an opposition to Fascism based on their identity as victims of oppression. This, however, was still an intellectual attitude which had yet to mature into political practice.

The period between 1938 and 1944 is, after that of his maturity as a chemist and a writer, the most detailed part of Levi's autobiographical construct. Here, in contrast to the representation of his adult self, he describes his feelings, his confusion about the present, his fears about the future, his political consciousness and his personal insecurities. In 'Ferro' (Iron), the fourth story in Il sistema periodico, set in 1939, Levi's positivist view of science – specifically chemistry – as order and truth is connected to his narrated self's growing opposition to Fascism. The reports set for his second-year course in qualitative analysis 'were, every time, a choice, a deliberation; a mature and responsible undertaking, for which Fascism had not prepared us' (I: 463); chemistry and physics 'were the antidote to Fascism ... because they were clear and well-defined and verifiable at every step, and not a tissue of lies and waffle, like the radio and newspapers' (I: 466–7).[18]

In this story – one of the most powerful of Il sistema periodico, and one of the best-known of Levi's writings – the iron of the title has multiple metaphorical meanings: philosophical, historical, and personal. As a chemical element, it is physical matter, which, in the narrated self's youthful positivist view of things, must be examined and understood because 'understanding matter is necessary in order to understand the universe and ourselves' (I: 466). It stands for the physical tempering of Levi's body and mind in mountain climbing expeditions, which lead him to test himself against nature, discovering his physical limits and attempting to transcend them. It also represents the hard times ahead for all Italians: 'an iron future, drawing closer month by month' (I: 469). Finally, it symbolises the physical and psychological strength of the other protagonist of the story, Levi's fellow student Sandro Delmastro, 'bound to iron by ancient kinship ties' through his blacksmith ancestors, empathically close to animals and mountains, laconically self-sufficient, willing to become close to a Jew at the time of the racial laws, prepared to accept the intellectual leadership of his middle-class friend but determined to introduce him, through challenging expeditions, to 'the taste of being strong and free, free also to make mistakes, and of being masters of our destiny' (I: 473). The story ends with brief details about Sandro's own destiny: one of the first members of the Piedmontese Resistance, he was arrested in 1944 and shot while trying to escape.

Levi graduated in July 1941. The early events of the Second World War, Italy's entry in June 1940 and the defeats of the Allies on all fronts, had filled him and his friends with despair. 'Our resistance at the time was passive', he says in 'Potassio' (Potassium), the story which follows 'Ferro': 'it was limited to rejecting Fascism, isolating ourselves from it, not letting ourselves be contaminated' (I: 475). With other young Jews, Levi sought answers in the Bible. The religious aspect of Jewish culture, however, is explicitly rejected even as it is mentioned: 'But where was Kadosh Barukhú, "the Holy One, Blessed be He", he who breaks the slaves' chains and submerges the chariots of the Egyptians? . . . the sky above us was silent and empty . . . we were alone, we had no allies we could rely on, neither on earth nor in heaven' (I: 475–6).

For Levi's narrated self, answers and certainties could still be sought in science. Physics, with its demonstrable theorems, seemed to him more reliable than chemistry, and a lecturer in physics[19] was the only one who agreed, in spite of the racial laws, to supervise his honours thesis. The thesis, which consisted of a shorter section on chemistry and a longer experimental section on physics, resulted in a final mark of 110/ 110 *cum laude*, the highest possible honour, for which the unanimous consensus of the examining board was needed. The fact that this recognition was given to a student 'of the Jewish race', as the degree certificate specified, is indicative both of the quality of Levi's research and of the wish of many university lecturers to express some dissent, however limited and timid, from the racial laws.

For six months, between the end of 1941 and the summer of 1942, he worked, with no papers and no prospects, in an asbestos quarry in the hills northwest of Turin. His job was to attempt to extract nickel from the rocks of the quarry. He enthusiastically set himself to formulating hypotheses and experimenting with methods, once again positivistically testing himself against the complexity of nature, until the hopelessness of his efforts became clear to him and his employers.[20] He then moved to Milan to work for Wander, a Swiss drug company, carrying out experiments with phosphorus in an ill-advised attempt to discover a drug against diabetes.[21] His prevailing feeling was intense personal loneliness: he felt an unrequited attraction towards a Gentile colleague, and believed that '[his] inability to approach a woman was a sentence without appeal, that would accompany [him] to [his] death, restricting [him] to a barren, pointless life poisoned by jealousies and abstract desires.' (I: 544). He was, however, part of a group of seven young, mostly Jewish friends from Turin who were alienated and made 'superficial, passive and cynical' (I: 547) by their condition as outcasts and by what Levi calls the *'danse macabre'* of the war.[22] They knew of the existence of the death camps from reports published in the Swiss papers, and from the testimonies of Italian soldiers who had fought in Greece or the Soviet Union and of Croatian and Polish Jews who had sought refuge in Italy.[23] They were still, however, unable to take action: 'our ignorance allowed us to live, as when you are on a climb and your rope is frayed and about to break, but you don't know and feel safe' (I: 548).

The turning point of the war in the winter of 1942–3, with the Allied victories in Northern Africa and the defeat of the Germans at Stalingrad, led to a resurgence of anti-Fascist activity throughout Europe. In Italy, the political parties which had been outlawed in 1926 resumed their activities underground. Among them was a new party, the Partito d'Azione, founded in 1942, whose program was largely inspired by the principles of *Giustizia e Libertà*, and whose members included many of the Northern Italian Jews arrested in the 1930s.[24] In Milan, Levi and his friends made contact with anti-

Fascist leaders, and joined the underground organisations of different parties. Levi chose to join the Partito d'Azione – probably because he identified with its mainly middle-class and intellectual membership and its emphasis on the moral aspect of political commitment – and became part of the network of contacts of what was to become the CLN (Comitati di Liberazione Nazionale), the national coalition of all anti-Fascist parties. In the story 'Oro' (Gold) of *Il sistema periodico* he lucidly and concisely recalls both the swift political growth of his generation of anti-Fascists, and their tragic underrating of the need for military as well as political training:

> Out of the shadows came men – lawyers, professors, and workers – whom Fascism had not crushed, and we recognised them as our teachers, those whose teachings we had until then vainly sought in the Bible, in chemistry, and on the mountains. Fascism had silenced them for twenty years, and they explained to us that Fascism was not only grotesque, improvident bad government, but negation of justice . . .. They told us that our mocking distaste was not enough; it needed to turn into anger, and the anger needed to be channelled into well-planned and swift revolt; but they did not teach us how to make a bomb, or how to fire a rifle (I: 548).

Events were moving too quickly for the Italian people to foresee the extent of the tragedy ahead, or to be fully prepared for it. On 25 July 1943, Mussolini was deposed by the Fascist hierarchs and placed under arrest by the King, and on 8 September the armistice between Italy and the Allies was made public. By that time the south of the Italian peninsula was occupied by the Allies, who had landed at several points in September. The north and the centre were occupied by the Germans, who after 25 July had been sending troops into Italy, and in September the latter rescued Mussolini and made him head of the new puppet Italian Social Republic in northern Italy.

For all Italians who found themselves under Nazi rule, the time that followed 8 September was a time of individual choice: to wait passively for events to run their course, to support the Nazis and the Fascists, or to act against them. That choice was far more dramatic for the forty thousand Jews then living in Italy,[25] as the SS and the Gestapo began to carry out round-ups of Jews in Rome and in smaller northern communities on the basis of the registers drawn up in 1938. On 17 November 1943, the Italian Social Republic declared all Jews to be 'foreigners' and 'enemy nationals' for the period of the war: on 30 November the Minister of the Interior issued a police order for the arrest and internment of all Jews living within the Italian territory and the confiscation of all their property. This meant that from that date onward Jews could be arrested by the Italian authorities as well (see Cavaglion 1986: 118–19; Zuccotti 1987: 167–70; Picciotto Fargion 1991: 825–6).

Some Italian Jews fled, mainly to Switzerland. Many went into hiding, sheltered by Gentile families or by Catholic priests and members of religious orders, who often supplied them with false papers.[26] Levi's mother – his father had died in 1942 – hid in the mountain region of Val d'Aosta, north of Turin, until the end of the war. Others chose the path of armed resistance. Although they never, unlike the Jews in France, fought in separate units, statistics show that the proportion of Italian Jews who chose to fight was higher than both the numerical proportion of Jews in Italy and the proportion of non-Jewish resistance fighters.[27]

What was to become the Italian Resistance[28] started off mainly as groups of young volunteers. They had no connections with either the CLN or what was left of the former Italian army, no military training and no organisational networks to supply them with shelter, food, clothes, and weapons. Yet they were determined to fight Fascism, mainly from a class perspective if they were peasants and factory workers, or for intellectual and moral motives, if they came from middle-class backgrounds (see Quazza 1976: 105–27). In 'Oro', Levi sums up their situation in a poignant and painfully honest assessment, understating the courage and determination he and his companions showed in their attempt:

> Thus, after the long intoxication with words, certain of the rightness of our choice, extremely unsure of our means, with far more despair than hope in our hearts, and against the backdrop of a defeated, divided country, we went into battle to test ourselves against the enemy (I: 549).

Levi's sister Annamaria became a courier for the units connected to the *Giustizia e Libertà* movement and the Partito d'Azione.[29] Levi joined a small group of partisans based near Brusson, in the Val d'Aosta. They did not get a chance to fight:

the local units had been infiltrated by some former army officers, who worked for the Fascist Militia and who led a raid on the partisan hideouts on 13 December 1943 (see Nicco 1990: 26–34). Three hundred militiamen surrounded eleven partisans; five – all Jewish – were arrested and taken to the militia headquarters in Aosta.[30]

Levi was carrying obviously false papers, and was rumoured to be a Jew. The Fascist officer who interrogated him told him that he could choose between declaring himself a partisan, which would mean execution, or declaring himself a Jew, which would, according to the police order of 30 November, result in his being kept in an internment camp until the end of the war. Although he strongly suspected that all Jews in internment camps would sooner or later fall into the hands of the Germans, Levi chose to reveal his real identity: 'partly because I was tired, and partly out of an irrational surge of stubborn pride' (I: 552). He later rationalised this 'stubborn pride' in an interview with Ferdinando Camon: 'I did not want it to remain unknown that I, a very incompetent partisan . . . but a partisan nonetheless, was a Jew: that therefore Jews too can find the strength to fight' (Camon 1987: 16).

On 17 February 1944 he was transferred to Fossoli, the main Italian internment camp, near the town of Modena in Emilia. Until 8 February, Fossoli had been run by the Italian authorities and no Jews had been deported. On that date the camp was taken over by the SS, who immediately began to organise deportation trains (Zuccotti 1987: 170–1; Picciotto Fargion 1991: 45–6). Most of the over 8,000 Jews deported from Italy between October 1943 and December 1944[31] left from Fossoli. Levi was on the eighth train, which departed on 22 February and reached Auschwitz four days later. The sealed wagons contained approximately 500 people, including thirty-one children (the youngest was one) and eighteen old people (the oldest was eighty-nine). The first selection was carried out as soon as the deportees stepped off the train: all but twenty-nine women and ninety-five men were sent directly to the gas chambers. The men who were not gassed were tattooed with matriculation numbers which went from 174,471 to 174,565 (Picciotto Fargion 1991: 46). Primo Levi became number 174,517.

Notes to Chapter One

1. See Milano (1992: 144–6, 272–6 and 306–8). A collection of documents on the Jews in Piedmont between 1297 and 1798 can be found in R. Segre (1986).
2. Luigi Luzzatti was Prime Minister in 1910–11; Claudio Treves and Giuseppe Emanuele Modigliani were Socialist deputies in the first two decades of the century.
3. General Giuseppe Ottolenghi was the Minister of War in 1902.
4. Some of the most important figures were the linguists Graziadio Isaia Ascoli and Benvenuto Terracini, the sociologists Leopoldo Franchetti and Cesare Lombroso and the anatomy professor Giuseppe Levi, the father of the writer Natalia Ginzburg.
5. See the evaluations in the memoirs of two well-known Piedmontese intellectuals, the half-Jewish Arturo Carlo Jemolo (1969: 53–4) and the observant Jew Augusto Segre (1979: 42).
6. Quoted in De Felice (1977: 108–9).
7. In a television interview Levi admitted that his recollections had been based on the 'collective memories' not only of his own family but also of other Piedmontese Jewish families (see Poli and Calcagno 1992: 223).
8. Published in *L'altrui mestiere*. In the English translation, it appears in *Other People's Trades*.
9. In the story 'Un lungo duello' (A Long Duel) Levi recollects that his father would immediately buy him any book he requested, with the exception only of the adventure novels by the prolific popular writer Emilio Salgari (III: 803).
10. See particularly 'La mia casa' (My House) and 'Un lungo duello' in *L'altrui mestiere* and 'Ranocchi sulla luna' (Frogs on the Moon) and 'Meccano d'amore' (Love's Erector Set) in *Racconti e saggi*. In the English translation, all four stories appear in *Other People's Trades*.
11. The Italian *liceo classico* is a highly academic secondary school, where somewhat greater emphasis is given to the humanities than to the sciences.
12. *Giustizia e Libertà* was a movement founded by anti-Fascist exiles in France in 1929. It consisted mainly of middle-class intellectuals; its main aims were the overthrow not only of

Fascism but also of the monarchy and the establishment of a parliamentary democracy committed to radical social and economic reforms. See Salvatorelli and Mira (1969, vol. II), Quazza (1976: 120–1) and De Luna (1982: 28–33).

13. Mario Levi, one of the brothers of Natalia Ginzburg, was not related to Primo Levi's family.

14. See Levi's interview with Giorgio De Rienzo (*Famiglia Cristiana*, 20 July 1975, p. 43).

15. There are several contradictory versions of this. Levi himself (1986d) does not mention the essay topic and says that he wrote a 'thin, silly piece' because he was in shock after hearing that he was about to be drafted into the Navy.

16. For detailed descriptions and analyses in Italian of the anti-Semitic campaign and the racial laws, see Caffaz (1975, 1988), De Felice (1977), Cavaglion and Romagnani (1988) and Milano (1992). An excellent treatment in English is to be found in Zuccotti (1987). Gunzberg (1992) offers a different perspective; she argues convincingly that the racial laws revived a centuries-old tradition of anti-Semitism in Italy (see especially Chapter 5).

17. The national figures were approximately 47,000 Italian Jews, just over one in one thousand in a population of forty-five million (Zuccotti 1987: 5). About 10 per cent (4,700) lived in Turin, working mainly in the professions and in the textile trade (Fabio Levi 1991: 24; Genovese 1991: 139–40).

18. In his dialogue with Tullio Regge, Levi said that in those years he also saw science as the antidote to the notion – inspired by the idealist philosophers Croce and Gentile – that scientific knowledge is a 'pseudoconcept', of practical utility but useless for understanding the world (Levi and Regge 1984: 13–15).

19. Most of the people mentioned in *Il sistema periodico* are identified only by first name, initials or nicknames. Levi's supervisor, Professor Dalla Porta, is referred to as 'the Assistant Lecturer' (see Levi and Regge 1984: 18–19).

20. See the story 'Nichel' (Nickel) in *Il sistema periodico*.

21. See the story 'Fosforo' (Phosphorus) in *Il sistema periodico*.

22. See the story 'Oro' (Gold) in *Il sistema periodico*, and Guadagni (1993). Levi's friends were Silvio Ortona, who was a Resistance leader and later a Communist Party MP; Eugenio Gentili Tedeschi; Emilio Diena; Carla Consonni, the

only Gentile of the group; Ada Della Torre, Levi's cousin, who was a courier in the Resistance and married Silvio Ortona; and Vanda Maestro, who had been at university with Levi, was captured and deported with him, and did not return from Auschwitz.

23. On 3 May 1971 Levi gave evidence at the trial against Friedrich Bosshammer, whom Adolf Eichmann had put in charge of anti-Jewish activities in Italy. Levi stated that by 1942–3 he had gathered information about the death camps from the Swiss press, from clandestinely listening to radio broadcasts from London, and from a British White Paper which had been smuggled to him and which he had translated into Italian (see Picciotto Fargion 1991: 841).

24. On the Partito d'Azione, see Quazza (1976) and De Luna (1982, 1985). A brief account in English is found in Ginsborg (1990: 15).

25. According to Picciotto Fargion (1991: 793), by 25 July 1943 there were 40,157 Jews in Italy, including 6,500 Jews of other nationalities who had sought refuge there.

26. An exhaustive account can be found in Zuccotti (1987); see especially chapters 7 and 9.

27. Zuccotti (1987: 248) states that the highest estimate of general Italian participation in the Resistance is 0.5 per cent of the national population, while the most conservative estimate of Jewish participation is 1,000 (about 2 per cent of the total Jewish population). See also Cavaglion (1989: 78–9) and Segrè (1990).

28. The literature on the Italian Resistance is extensive. The most recent and deepest analysis is Pavone (1991). Other authoritative accounts are Battaglia (1964) and Quazza (1966). A lucid summary in English is found in chapter 2 of Ginsborg (1990).

29. See the story 'Il mitra sotto il letto' (The Tommy Gun under the Bed) in *Racconti e saggi*. The English translation is in *The Mirror Maker*.

30. Levi repeatedly stated that he considered his participation in the Resistance an unheroic, in fact 'the least brilliant', episode in his life. In the first page of *Se questo è un uomo*, he says sternly that when he joined his fledgling group '[he] had not yet been taught the lesson [he] was later to learn swiftly in Auschwitz: that man's first duty is to pursue his

ends by suitable means, and those who make mistakes pay for them' (I: 5). On 26 June 1980 he wrote to the Director of the Aosta Research Centre on the Resistance, who had asked him to provide details on the activities of his group: 'It is a story of well-meaning, but careless and foolish, young people, and it is best forgotten.'

31. The figures in Caffaz (1988: 80–4) come to 8,369. Zuccotti's (1987: 146) and Picciotto Fargion's (1991: 835–53) estimate is 8,716. Only 686 returned.

2

174517

*A*uschwitz had been built at the end of 1943, when the lack of workers in German industry had become so acute that the regime decided to make use of all available human resources, including the Jews. Auschwitz was therefore, in Levi's own words, 'a hybrid camp, in fact a hybrid "empire" of camps: extermination plus exploitation, in fact extermination through exploitation' (Camon 1987: 38).[1] The most succinct summary of the organisational structure of Auschwitz is given by Levi himself:

> There was not one camp at Auschwitz: there were thirty-nine of them. There was the town of Auschwitz and inside it there was a camp, which was Auschwitz proper, that is to say, the capital of the system. Two kilometres further down there was Birkenau, that is to say Auschwitz II, where the gas chambers were. This was a huge camp, subdivided into four – six adjoining camps. Further up there was the factory, and by the factory there was Monowitz, or Auschwitz III. That is where I was. This camp belonged to the factory, which had financed it . . .. In my camp there were about 10,000 of us; in Auschwitz I there were 15 or 20,000; in Birkenau many more, 70 or 80,000 . . ... The camps' central Administration was in Auschwitz I, and the death camp was Birkenau. The system in Auschwitz resulted from the experience gained in all the other camps with regard to both forced labour and the extermination of the prisoners (Camon 1987: 65–6).

Of the over eight thousand Jews deported from Italy, 5,951 were taken to Auschwitz. Only 356 of these returned (Picciotto Fargion 1991: 25–32). Levi – prisoner 174517 – attributed his own survival to a variety of factors, the main ones being his relatively late arrival and his being fit enough to be made part of the forced labour system. He always stressed, however, that luck played an essential role (Roth 1986: 40; Camon 1987: 71).

Levi started taking notes on his experience while still a

prisoner, working in one of the laboratories of Buna, the Monowitz rubber factory, owned by the industrial giant IG-Farbenindustrie. Since writing anything was extremely dangerous, he destroyed these notes immediately, but he knew that if he were ever to return home, he would bear witness; in fact he would strive to return in order to bear witness.[2]

In January 1945 the German troops, threatened by the impending arrival of the Soviet Army, evacuated all the healthy prisoners from Auschwitz. Nearly all died during the evacuation march, or later in Buchenwald and Mauthausen. Levi, ill with scarlet fever, was left behind. What happened to him and to the other prisoners in the ten days before the Red Army entered Auschwitz on 27 January is related in the last chapter of *Se questo è un uomo*.

Nine months elapsed before Levi could return to Turin. He and the other survivors spent five months in the transit camp at Katowice in Poland, and then two months at Staryie Doroghi in the Soviet Union, where the Italians were 'clearly held as hostages by the Soviet Army, which was waiting to see how things would end'.[3] The long and slow journey back through the Soviet Union, Rumania, Hungary, Austria and Bavaria is recounted in *La tregua* (*The Truce*).

Levi returned to an Italy which the war and the German occupation had devastated physically, socially and economically.[4] In Turin, 30 per cent of housing had been destroyed or badly damaged, and so had more than 50 per cent of the streets, roads, bridges, and public transport. Unemployment was high; Levi had to wait three months before finding work in January 1946 with Duco-Montecatini, a paint factory near Lake Avigliana, a short distance from Turin. Almost thirty years later, in the story 'Cromo' (Chromium) of *Il sistema periodico*, he represented, in the context of socially and economically shattered Northern Italy, his need to force everyone around him to face what he had suffered:

> The things I had seen and suffered were burning inside me; I felt closer to the dead than to the living, and felt guilty for being a man, because men had built Auschwitz . . .. It seemed to me that I would be purified if I told my story, and I felt like Coleridge's Ancient Mariner, who on the streets waylays the wedding guests going to the feast . . .. Nobody took much notice of me: colleagues, the manager, and workers had other things to think about – a son who had not returned from Russia, a stove without wood, shoes without soles,

warehouses without stocks, windows without panes, the freezing cold which split the pipes, inflation, food shortages, and the virulent local feuds (I: 570).[5]

The urgent need to communicate took on different forms. As a scientist, together with another scientist – the doctor and Auschwitz survivor Leonardo De Benedetti, the 'Leonardo' of *La tregua* – he informed the scientific community by means of a report on the health organisation in Monowitz, which appeared in the authoritative medical journal *Minerva Medica* (Levi and De Benedetti 1946). Its purpose was the strictly referential communication of the manner in which the physical destruction of thousands of human beings had been accomplished. It concentrates on factual details about the prisoners' diet and diseases, and about the organisation and functioning of the gas chambers and the crematorium ovens, without taking an explicit moral stand.[6]

Levi's emotions of anger and despair, subdued in the report, were expressed for himself and the people closest to him in 'concise and gruesome poems' (I: 570).[7] The desire to reach as many people as possible, and to make them reflect on the collective dimension of the 'final solution', led him to elaborate his memories into a book. In 'Cromo' Levi describes the development of this book, from something 'which grew in [his] hands almost spontaneously, without plan or system, tangled and teeming like a nest of termites' (I: 570) into a conscious intellectual construct, defined in an explicit comparison to his main profession: 'the work of a chemist who weighs and divides, measures and judges on the basis of definite evidence, and endeavours to answer questions' (I: 572). The story also tells how Levi's creativity, and his overall confidence, were increased by the newly-found closeness with the 'patient, wise and confident' woman with whom he had fallen in love: Lucia Morpurgo, a friend of his sister.

In the spring of 1947 parts of this book, with the provisional title 'Sul fondo' (On the Bottom), appeared in the Piedmontese Communist Party weekly *L'amico del popolo*, edited by his friend Silvio Ortona. Its positive reception encouraged Levi to submit the completed manuscript to the publishing firm Einaudi, considered the anti-Fascist publisher *par excellence* since its foundation in 1933. The manuscript was read by several people, including the writers Cesare Pavese and Natalia Ginzburg; Ginzburg informed Levi that Einaudi was not interested in it.

This may have been due to a number of factors. Levi, a scientist, unfamiliar with and unknown in literary circles, may have seemed too much of an oddity to justify Einaudi gambling on his book. The book may have been judged just one among the many prison and concentration camp memoirs which in those years were being published by a proliferation of small, politically committed and usually short-lived firms. The writers who assessed it may have been affected by the desire, widespread throughout the country and typical of any nation recovering from war and civil war, to look to the future rather than the past.[8] Levi then submitted his manuscript to De Silva, a small Turin firm directed by the former partisan Franco Antonicelli, who published it in a series of memoirs after persuading Levi to change the title from *I sommersi e i salvati* (*The Submerged and the Saved*)[9] – which was left as the title of the central chapter – to *Se questo è un uomo*, a line from the poem chosen as its epigraph. The print run was 2,500 copies, of which under 2,000 were sold, mainly to other ex-deportees.[10] The rest were stored in a warehouse in Florence, where they were lost in the flood of November 1966.

In June 1947 Levi decided to leave Duco-Montecatini and to establish himself as a freelance chemical consultant. His farewell to his employer and colleagues was a lighthearted satirical poem.[11] For a few months – as he later described in the stories 'Arsenico', 'Azoto' and 'Stagno' (Arsenic, Nitrogen and Tin) in *Il sistema periodico* – he attempted, in partnership with his friend Alberto Salmoni,[12] to make a living through consultancy work and the production of chemicals in makeshift laboratories. By the end of the year the experiment had failed and Levi – who had married Lucia Morpurgo in September – went back to salaried employment. He joined SIVA (Società Industriale Vernici e Affini), a firm specialising in the production and development of synthetic resins and insulating enamels, with responsibility for quality control and the development of new products. At the beginning of the 1950s, when SIVA expanded and moved to the nearby town of Settimo Torinese, Levi became its technical manager.

Now a family man – his daughter Lisa Lorenza was born in 1948 and his son Renzo in 1957[13] – and working as a chemist,

Levi nevertheless continued to bear witness. In 1953 he and Lello Perugia (the 'Cesare' of *La tregua*) won a compensation court case against IG-Farbenindustrie. This was also a political trial, because the two survivors wanted to demonstrate that firms which had collaborated with the Nazi regime were still thriving after the war, and had not really paid for their involvement (Guadagni 1993). In 1955 he wrote an article for the tenth anniversary of the deportees' return. He spoke strongly against the guilty conscience of those who

> try in every way to change the subject by referring to nuclear weapons, the indiscriminate bombings [of German cities by the Allies], the Nuremberg trials, and the problematic Soviet labour camps: these arguments are not without weight, but they are totally irrelevant as moral justifications of Fascist crimes, which, because of their character and magnitude, are a monument to cruelty, unprecedented in human history (Levi 1955: 53).

He also discussed the theme of the survivors' sense of shame, which had been 'burning inside him' since his return, and which he was to analyse in depth thirty years later in *I sommersi e i salvati*:

> We are men, we belong to the same human family as our slaughterers . . .. It is vain to call the death of the countless victims of the camps glorious. It was not glorious: it was a defenceless and naked death, ignominious and obscene. Neither is slavery honourable . . . it is in its essence an ignoble condition, the source of almost irreparable degradation and of moral disintegration. . . . This does not diminish the crime of the Fascists and the Nazis, in fact it makes it a hundred times worse (Levi 1955: 53–4).

By the end of the 1950s, however, the political and cultural climate had changed. Italians who had lived through Fascism and the war and had experienced German occupation, prison or deportation were facing a new generation which knew very little about them, because school history curricula stopped at the end of the First World War. This, and the need to oppose the resurgency of neo-Fascist and neo-Nazi movements in Western Europe, led to numerous broad-based initiatives, including series of lectures on Fascism and anti-Fascism and publication of war and prison diaries (including *The Diary of Anne Frank*). All of these aimed at encouraging people to think about and discuss the reasons for, and the consequences of, the events of twenty years earlier. Levi approached Einaudi again, and *Se questo è un uomo* – rewritten and expanded[14] – was published in 1958. The reception was extremely positive, and resulted a few months later in an exhibition of items and documents on deportation in Turin. The first edition (2,000 copies) sold out within a few months, as did three reprints between 1958 and 1963. It has never been out of print, and by 1987 it had sold nearly 750,000 copies (Einaudi 1990: 32).

Se questo è un uomo is a difficult book to label. It clearly belongs to the main stream of 'Holocaust literature', survivors' accounts of their experiences in the death camps.[15] These accounts are a necessarily diverse genre because of their authors' differing social and political experiences prior to deportation, differing experiences in the camps and differing literary and narrative skills. Most memoirs, however, have similar structures in that they describe the same sequence of events (arrest, journey to the camp, arrival, initiation, conditions, liberation) and, although with a different focus, they have similar themes (work, selections for the gas chambers, linguistic chaos, effects of the camp conditions on the prisoners' minds and behaviour) (see Haft 1973, Bravo and Jalla 1986, and Bravo and Jalla 1994). As Haft points out, the narrations which strictly adhere to factual details are the least effective, because of the lack of pre-existing social or historical frames of reference in which Holocaust memories can be placed (1973: 79). *Se questo è un uomo* stands out among these, and is generally considered – with Robert Antelme's *L'espèce humaine* (*the Human Race*) and Elie Wiesel's *La nuit* (*Night*) – one of the most compelling because its structure, content and language make it at one and the same time a philosophical and sociological examination of the death camps and a unique literary text. It is frequently quoted in both historical monographs (such as Giuntella 1979) and psychological and moral analyses of the camps (such as Devoto and Martini 1981, and Todorov 1992) because Levi's shaping of his experience into literary form is more effective than any purely historical account.

'This book of mine,' Levi states in the preface, 'has not been written in order to formulate new accusations; it may, rather, provide evidence for a dispassionate study of some aspects of the human mind' (I: 3). This statement of intent is expanded at the beginning of the chapter 'I sommersi e i salvati':[16] 'It is my conviction that no human experience lacks meaning and is unworthy of analysis' (I: 88). From the outset, therefore, Levi's discourse differentiates itself from specifically Jewish discourses such as Wiesel's, and from discourses restricted to the time and places of the death camps, such as most of the published memoirs by Italian survivors.[17] The preface also alerts the readers to the relevance of the Auschwitz experience for the present and the future – the feature that characterises all Levi's writings on the Holocaust:

> Many individuals or many nations may believe, more or less consciously, that 'every stranger is an enemy' . . .. But . . . when the unspoken dogma becomes the major premise of a syllogism, then, at the end of the chain, there is the concentration camp. It is the product of a view of the world carried rigorously to its consistent conclusion: as long as this view remains, its conclusions are a threat to us. The story of the death camps should be understood by everyone as a sinister danger signal (I: 3).

The book's title may at first sight recall that of Antelme's *L'espèce humaine*, since both sum up the central theme of both texts, the human traits which survive, or are crushed, in the camps. The similarity, however, is only apparent. While Antelme's abstract expression focuses on the humanity shared and lost by both the oppressors and the victims, Levi's indirect question highlights the victims: it asks what human features are left after they have been deprived of their identities and of their collective social and moral codes, and how these features manifest themselves under the conditions of the camps.

'If this is a man' is a line from 'Shema', a poem Levi wrote in 1946 and chose as the book's epigraph. The title ('Hear', in Hebrew) immediately recalls *Shema Israel*, the most common of Jewish prayers, central to the identity of every Jew, the prayer that Jewish martyrs have traditionally recited at the moment of death.[18] In the poem, the prayer is both recontextualised for the world after Auschwitz and strongly problematised. Levi's words address humankind at large rather than only the people of Israel, and command them – on pain of being accursed – to meditate on the fate of human beings rather than to believe in God and love him, and to pass on their knowledge to future generations.

You who live secure
In your warm houses
 . . . Consider if this is a man
 Who labours in the mud
 Who knows no peace
 Who fights for a crust of bread
 Who dies at a yes or a no
. . . Consider that this came about:
I command these words to you.
Engrave them on your hearts
When you sit at home, when you walk by the way,
When you go to bed, when you rise;
Repeat them to your children.
 Or may your house crumble,
 May disease cripple you,
 May your children turn their faces from you (I: 1).

The book is arranged chronologically only in the opening chapters (which describe Levi's arrest, the transit camp at Fossoli, the journey to Auschwitz and the prisoners' initiation) and in the final chapter, which describes the last ten days of Auschwitz in diary form.[19] The central chapters are simultaneously successive stages of Levi's time in the camp and analyses of aspects of Auschwitz as an institution (see Mengaldo 1990: xxxix); they have general titles such as 'Our Nights', 'Work', 'A Good Day', which are all the more striking for their 'normality'.

Unlike other anti-Fascist survivors (Caleffi 1955; Pappalettera 1965), Levi says very little about his resistance activities which led to his arrest. This is consistent both with his stated ethical and social purposes, and his embarrassment at his involvement having been so brief and uneventful. The self-deprecating autobiographical sketch which opens the first chapter ('I was twenty-four and had little wisdom, no experience, and a strong tendency . . . to live in a world of my own, which was unreal and inhabited by civilised Cartesian shadows . . . I cultivated a moderate and abstract sense of rebellion', I: 5) highlights one of the central themes of the book: Levi's own education, his experience of unlearning some of his naive assumptions and of learning about human nature, identity, language and, above all, power.[20]

The learning experience is both individual and collective.

Collective learning is represented in negative terms, as adjustment to the conditions in the camp and resignation to present pain and impending death. The chapter 'Sul fondo' (On the Bottom) is an extended representation of the initial process of induction of the Italian prisoners. The process begins with the prisoners' first questions to the Germans, who contemptuously refuse to answer, and to the other prisoners, whose explanations are mysteriously sinister. At the end Levi sums up the new collective knowledge, repeating 'We have learned' before describing the history and topography of the camp, the categories of prisoners, the value of food and the camp regulations, and concluding with the last thing the newcomers have learned, 'to wipe out the past and the future'. By the chapter 'L'ultimo' (The Last One) the learning process is completed. The description of the public hanging of one of the few who took part in a revolt is framed by two exchanges between Levi and his friend Alberto.[21] The first is Levi's proud account of some of the methods of petty theft perfected by the two of them to add to their daily bread rations. The chapter ends with the word 'shame': the shame that overwhelms both of them after they realise that, unlike the executed man and like everyone else, they have adjusted to the system of the camp and have lost all strength to rebel. This same episode appears also in Wiesel's *La nuit*, but with a very different focus: Wiesel dramatically emphasises the prisoners' loss of faith in God in the face of the abomination they have witnessed (' Where is He? Here He is – He is hanging here on this gallows . . .' Wiesel 1981: 77), while Levi emphasises the prisoners' awareness of the change that has taken place within them ('To destroy a man is difficult, almost as difficult as to create one; it has not been easy, it has not been quick, but you Germans have succeeded. Here we are, docile under your gaze; you have nothing more to fear from us; no acts of rebellion, no words of defiance, not even a look of judgement' I: 155).

Unlike collective learning, individual learning – specifically, Levi's – is always connected to the preservation of personal identity and dignity.[22] 'Dignity' in the context of the camps has best been defined by Todorov as 'continuing to be a subject in possession of his or her own free will, capable of making decisions followed by action' (1992: 21 and 63). In a much-quoted scene in the chapter 'Iniziazione' (Initiation), the Austrian soldier

Steinlauf tells Levi that the effort to keep clean is essential, because 'to survive we must endeavour to save at least the skeleton, the scaffolding, the form of civilisation', and that cleanliness is a symbol of the prisoners' power to refuse their consent to the system of the camp. This moral lesson, however, is presented ambivalently: while acknowledging its wisdom and virtue, Levi expresses both his doubts as to its applicability in the 'complicated infernal world' of Auschwitz, and his awareness that new moral systems may have to be elaborated, or that no moral system is possible (I: 34–6). A more poignant and bitter contrast is represented in the chapter understatingly entitled 'Esame di chimica' (Chemistry Examination). To be chosen for a unit of chemical specialists, that is to say to be able to survive the winter, Levi must demonstrate his professional competence to Doktor Pannwitz, one of the chemists managing the rubber plant attached to Monowitz. As the two men look at each other, Pannwitz becomes a symbol of the whole Third Reich, dominated by the logical necessity of ascertaining whether the subhuman specimen facing him has any knowledge worth exploiting. To face Pannwitz as a subject rather than an object, Levi concentrates on recalling his training and competence. As these gradually re-emerge, his identity and dignity are reinforced, which enables him not only to perform well, but also to pass judgement both on Pannwitz and on the other face of the same coin, the German foreman who, after the examination is over, cleans his dirty hand on Levi's shoulder.

Recalling the experience over ten years later, Levi wrote, using the present tense: 'If I now knew how to explain fully the nature of that look, exchanged as if through the glass wall of an aquarium between two beings who live in different worlds, I would also have managed to explain the essence of the great insanity of the third Germany' (I: 109). This is one of the central themes of the book, and of Levi's writings on the Holocaust: the tension between the nature of the hell surrounding him, which is a deliberate challenge to any attempt to ask or answer questions, and his desire and ceaseless efforts to make sense of it and to convey to others what he has understood. On his first day in Monowitz, Levi, driven by thirst, grabs an icicle; a guard promptly snatches it from him. Levi's question *'Warum?'* (Why?) is instantly answered by a terse summing up of the law of the camp: *'Hier ist kein Warum'* (There's no why here) (I: 23). Some prisoners internalise the law, giving up their identity: on the bottom of their bowls, most carve their numbers, Levi his name, and another man *'ne pas chercher à comprendre'* (do not try to understand) (I: 107). Yet asking questions, and reflecting on the answers, is vital in order to grasp the full measure of what is happening. This Levi learns from another prisoner:

> 'Show me your number: you are 174517. This numbering began eighteen months ago and applies to Auschwitz and all the satellite camps. There are ten thousand of us now here in Buna-Monowitz; perhaps thirty thousand between Auschwitz and Birkenau. *Wo sind die andere?* Where are the others?'
> 'Perhaps transferred to other camps . . .?' I suggest.
> Schmulek shakes his head, turns to Walter:
> *'Er will nix verstayen'*, he does not want to understand (I: 48–9).

Levi does begin to understand when Schmulek is selected for the gas chamber on the following day.

The chapter 'Al di qua del bene e del male' (This Side of Good and Evil) describes with scientific objectivity the manifold forms of theft and graft within Auschwitz, and immediately afterwards directly addresses the readers and encourages them to understand and learn on the basis of the evidence provided:

> In conclusion: theft in Buna, punished by the civilian authorities, is allowed and encouraged by the SS; theft in the camp, severely repressed by the SS, is considered a normal exchange operation by the civilians; theft among prisoners is generally punished, but the punishment strikes the thief and the victim with equal gravity. The reader is now invited to consider what the words 'good' and 'evil', 'just' and 'unjust' could possibly mean in the camp; let everybody judge, on the basis of the picture I have outlined and of the examples given above, how much of our ordinary moral world could survive on this side of the barbed wire (I: 87).

The basic paradox which underlies all discourses on the Holocaust is that, while trying to describe the indescribable, they also must point out that language is inadequate to convey the *univers concentrationnaire*.[23] In *Se questo è un uomo*, the inadequacy of language is one of the first realities the prisoners encounter collectively: 'For the first time we realised that our language lacks words to express this offence, the demolition of a man' (I: 20). Abstract words, denoting universal human experiences, are particularly alien to the reality of Auschwitz, which can only be represented as 'something else', as total 'otherness':

> We say 'hunger', we say 'tiredness', 'fear', and 'pain', we say 'winter', and they are something else. They are free words, created and used by free men who used to live, happily and sadly, in their own homes. If the camps had lasted longer, a new, harsh language would have been born (I: 126–7).

Levi's own language reflects this paradox, and attempts to solve it through a range of strategies. The first is the use of a variety of biblical and literary references which, however, are problematised at the very time they are used.[24] Biblical images are explicitly and powerfully reclaimed as a collective parallel to the exile and oppression of the people of Israel: the Italian Jews in Fossoli, waiting to be deported, experience 'the ancient grief of the people that has no land' (I: 8) and the stories the prisoners tell one another are 'stories of a new Bible' (I: 64). Yet the religious dimension of Judaism is consistently denied, even in passages which directly refer to divine justice and power. The Carbide Tower, called the Tower of Babel by the prisoners who built it, symbolises

> the insane dream of grandeur of our masters, their contempt for God and men . . .. Just as in the ancient fable, we all feel, and the Germans themselves feel, that a curse – not a transcendent, divine one, but an immanent, historical one – hangs over the arrogant building, founded on the confusion of languages and erected in defiance of heaven, like a stone blasphemy (I: 72).

The most explicit example of this tension is in the final chapter, in the description of the prisoners' first awareness that their oppressors have fled:

> The Germans were no longer there. The watchtowers were empty.

> Today I think that, if for no other reason than that an Auschwitz existed, no one in our age should speak of Providence. Yet without doubt in that hour the memory of biblical salvations in extreme adversities passed like a wind through all our minds (I: 164).

The attempt to describe the indescribable through biblical references, despite the awareness that they are not applicable to Auschwitz, is evident in the numerous echoes of the language of the Bible, particularly iteration and the anaphora of *and*.

Especially in the first chapter, 'Il viaggio' (The Journey), these echoes transform the narration into a biblical intertext:

> The time for meditating, the time for deciding was over . . ..
> Old Gattegno lived in Hut 6A, with his wife and many children and grandchildren and sons-in-law and bustling daughters-in-law. . . . Their women were the first of us to complete the preparations for the journey, silently and swiftly, so that there would be time for mourning; and when everything was ready, the bread baked, the bundles tied together, then they bared their feet, let down their hair, and placed the funeral candles on the ground, and lit them according to the custom of their fathers, and sat on the ground in a circle for their lamentation, and all night long they prayed and wept. Many of us paused before their door, and, for the first time, the ancient grief of the people that has no land, the hopeless grief of the exodus which is renewed every century, descended into our souls (I: 8).

The chapter ends with the prisoners who have survived the first selection – carried out as soon as they got off the sealed wagons – moving off towards the main camp. The verb tense suddenly shifts from the past historic to the present, both to signify that biblical recollections are no longer applicable to the new experience, and to make the memory relevant to the present and the future. From this point on, the present tense prevails throughout the text. It gives dramatic immediacy to the narration and the events; it is used meta-narratively to convey Levi's reflections on what he is telling ('Today, this very day when I am sitting at a table writing this, I myself am not convinced that these things really happened', I: 106); and it has the gnomic function of formulating general observations on human nature ('The human capacity to dig a burrow around oneself, to secrete a shell, to erect a tenuous barrier of defence around oneself, even in apparently desperate circumstances, is amazing, and should be studied carefully', I: 53; 'Human nature is such that pains and sorrows suffered simultaneously do not accumulate to form a whole in our consciousness, but the lesser ones hide behind the greater ones according to a clearly-defined law of perspective. This is fortunate, and it is what allows us to survive in the camp', I: 73).[25]

The same conceptual and linguistic problematisation applies to the many literary references in the text, which are both explicit and implicit and range from Homer to Sophocles, from morality plays to Jack London. The main source, however, is Dante's *Inferno*, which is one of the literary texts studied in the first year of *liceo* and therefore familiar to all Italians who progress beyond compulsory school age. Levi quotes and adapts a variety of passages from this Christian medieval account of Hell to attempt to convey the unspeakable degradation of Auschwitz, even if only by analogy. The discovery that in Auschwitz 'there is no why' is immediately followed by two lines from Canto XXI, where some demons sarcastically shout to a damned soul that Hell is not meant to be as enjoyable as his native town of Lucca, with its sacred icons and its pleasant river:

> No Sacred Face will help thee here! It's not
> A Serchio bathing party . . .[26]

Here the recollection from Dante helps Levi to understand the negative nature of Auschwitz, its *not* being like any previously known discourse or system of relations. More frequently, however, the reality of Auschwitz prevails upon the literary text. Levi implicitly compares the guard escorting the prisoners into Buna to the infernal ferryman Charon, but points out that, instead of shouting 'Woe to you, you wicked souls' like Charon, he asks them politely for their money or watches, which will be of no use to them 'afterwards' (I: 14). In the chapter 'Il canto di Ulisse' (The Canto of Ulysses), Levi decides to translate Dante's well-known episode for a French Jew, as the two of them are on their way to fetch their daily rations of soup. A profound emotional tension is created through the juxtaposition of the traditional, Romantic interpretation of Dante's Ulysses – the individual whose 'virtue' lies in his striving to push human 'knowledge' further, and who maintains his sense of identity even in Hell – and human existence in Auschwitz. As he quotes the central lines of the speech addressed by Ulysses to his comrades, Levi becomes intensely aware of the duty to remain rational beings and not to be submerged by the animal-like struggle for physical survival, and urgently tries to share this awareness with his companion:

> Now listen Pikolo, open your ears and your mind, you have to understand, I need you to:

174517

> Think of your breed; nature did not intend
> Mankind to live as brutes, but to pursue
> Virtue and knowledge to the very end.

As if I were hearing it for the first time: like the blast of a trumpet, like the voice of God. For a moment I have forgotten who I am and where I am (I: 117).

Immediately afterwards the two men arrive at their destination and queue up for their soup. The moment of rational detachment is over, and – like Ulysses and his followers in Dante's text, whose ship is overwhelmed and sunk by a higher power at the end of their journey – they sink again into the passive degradation of the camp, with soup as its symbol:

> We are now queuing for the soup, among the sordid, ragged crowd of soup-carriers from other Kommandos. Those just arrived are crowding behind us. 'Kraut und Rüben?' 'Kraut und Rüben.' The official announcement is made that the soup today is of cabbages and turnips. 'Choux et navets.' 'Kaposzta és répak.'

> . . . until the sea closed over us (I: 118).[27]

The fragments from many languages which are inserted into the text here, and also in the description of the rush for the rations of bread, 'of pane-Brot-Broit-chleb-pain-lechem-kenyér' (I: 33) and in the history of the Carbide Tower ('its bricks have been called Ziegel, briques, tegula, cegli, kamenny, mattoni, téglak, and have been cemented together by hate', I: 72), are more than just a representation of the multilingual chaos of Auschwitz. They are symbols of the various cultures of the oppressed peoples, which are reduced to scraps of lexical items connected with the minutiae of daily existence, and combined with fragments of the oppressors' languages. Yiddish, the common language of Eastern European Jews, is represented as the immediate marker of their shared identity, from which Italian Jews, who neither speak nor understand it, are excluded. German is seen as occasionally uncontaminated by the surrounding reality ('*Heimweh* is what they call this pain in German; it is a beautiful word, it means "homesickness"', I: 51), although more often it is degraded by the reality it simultaneously reflects and conditions: '"Wieviel Stück?" the sergeant asked; and the corporal saluted smartly and replied that there were six hundred and fifty "head"

{ 35 }

and that all was in order' (I: 9); 'this way of eating on our feet, furiously, burning our mouths and throats, without the time to breathe, is *fressen*, the way animals eat, and certainly not *essen*, the way human beings eat' (I: 75). The Polish word for the morning order to get up, *Wstawac'*, is 'the daily sentence', the condensation of the ever-repeated offence to humanity.

Levi also endeavours to overcome the inadequacy of language by generally avoiding expressions of overt anger and despair, and by choosing instead to convey the reality of Auschwitz through individual examples rather than through descriptions of mass atrocities. His discourse often takes the form of inductive and deductive arguments, which are always presented through concrete instances in the form of brief sketches of individual prisoners. These men are introduced and their symbolic function is highlighted by the fact that they are identified only by their first name or by a nickname; their relevant characteristics are outlined and general principles are drawn from Levi's observation of them. Null Achtzehn (Zero-eighteen), who has given up even his name and is identified only by the last three figures of his number, the first of which is a very symbolic zero,[28] and who passively follows orders without trying to avoid work or to acquire extra food, becomes a powerful lesson of how to lose one's humanity and not survive (I: 37–8). The naive and clumsy newcomer Kraus, to whom Levi recounts a fictitious and comforting dream, represents the rare, fleeting moments of human solidarity and communication (I: 138–9). At the close of the chapter 'Ottobre 1944' (October 1944), after a factual description of a selection for the gas chambers, old Kuhn, who thanks God for having been spared, provides occasion for Levi's rejection of any religious perspective and, something unusual, his angry moral judgement:

> Kuhn is out of his mind. Doesn't he see, in the bunk next to his, Beppo the Greek, who is twenty years old, and will be gassed the day after tomorrow, and knows it, and is lying there staring at the light bulb without saying anything and without thinking about anything any more? Doesn't Kuhn realize that next time it will be his turn? Doesn't Kuhn understand that what has happened today is an abomination that no propitiatory prayer, no pardon, no atonement by the guilty, nothing at all in the power of man can ever heal again?
>
> If I were God, I would spit Kuhn's prayer out to the ground (I: 133–4).

More frequently, general principles are first stated and subsequently demonstrated through specific examples. The central chapter, 'I sommersi e i salvati' (The Submerged and the Saved), is an extended deductive argument. It begins with a universal scientific statement: '. . . the concentration camps were, also and strikingly so, a gigantic biological and social experiment': by observing thousands of individuals of different ages, backgrounds, languages and habits, forced to live under identical conditions of deprivation, it can be possible 'to establish what is essential and what is acquired in the behaviour of the human animal in the struggle for life' (I: 88). Levi then proceeds to examine in detail the distinction – far more clear-cut in the death camps than anywhere else – between two categories of prisoners, those doomed to perish and those likely to survive, and comes to the conclusion that 'survival without giving up anything of one's own moral world was granted only to very few superior individuals, made of the stuff of martyrs and saints' (I: 94). This general principle is demonstrated through four specific examples: Schepschel, who learned to scrounge a little extra food through petty theft, occasional services, and occasional cruelty; Alfred L., who succeeded in becoming a privileged prisoner by managing, with iron self-discipline, to look clean and hard-working; Elias, who was among the fittest to survive in the camps because he was exceptionally strong, virtually insane, and devoid of any moral scruples; and Henri, who learned a variety of calculating, detached ways to manipulate and use anyone who could protect him.

The rarer instances of moral and spiritual survival are described in a less detached fashion, as positive lessons Levi learned and by which he was helped in Auschwitz and afterwards. His friend Alberto, who was to die during the evacuation march, is consistently depicted in positive terms, as 'unscathed and uncorrupted', and capable of remaining everybody's friend while using his intelligence and intuition in the daily struggle for existence: 'I always saw, and still see, him as the rare image of the man who is strong and gentle, against whom the weapons of night are blunted' (I: 54).[29] The highest tribute is paid to the civilian worker Lorenzo,[30] who – at considerable risk to himself, and without asking for anything in return – gave Levi some food every day for six months, and once managed to write to Levi's family on his behalf:

However little sense there may be in attempting to ascertain why I, among thousands of others in the same conditions, managed to survive the test, I believe that it is thanks to Lorenzo that I am alive today. This was not so much for the concrete assistance he gave me, as for his having constantly reminded me, with his presence, with his easy, matter-of-fact way of being good, that there still existed a just world outside ours . . .. Lorenzo was a man: his humanity was pure and untainted, he was outside this world of negation. Thanks to Lorenzo, I managed not to forget that I myself was a man (I: 125).

The final chapter, 'Storia di dieci giorni' (The Story of Ten Days), describes Auschwitz between the flight of the Germans and the arrival of the Red Army. The first, tentative human actions of cooperation and altruism are described against the background of spreading disease, death and total disintegration:

> And then Towarowski . . . proposed to the other sick men that each give a slice of bread to the three of us who had been working, and the others agreed.
> Only a day before, such an event would not have been conceivable. The law of the camp was: 'eat your own bread, and, if you can, your neighbour's', and left no room for gratitude. That meant that Auschwitz was indeed dead. . . . I believe that that moment can be pinpointed as the beginning of the process by which we who had not died slowly changed from *Häftlinge* [prisoners] back to men (I: 166–7).

The moment of liberation, with the arrival of the soldiers of the Red Army, is a brief, silent and understated scene, with none of the elation and gratitude described in many other accounts:

> The Russians arrived while Charles and I were carrying Sómogyi not far from our barracks. He was very light. We overturned the stretcher onto the grey snow.
> Charles took off his cap. I regretted that I did not have a cap (I: 181).

In 1963, the year of publication of *La tregua*, Levi was sent a copy of an adaptation of *Se questo è un uomo* for a Canadian radio station. He appreciated its tone of 'spoken meditation' and its attempt to convey the Babel-like confusion of languages through scenes in which several languages were spoken by the various characters (Marché and Levi 1966: 7). A few months later he wrote his own radio adaptation, which was broadcast on 24 April 1964. It consisted of the central episodes of the book, from the arrival at Auschwitz to the last ten days, linked by a narrator's comments and judgements. Levi's adaptation, like the Canadian one, used multilingual dialogues with German, French, Polish, Yiddish and Russian spoken by authentic native speakers who were not professional actors.

Multilingualism is also one of the main features of the theatre adaptation which Levi – after overcoming considerable doubts – agreed to write together with a friend, the actor Pieralberto Marché. Directed by Gianfranco de Bosio and performed by the Turin Theatre Company, using fifty-three actors of seven nationalities, it was first performed at Teatro Carignano on 18 November 1966.[31] Like the radio adaptation, the theatre version begins and ends with the poem 'Shema', recited line by line by different actors. The main episodes of the book are recreated as a quick succession of brief scenes, and the authorial narration and descriptions become choral comments, with the actors taking turns to speak. The dramatisation is more effective in scenes where a few characters communicate with, or confront, each other – such as the 'chemistry examination' – than in scenes – such as that of the Canto of Ulysses – which recreate states of mind or collective experiences, since in the latter scenes the moral issues tend to be explicitly 'told' rather than 'shown'. Most reviewers in fact pointed out that Levi's understated discourse, when translated for the stage, becomes overstated and at times rhetorical, and made unfavourable comparisons with the starkness of the court evidence which constitutes the text of a play dealing with a similar theme, Peter Weiss's *Die Ermittlung* (The Investigation) (Capriolo 1966; Blandi 1966).[32]

When *La tregua* was published in April 1963, Levi's life centred mainly around his family and his work at SIVA. He had, however, become fairly well known as one of the most willing and effective witnesses of the Holocaust. In the late 1950s he started giving talks to secondary school students and encouraging other ex-deportees to visit schools in spite of objections from school authorities.[33] He was to continue doing this for over twenty years. He also spoke on the concentration camps at a number of public meetings, most notably in February 1961 at the time of the trial of Adolf Eichmann in Jerusalem.[34] Writing was something he did in his spare time, every night after work: mainly science fiction stories, which appeared in several

Italian papers, and a variety of stories and short essays for the Turin daily *La Stampa*, for which he wrote on an irregular freelance basis from 1960 to his death. He did not belong to any literary circles, and still saw himself as an 'occasional writer' (Poli and Calcagno 1992: 17).

Nevertheless his decision, after the publication of *Se questo è un uomo*, to write an account of his nine-month odyssey following the entry of the Red Army into Auschwitz was primarily born of a wish to produce a work that was a full literary construct, and to prove to himself and his readers that he had authentic narrative and stylistic ability. He explained this clearly in a 1986 interview with Philip Roth:

> I had recounted each adventure many times, to people at widely different cultural levels (to friends mainly and to secondary school boys and girls), and I had retouched it en route so as to arouse their most favourable reactions. When *If This Is a Man* began to achieve some success, and I began to see a future for my writing, I set out to put these adventures on paper. I aimed at having fun in writing and at amusing my prospective readers (Roth 1986: 41).

The literary motivations which led Levi to write *La tregua* could also be connected to a general cultural and literary trend at the end of the 1950s and the beginning of the 1960s: a movement away from the unmediated testimony and populist naiveté of neo-realism and towards more complex notions of 'realism' and of the relationships between individuals and historical processes.[35] Another less obvious factor was the widespread awareness of the changes taking place in the national and international political climate. The beginning of the gradual 'thawing' of relations between the capitalist and the socialist blocs at the beginning of the 1960s caused Levi to feel that 'in Italy, for the first time, it was possible to talk about the Soviet Union in objective terms, without being accused of Communist leanings by the Right and of reactionary bias by the powerful Italian Communist Party' (Poli and Calcagno 1992: 24–5).[36] The cautious optimism and hopes of those years affected Levi's writing of his experiences:

> I gave emphasis to strange, exotic, cheerful episodes – mainly to the Russians seen close up – and I relegated to the first and last pages the mood ... 'of mourning and inconsolable despair' (Roth 1986: 41).

The first page lucidly and solemnly opens where *Se questo è un uomo* ends, highlighting the central theme of Levi's writings on the Holocaust – the offence to humanity – and anticipates the pessimistic reflections of *I sommersi e i salvati*. The four young Russian soldiers who first enter Auschwitz silently share with Levi and the other survivors 'the shame that the Germans did not know, the shame the just man experiences at another man's wrongdoing, and the guilt that such a wrong should exist, that it should have irrevocably been brought into the world of things that exist' (I: 216). Just as in the episode of Kuhn in the earlier text, the offence is clearly defined as 'unhealable', and as 'an inexhaustible source of evil' for humankind as a whole: 'it breaks the body and soul of the submerged, it extinguishes them and renders them abject; it reverts to the oppressors as infamy, it lives on in the survivors as hatred, and it is ever present in a thousand ways, against everyone's will, as thirst for revenge, as moral capitulation, as negation, as weariness, as surrender' (I: 217).

The last pages describe a recurring dream, which opens in the present tense: peaceful everyday situations disintegrate, and Levi finds himself 'at the centre of a grey and murky nothingness' and 'knows' that he is again in the camp, 'and nothing was true outside the camp. The rest was a brief respite, or a deception of the senses, a dream' (I: 423). Auschwitz represents the entire human condition, and the homeward journey of Levi and his companions becomes a symbol of the provisional nature of life: all that can be hoped for is the occasional 'truce' between past and future battles. This sense of despair recurs at various points in the text. The survivors' initial hope for 'an upright and just world, miraculously re-established on its natural foundations' is with hindsight defined as 'naive' (I: 242). Levi's equally naive belief that the war is finally and definitively over is contradicted by a Polish lawyer, all too conscious that anti-Semitism lives on in his country and elsewhere, and by Mordo Nahum, a cold and ruthless Greek survivor who laconically informs Levi that 'War is forever' (I: 256). The sight of Austria and Bavaria defeated and devastated fills the victims of Nazism neither with joy nor with compassion, but rather with 'the heavy, threatening sense of an evil, irreparable and ultimate, present everywhere, nestling like gangrene in the gut of Europe and the world, the seed of future destruction' (I: 416).[37] This foreboding is also the theme of the epigraph, the poem 'Alzarsi' (Get up) which Levi had written in 1946:

Now we have found our homes again,
Our bellies are full,
We have finished telling our story.
It is time. Soon we will hear again
The foreigner's command:
'*Wstawac*'.

Between the initial despair and the final premonition, however, the journey home is also a picaresque sequence of encounters and adventures against an ever-changing background of black markets, railway stations, transit camps, barrack rooms, steppes and forests.[38] The contacts with other lands and other people lead the ex-deportees to making discoveries about one another and themselves, continuing the learning process which began with deportation. This time, however, the education process is mostly positive. With few rules and certainties, the survivors retrieve and confirm their sense of self by exchanging various kinds of knowledge as well as goods and by practising the skills, legal and otherwise, they had learned before deportation. By relearning how to make decisions and choices which are to varying extents free, they rediscover their autonomy and dignity, the systematic destruction of which had been one of the main aims of the *univers concentrationnaire*.[39] Thus the journey home also becomes, in the tradition of the Enlightenment, a process of intellectual and moral education, a journey upwards in spite of – possibly because of – the survivors' displacement, memories of the past and forebodings about the future. This is reflected in the book's structure: the chapters are no longer, as in *Se questo è un uomo*, general descriptions but are rather a chronological narration of the successive stages of the journey, mainly in brief episodes and vignettes; their titles are mainly names of people and places, which occasionally have a metaphoric as well as a literal meaning ('Il bosco e la via' (The Forest and the Path); 'Vacanza' (Holiday)).

The necessary – although not sufficient – condition for learning is communication. The entire book pulsates with the need to communicate, to create links between languages, cultures, and human beings. The language of the first chapters, in their biblical echoes and anaphoras reminiscent of *Se questo è un uomo*, establishes the survivors' urgent need to become full human beings again through the 'free words created and used by free men', which they had been denied in Auschwitz. A memorable symbol of this need is Levi's haunting description of the three-year-old Hurbinek, whom nobody had taught to speak, and who dies soon after being freed, at the end of a desperate struggle to utter meaningful sounds.

> Hurbinek, who was three years old and had perhaps been born in Auschwitz and had never seen a tree; Hurbinek, who had fought like a man, to his last breath, to win his entry into the world of men, from which a bestial power had excluded him; Hurbinek, the nameless, whose tiny forearm had also been branded with the tattoo of Auschwitz; Hurbinek died in the first days of March 1945, free but not redeemed. Nothing is left of him: he bears witness through these words of mine (I: 228).

The many languages the ex-prisoners speak and the various scraps of languages they manage to acquire in their wanderings are the central element in Levi's representation of attempts to communicate with, and learn from, people of different nations and cultures. The successful efforts to find shared meanings are mainly represented as brief episodes whose dominant emotion is delight at the satisfaction of one of the most basic human needs, that for free contact with other human beings. This applies to Levi's description of his picking up fragments of Polish to carry out transactions in the market of Cracow ('I returned from my survey ... with many haphazard snippets of linguistic knowledge ... which filled me with a foolish and childish joy', I: 253); to a dialogue between Levi and a Polish priest carried out in the only language they have in common, Latin; and to a hilarious nocturnal encounter in the middle of the Russian steppe between Levi, who is with his friend Cesare, and the people of a tiny village, where all kinds of linguistic and non-linguistic communication are attempted before, to everyone's satisfaction, six plates are exchanged for a chicken.

The ex-prisoners' rediscovery of their sense of self is reflected in another major difference between *Se questo è un uomo* and *La tregua*: the presence in the latter of different types of character constructs, some in the form of one-off sketches, some recurring throughout the text, but always with one dominant characteristic highlighted, and some developed cumulatively.

The characters who only appear once are mainly symbolic instances of general phenomena, above all of incongruous ways of behaving which Levi represents as the logical consequence of the ex-deportees' past experiences. Frau Vita, rendered psychologically unstable by her memories, tries to exorcise them with frantic activity and is 'hungry for words, for intimacy, for human warmth' (I: 234). D'Agata, 'a small, sober, reserved and very clean Sicilian bricklayer', who is engaged in an obsessive and hopeless war against bedbugs, is both pitied and envied by his companions because he is 'the only one whose enemy was concrete, present, tangible, and could be fought, beaten, crushed against the wall' (I: 312). Velletrano, born in the overcrowded ghetto of Rome, after surviving Auschwitz has reverted to the wild state in the Russian forest, living by hunting and gathering; however, 'being all the same a son of man, in his own way he pursued virtue and knowledge . . . he made himself a knife, then a spear and an axe, and I do not doubt that, had he had the time, he would have rediscovered agriculture and cattle-raising' (I: 359). Most of the female characters are sketches of this kind, and are represented in terms of their sexual connections to men rather than as autonomous beings able to make personal choices. Two Wehrmacht auxiliaries used as prostitutes by the ex-deportees are identified merely as 'the girls in the forest' and as a wild and mysterious 'alternative to celibacy' (I: 358); two 'wooden, grumpy-looking' female Russian soldiers are easily seduced away from their guard duty by two 'hardboiled' Italian men who 'consciously sacrifice themselves for the common good' (I: 408). Flora, an Italian woman Levi had met in Auschwitz, is also represented first in terms of idealised desire ('she seemed beautiful, mysterious, incorporeal', I: 374) and then, after the discovery that she is a prostitute, in terms of disenchantment ('acute discomfort, an absurd and impotent mixture of jealousy and disillusionment', I: 375).

In the case of the characters who appear at various points in the text with one dominant characteristic highlighted, this characteristic is usually a positive one, an aspect of human initiative aimed at cooperation and mutual help rather than at individual survival against everyone else. Levi's friend, the physician Leonardo, is represented in terms of his unselfish courage which is 'silent, not innate, not religious, not transcendent, but rather deliberate and striven for hour by hour' (I: 267). Another doctor and Auschwitz survivor, Gottlieb, is consistently characterised as 'sharp as a sword', overcoming shortages and bureaucracies with his 'nerve, his soaring imagination, his rapier-like quickness' (I: 318–19). Eighteen-year-old Galina, a Russian girl who assists Levi in the makeshift pharmacy of a transit camp, represents femininity in Levi's consciously masculine discourse ('the only one among her female companions to dress with a certain elegance, and to have shoulders, hands and feet of acceptable dimensions', I: 270). While she is granted 'the same dignity as her comrades and boyfriends, the dignity of those who work and know why, of those who fight and know they are in the right, of those who have their lives ahead of them' (I: 271), she is mainly an object of Levi's longing for tenderness and comfort, and remains in his mind as a bittersweet memory of 'things not said, opportunities not grasped' (I: 401). The only female character presented as independent of male desire, the middle-aged Russian nurse Marja, is constructed as resourceful, pragmatic, helpful, tough and basically sexless.

The identities of the characters developed cumulatively are constructed through their reactions to different circumstances and to one another. This applies particularly to Levi's autobiographical persona. His narrated self is one of the characters in his narration and, like everyone else, he is at different times bewildered, hopeful, frightened, curious and oppressed by memories. However, at the same time he is primarily an observer: he compares his interest in individual and collective behaviour in extraordinary circumstances to that of 'a natural scientist studying the activities of an animal with complex instincts' (I: 265). Just as in *Se questo è un uomo*, he uses the natural scientist's inductive method to draw philosophical and ethical reflections from concrete, even trivial experiences and encounters:

> I was meditating . . . that nature rarely grants compensations, and so does human society, because it is timid and hesitates to abandon nature's grand order of things; and what a conquest it is, in the history of human thought, the moment when nature is seen no longer as a model to be imitated, but as a shapeless block to be sculpted, or an enemy to be fought (I: 243).

Moral codes, all of them, are rigid by definition . . . they must be accepted or rejected as a whole. This is one of the main reasons why man is gregarious, and seeks more or less consciously the company not of anyone in general, but only of those who share his profound beliefs (or lack of them) (I: 250).

Levi's precise observation also produces many humorous pages, with the humour resulting from the contrast between various types of illogical or incongruous behaviour and his logical and rational, if sympathetic, description. His depiction of a football match between a makeshift team of Italian ex-prisoners and a Polish team, refereed by a Russian captain, and of the enthusiastically rowdy response of Russian soldiers to the showing of adventure films, are comic masterpieces. The 'normal' assumptions that the rules of a game will be observed, or that the audience of a film will remain uninvolved, are sharply overturned and the resulting chaos is wryly presented as totally logical.

A humorous function, as well as an enrichment of Levi's autobiographical construct, is achieved by his use of literary references. Those in *La tregua* come mainly from the nineteenth-century classics (Jules Verne's *Michael Strogoff, The Brothers Karamazov* and Alessandro Manzoni's *I promessi sposi (The Betrothed)*) which were part of the cultural background of middle-class Italian youth of his generation. They do not, as in *Se questo è un uomo*, provide parallels for a reality which is unspeakable, but rather highlight the incongruity of the situations in which Levi and his companions find themselves, and the distance between Levi's background and the ex-deportees' struggle to survive on the streets of Eastern European cities and in the Russian forests and steppes. In the barter encounter with the Russian peasants, Levi uses an (unacknowledged) quotation from *I promessi sposi* to make a self-mocking comparison. His own attempt to apply deductive methods to linguistic communication, which results in total failure, is implicitly compared with the way of reasoning of a minor character in Manzoni's novel, who deductively argues that, since the plague is entirely due to the influence of planetary conjunctions, there can be no cure against it, and consequently takes no precautions and dies of it:

174517

Russian, they say, is an Indo-European language, and chickens must have been known to our common ancestors in a period certainly preceding their subdivision into the various modern ethnic groups. *'His fretus', that is to say on these fine foundations*, I tried to say 'chicken' and 'bird' in all the ways known to me, but I obtained no visible results (I: 343; my italics).[40]

Levi's autobiographical construct is also developed through the narration of the associations between Levi's narrated self and two men, the Greek Mordo Nahum and the Roman Cesare, who are explicitly compared and contrasted with Levi and with each other. Through a variety of shared adventures, both the Greek and the Roman are constructed as cunning, experienced in deals – both honest and otherwise – and endowed with leadership skills. Compared with them, Levi's persona is represented as cautious, lacking in practical knowledge and more inclined to speculate than to take initiatives. They are also sharply contrasting human types, and, by implication, examples of differences between national cultures:

For Cesare, 'work' was at different times an unpleasant necessity or an amusing opportunity to meet people, and not a frigid obsession, or a Lucifer-like self-assertion. One was free, the other a slave to himself; one was miserly and rational, the other prodigal and volatile. The Greek was a lone wolf, in constant war against everyone, old before his time, enclosed within the circle of his malevolent ambition; Cesare was a child of the sun, a friend to the whole world, knew neither hatred nor contempt, he was as changeable as the sky, cheerful, sly and naive, foolhardy and cautious, very ignorant, very innocent and very civilised (I: 285–6).

The differences both between and within people of various nationalities are one of the recurring themes of *La tregua*. One of the most striking features of the text is its representation of the Russian people. They are depicted, wryly but sympathetically, as tough, compassionate, naive, pragmatic and above all easy-going, and are often explicitly contrasted with the 'demonic' Germans and the 'functional, technological' Americans. The Red Army officers are consistently represented as disorganised and blundering, yet never unkindly, authorities who 'seemed to love bureaucracy with that Platonic, spiritual love which neither attains nor desires possession' (I: 266). The overall judgement is positive, and firmly founded in the historical context of the victory over the Germans:

Yet, beneath their slovenly and anarchical appearance, it was easy to see in them, in each of those rough, open faces, the good soldiers of the Red Army, the valiant men of old and new Russia, gentle in peacetime and savage in war, strong from an inner discipline born out of consensus, love for one another and love for their country; a discipline that was stronger, because it came from within, than the mechanical, servile discipline of the Germans. It was easy to understand, living among them, why it was their discipline, and not the other, that had ultimately prevailed (I: 264).

The construction of Jewish identity is as gradual as that of Russian identity, but it is inevitably more complex. The religious aspect is present only in the form of a few biblical references, which serve mainly as terms of comparison to the survivors' wanderings in search of their homes. Diaspora Jews from many European nations (the Greek Mordo Nahum, the Russian captain who doubles as a kitchen inspector and a football referee, Dr Gottlieb, who 'came from Rieka, Vienna, Zagreb and Auschwitz' (I: 303), Cesare from the slums of the Rome ghetto) are represented in terms of their national cultures rather than in terms of a common history. This is consistent with Levi's view, which he would develop and articulate twenty years later,[41] that the essential feature of Jewish culture is its polycentric nature, and that Diaspora Jews are the 'centre of gravity' of Jewish identity. Language has, obviously, a central role in this conceptualisation. The multilingual skills acquired by many characters, such as Mordo Nahum, Dr Gottlieb and Levi's own narrated self, help them to communicate with one another and with the people of the countries they cross. This positive cooperation is implicitly contrasted with the linguistic chaos of the Darwinian struggle for survival in Auschwitz. Among the many 'haphazard snippets of linguistic knowledge' which Levi acquires, and in turn passes on and explains to his readers, are a few expressions from the dialect spoken by the Jews of Rome and a few Yiddish expressions. Yiddish, however, is problematised in an episode halfway through the book. Levi and three Italian companions meet two Russian Jewish girls, who bluntly tell them they can't be Jewish, since they speak no Yiddish ('Ihr sprecht keyn Jiddisch: ihr seyd ja keyne Jiden!').[42] This identification of Yiddish, the common language of unassimilated Eastern European Jews, with Jewish identity has its negative corollary in that anyone – such as assimilated Western European Jews –

unable to speak it is inevitably seen as alien and 'other'. In *La tregua* this is presented as yet another – half-successful and half-failed – attempt at cross-cultural communication, but the role of Yiddish remained one of Levi's cultural preoccupations in his subsequent writings about Jewish identity.[43]

In the last chapter, the encounters of the survivors of Auschwitz with the German people in Munich ('deaf, blind and dumb, barricaded among their ruins as in a fortress of deliberate ignorance, still strong, still capable of hatred and contempt', I: 420) are immediately followed by a brief description of a group of young Eastern European Zionists heading for Palestine, 'immensely strong, masters of the world and their destinies' (I: 421). Just as the reflections on the Germans are echoed in most of Levi's subsequent writings until the final summing-up of *I sommersi e i salvati*, so the determined young Zionists anticipate the motley band of partisans, survivors of destroyed Eastern European cultures, who move towards an uncertain future in Palestine in *Se non ora, quando?*

Unlike *Se questo è un uomo*, *La tregua* had immediate critical and popular success. Italian reviewers unanimously praised its calm and lucid language and its concise sketches of people and landscapes, and appreciated its moral and historical judgements. In 1963, the year of its publication, it won third place in the Strega Prize, the most prestigious Italian literary award; this, however, is reputed to be affected by the wishes of large publishing houses. It also won the newly-established Campiello Prize, where five books selected by literary critics are ranked on the basis of a secret ballot held among a randomly-selected sample of 300 readers. This victory was particularly significant because it confirmed that Levi – a full-time chemist who wrote in his spare time and who had no connections with literary circles, powerful publishers or political spheres – had narrative skills that appealed to readers and could use his scientist's rigorous observation to depict lighthearted or tender moments as well as mass scenes and dramatic passages.

Within four years *La tregua* had been translated into German, English, Dutch and French. Outside Italy it was not, until the 1980s, read as anything other than a sequel to *Se questo è un uomo*, and therefore judged within the parameters of Holocaust literature, but Levi's international success in the 1980s led to its being translated into six other languages and being seen as a work in its own right. In some recent evaluations of Levi's work (Howe 1985: 14; Fortini 1987; Mengaldo 1989: 97) *La tregua* has been called Levi's masterpiece, for its picaresque structure, humour, rhythm and its elements of hope. This evaluation is problematic because it may indicate a tendency to downplay Levi's testimony in favour of his skills as a writer; but it is nevertheless significant, because it fully recognises the literary value of the book as well as its moral and historical tensions.

La tregua was also a turning point in Levi's own life and self-definition. As he himself put it in a brief recollection nearly twenty years later, the success of the book and his winning the Campiello Prize encouraged him to see himself as a writer who could go on to produce texts unconnected with his experience of deportation, and to envisage a future as a writer rather than as a chemist:

> It [the prize] was a second professional qualification, at an age when many begin to lower their sails, it was the passport into a new world, full of stimulation and risk: and, at forty-four, I had not yet lost my taste for risk. I did not abandon the security of the factory straight away, but I accepted the label of writer, and I planned a new life: some time or other, I would leave my trade as a transformer of matter and I would start a new one. It was as if I was preparing myself to be born a second time (Levi 1982b: 3).

Notes to Chapter Two

1. The research output on the death camps is by now immense. An introductory bibliography can be found in Shimoni (1991). Invaluable introductory works are Dawidowicz (1975, 1976), Hilberg (1985: 555–69) and Marrus (1987). Specifically on Auschwitz, see Czech (1990).
2. See the interview with Balbi (1982b) and Bravo and Jalla (1986: 259).
3. See the interview with Goria (1982c).
4. For details about the conditions of Italy in the immediate post-war period, see chapter 3 of Ginsborg (1990).
5. Levi also described his state of mind in that period in several interviews. See especially those with Philip Roth (1986) and Risa Sodi (1987).

6. For a detailed analysis of this report, see Cavaglion (1992, 1993a, 1993b: 38–41).
7. The poems were originally distributed privately to Levi's friends. In 1975 twenty-seven of them were published by Scheiwiller under the title *L'osteria di Brema*; they later became part of Levi's collected poems, *Ad ora incerta* (*At an Uncertain Hour*). All Levi's poetry is discussed in chapter 5.
8. See Orengo (1985, 1987), Bravo (1986: 72) and the overview of the historical background to Italian war and prison camp memoirs in Cereja (1986).
9. In both Stuart Woolf's translation of *Se questo è un uomo* and Raymond Rosenthal's translation of Levi's last book the first element of the pair, *i sommersi*, is translated as 'the drowned'. I believe 'the submerged' to be closer to the original Italian as well as to the line from Dante's *Inferno* from which it is taken (see chapter 5).
10. Among the few readers who realised the importance of the book was Italo Calvino, who reviewed it for the Communist daily paper *L'Unità* and praised it not only for the effectiveness of the testimony but also for its narrative power (Calvino 1948).
11. The full text of the poem, 'Il testamento del vicecapolaboratorio' (Last Will and Testament of the Deputy Head of the Laboratory), is in no. 6 (May 1987) of the Montedison periodical *Montedison. Progetto Cultura* (p. 6).
12. In *Il sistema periodico* Salmoni is called Emilio.
13. In an interview with Dvorah Getzler (Getzler 1986) Levi said that his son had been named after Lorenzo Perrone, the man who – as related in *Se questo è un uomo* and in the story 'Il ritorno di Lorenzo' (Lorenzo's Return) in *Lilít* – when Levi was in Auschwitz, brought him food and contacted his family at great risk to himself. His daughter's second name is also probably a tribute to Perrone.
14. The additions are details on Levi's arrest, the chapter 'Iniziazione' (Initiation) and references to the mix of languages in the camp. The spelling and morphology of non-Italian words and factual information and data were also checked and corrected. For an extended examination of differences and variants between the De Silva and Einaudi editions, see Tesio (1977), who points out that the second version is not only more precise – as befits testimony – but

also more poetic and more stylistically refined.

15. For comprehensive analyses of Holocaust literature, see Langer (1975), Rosenfeld (1980) and Ezrahi (1980). Todorov's (1992) study of moral issues arising from the death camps also contains relevant and perceptive discussions of the most significant texts. For analyses focusing specifically on Italian texts, see Devoto and Martini (1981), Bravo (1986) and Cereja (1986). Bravo and Jalla have compiled a bibliography of memoirs by Italian survivors (1990), which they subsequently expanded with a lucid introduction on the value of testimony in historiography (1994).

16. See note 9.

17. See, among many others, Vasari (1945), Tedeschi (1946) and Caleffi (1955).

18. The full text of the prayer is in Deuteronomy 6: 4–7:

> Hear, O Israel: The Lord our God, the Lord is one. Love the Lord our God with all your heart, and with all your soul, and with all your strength. And these words, which I command you this day, shall be upon your heart, and you shall teach them diligently to your children, and you shall repeat them when you sit in your house, and when you walk by the way, and when you go to bed, and when you rise. And you shall bind them upon your arm, and you shall wear them on your foreheads between your eyes as a reminder. And you shall write them on the door-posts of your house and on your gates.

19. This chapter was the first part of the book to be written by Levi. See Cavaglion (1993: 28–9).

20. *Se questo è uomo* has been read as a 'reverse *Bildungsroman*', a narrative of unlearning previous knowledge and learning from scratch about survival, by Langer (1975: 82–4) and Rosenfeld (1980: 57).

21. Alberto has been viewed by some critics as the first of several *alter egos* in Levi's works. See Frassica (1991).

22. For a stimulating analysis of the notion of personal identity in *Se questo è un uomo*, see Gilliland (1992).

23. The expression *univers concentrationnaire* was coined by the French writer David Rousset and used as the title of his memoirs (1947).

   For an analysis of Levi's view of the role of language in *Se questo è uomo* see Epstein (1987), Girelli-Carasi (1990a) and Gilman (1991: 295–7).

24. For an extended discussion, see Girelli-Carasi (1990a, especially pp. 52–4). Rosenfeld (1980: 31) points out that many texts of Holocaust literature use literary models but turn them against themselves, 'overturning the reigning conceptions of man and his world that speak in and through the major writings of our literary traditions'.
25. For the use of tenses in *Se questo è uomo* see Motola (1987: 260–1), Biasin (1989: 10), Toscani (1990: 38–43), and Mengaldo (1990: xli–xliii).
26. The Serchio is the river which flows through Lucca.
    A comprehensive analysis of this episode is in Gunzberg (1990). References to Dante in *Se questo è uomo* are identified and discussed in Gunzberg (1986), Gunzberg (1990), Sodi (1990), and Amsallem (1992).
27. *Inferno* XXVI, 118–20 and 242; the translation is by Geoffrey L. Bickersteth (1972), Oxford: Basil Blackwell.
28 Gunzberg (1986: 28) points out that in Hebrew the number 18 symbolises life. *Null Achtzehn* therefore could also be read as 'no life'.
29. 'The weapons of night' is an indirect reference to the 1953 novella *Les armes de la nuit* by Vercors (pseudonym of Jean Bruller). Levi mentioned this text again in *I sommersi e i salvati* in strongly critical terms, defining it as 'intolerably infected with aestheticism and literary self-indulgence' (I: 695).
30. See note 13.
31. The full text of the theatre adaptation is in Marché and Levi (1966).
32. See also the discussion by Davico Bonino (1991: 143–5).
33. Personal communication from Ferruccio Maruffi (January 1992). See also Maruffi (1991).
34. See the report ('Gli orrori di Auschwitz rievocati da quattro scampati') in *La Stampa*, 24 February 1961, p. 4.
35. See Manacorda (1967: 234–302) for an overview of the developments and crisis of neo-realism in the 1950s.
36. See also Levi (1984e: 384).
37. For a perceptive analysis of the conclusion of *La tregua*, see the review by Ferretti.
38. For an analysis of the picaresque elements of the book, see Mengaldo (1989: 97). Howe (1985: 16) argues instead that, while the text appears to have a picaresque structure, it is 'anti-picaresque' because of the 'strong nervous tension'

between the experience of freedom and the memories of the death camps.

39. See Todorov (1993: 61–8).

40. The quotation comes from the conclusion of chapter 37 of *I promessi sposi*. After reporting the deductions of Don Ferrante, the character in question, the narrator comments: '*His fretus*, that is to say on these fine foundations, he took no precautions whatever against the plague. He caught it in due course, took to his bed, and died.'

41. See the interview with Lerner (1984a), and chapter 4.

42. Since Levi at the time had little direct knowledge of Yiddish, the spelling and morphology of this reported saying are in fact closer to German than to Yiddish. When Levi quoted it again twenty years later, in *Se non ora, quando?*, his knowledge of Yiddish had improved, and the quotation was correct ('Redest keyn jiddisch, bist nit keyn jid') (II: 369).

43. For a discussion of Yiddish in *La tregua*, see Gilman (1991: 297–9).

3

'My Own Stories, Other People's, Everybody's and Nobody's'

The 1960s were a period of swift and deep change in Italian society. The Italian economy recovered from the damage caused by the war and grew – thanks to the production and export of consumer goods – at a fast rate, if not a consistent one.

Most of northern and central Italy experienced rising employment and unprecedented individual prosperity. Turin, through a steady flow of peasants from the south coming to work in its factories, nearly doubled its population between 1951 and 1967. In a few years, the northern tradition of the *operaio professionale* – the male worker who was proud of the skills acquired through a long apprenticeship and had a considerable degree of control over the products of his work – was replaced by that of the *operaio massa*, the unskilled assembly line worker who carried out repetitive motions at high speed with little training and little professional pride. These new workers were disaffected and angrily militant: in the early 1960s there were waves of mass strikes and violent confrontations with the police, especially in Turin, which was the heart of the Italian manufacturing industry.[1]

The late 1960s saw the rise of a movement which, although originally limited to student protests against the elitist and hierarchical structure of the universities, quickly developed into an analysis of the role of education within capitalism. This led to students seeking ways of cooperating with factory workers in labour disputes in order to challenge the entire economic and social system of the nation. Turin was, with Milan and Rome, one of the centres of very complex interactions between different political movements and tendencies arising out of this new militancy. In the summer and the 'hot autumn' of 1969, widespread strikes and new radical forms of action – such as factory occupations, disruption of assembly lines, industrial sabotage and damage to public and private property – took place in the major plants of northern Italy. The workers demanded not only better conditions but also greater control of the workplace, and the struggles were led by different revolutionary groups, the most important of which, *Lotta Continua* (Unceasing Struggle) and *Potere Operaio* (Workers' Power), had a widespread following in Turin. By the early 1970s the 'extra-parliamentary' movements were solidly established and had expanded their activities beyond individual workplaces, fighting for national reforms in housing and workers' conditions and responding angrily to revelations of contacts between extreme right-wing groups and members of the Italian armed forces and secret services.[2]

Primo Levi's political allegiance was with the traditional left rather than the new movements. However, he was never a member of any party, nor did he in those years take an open political stand. By the end of the 1960s he was general manager of SIVA, which had become part of SICME-SIVA-SCET, a three-plant complex producing enamelled electrical conductors for a variety of industrial uses. SIVA, the smallest of the three plants, was not strongly unionised and there were relatively few disputes between management and unions; Levi was personally liked and respected by the workers for his honesty and his unassuming manners. In addition to being in charge of quality control and coordinating research, Levi was responsible for customer service, explaining to customers the features of the resins and enamels produced by SIVA and helping them to identify and solve any problems connected with the supplied products. He was deeply involved with his work. Laboratory research – constructing or altering formulae for new insulating resins and varnishes and testing them to see whether they worked and whether they could be mass-produced – was a series of challenges to his imagination and to his principles of precision and rigour. In *La chiave a stella* (*The Wrench*), Levi's autobiographical persona explains the process of industrial molecular research through an amusing extended simile:

> We are . . . like some elephants who are given a small empty box with all the parts of a watch in it; we are very strong and patient,

and shake the box in every possible way and with all our strength. Maybe we even warm it up, because heating is another form of shaking. Well, sometimes, if the watch isn't very complicated, if we keep on shaking, we manage to put it together; but . . . it is more sensible to get there a bit at a time, first putting two pieces together, then adding a third, and so on (II: 152).

Customer service was probably less congenial to his reserved personality. 'Uranio' (Uranium), in *Il sistema periodico*, is a customer's tall story which is embedded in a wry description of the unwillingness of Levi's autobiographical persona to engage in the 'ritualised courtship dance' of customer relations:

There are some technical salesmen who seem to have been born that way, born to Customer Service like Athena. This is not so for me, and I am sadly aware of it. When I need to work in CS, either at my office or elsewhere, I do it unwillingly, half-heartedly, with hesitation and not much human warmth. Still worse: I tend to be abrupt and impatient with customers, who are themselves impatient and abrupt, and to be mild and compliant with suppliers, who, themselves engaging in CS, are compliant and mild with me. In short, I am not good at CS, and I am afraid that it is too late for me to learn (I: 609–10).

Customer service did, however, give Levi the opportunity to travel in Italy and abroad. He made several trips to Great Britain and West Germany, to arrange for the production of synthetic resins in cooperation with Ciba-Geigy in London and Bayer at Leverkusen. He worked with German industrial partners out of loyalty to his employers. However, he later related a few uneasy exchanges with German colleagues, who had reacted with embarrassment and coldness when he told them that he had learned German in Auschwitz.[3] At the beginning of the 1970s he made three trips to the Soviet Union, to promote a resin for brakes to the producers of Soviet versions of Fiat vehicles in Togliattigrad, an industrial town on the Volga. Some of his experiences on those trips provided ideas for his writings: 'a journey [he said in a 1982 interview] always leads to collecting raw materials, which are stored somewhere and can be useful later on'.[4]

In 1965 he returned to Auschwitz for a commemorative ceremony organised by the Polish government. It was, as he put it, 'less dramatic than one could have thought. . . . too much noise, little room for meditation, everything carefully tidied up, clean buildings, a lot of official speeches'.[5] During the Six Day War of June 1967 he made no public statement but was photographed with other Turin Jews, donating blood for Israel.[6] He made a single brief visit to Israel in 1968. His impressions were positive: he appreciated the vitality of the Israelis and their pride in the country they had built (see Dini and Jesurum 1992: 130–1).

His work, his family, and the network of friends he had made before his deportation and in the years after his return – the lawyers Bianca Guidetti Serra and Alessandro Galante Garrone, the political philosopher and anti-Fascist leader Norberto Bobbio and two writers, the former war prisoner Mario Rigoni Stern and the former Resistance fighter Nuto Revelli – were the intellectual and emotional centres of his life. He did not belong either to groups of Marxist intellectuals which had formed in the 1960s, such as the group around the journal *Quaderni rossi* (*Red Notebooks*) in Turin, or to literary circles. His scientific training, his profession and the fact that his writing had evolved from testimony meant that he kept his distance from both established circles (such as the groups of writers working for and being published by Einaudi) and avant-garde groups, (such as *Gruppo '63*, named after the year when it was formed) which rejected 'bourgeois rationality' and its reflections in traditional literature in favour of experimental, disruptive language which was meant to mirror and question the disintegration of advanced capitalist society.[7]

The most successful literary works of the early 1960s were reconstructions of individual and collective historical experiences which, like Giuseppe Tomasi di Lampedusa's *Il gattopardo* (*The Leopard*, 1958), attempted to gain insights into the present by examining the developments of the previous century or, like Natalia Ginzburg's *Lessico famigliare* (*Family Sayings*, 1963) and Giorgio Bassani's *Gli occhiali d'oro* (*The Gold-rimmed Spectacles*, 1958) and *Il giardino dei Finzi-Contini* (*The Garden of the Finzi-Continis*, 1962), recollected the Fascist period, representing and problematising aspects of Italian Jewish identity. In the same years, however, other writers – most notably Elio Vittorini and Paolo Volponi who, like Levi, worked full-time in industrial management – chose to focus on the condition of factory workers, generally sharing an explicit political commitment to represent their alienation in order to contribute to their process of liberation from it.[8]

The mid-1960s were also the years when intellectuals in Italy, as in other industrialised nations, began to analyse the role of science in society and culture and the relationship between science and literature. On the one hand writers – stimulated by C.P. Snow's 1959 pamphlet *The Two Cultures and the Scientific Revolution*, translated into Italian in 1964 – debated the fragmentation of knowledge, the limitations of humanistic and literary culture and the differences between scientific and literary languages.[9] Italo Calvino – possibly the Italian writer most open to the challenges posed to literature by scientific discourses – pointed out in 1967 the need for a global cultural and epistemological integration: 'We will not have a culture equal to the challenge until we compare against one another the basic problematics of science, philosophy, and literature, in order to call them all into question'.[10] On the other hand, scientists committed to social and political change began to question the ideological construction of scientific knowledge as an absolute cultural value. They made explicit connections between the process of asking scientific questions and the mechanisms which decided which questions should be asked, situated science firmly among social relations within the sphere of production, and rejected any automatic identification of scientific and technological progress with improvement for society as a whole.[11]

A reflection of this growing inquiry into the role and paradigms of science was the increasing interest of Italian readers in science fiction, particularly in those works which represented possible undesirable technological developments, or which produced effects of 'cognitive estrangement'[12] by confronting readers with uncomfortable aspects of their own society seen from the perspective of alien environments or characters. The fiction of writers such as Isaac Asimov, Robert A. Heinlein and Theodore Sturgeon was translated into Italian and quickly became very popular, as did a series of anthologies of science-fiction stories in translation published by Einaudi from 1958 on. A few well-known Italian writers published pessimistic visions of the future; notable examples are the fantasy tales *Sessanta racconti* (*Sixty Stories*, 1958) by Dino Buzzati, and *Il Medioevo prossimo venturo* (*The Middle Ages to Come*), an apocalyptic collection of pieces on future escalating technological catastrophes, one of the best-sellers of 1971 which was written by Roberto Vacca, a full-time systems engineer and a friend of Levi.

Levi had always been fascinated by the literary tradition which, from Thomas More through François Rabelais, Jonathan Swift, Jules Verne and H.G. Wells to Aldous Huxley, used space and time travels as estrangement devices in order to articulate critical discourses on society. In some of the essays in the collection *L'altrui mestiere* (*Other People's Trades*) he paid tribute to Rabelais[13] and Huxley. His 1981 'personal anthology' of the literary and non-literary texts most significant for his own development, *La ricerca delle radici* (*A Search for Roots*),[14] contains what he defines as 'many instances of things turned upside down' (I: 179): excerpts from *Gulliver's Travels* and from *Gargantua*, and the classic short-short story 'Sentry' by Fredric Brown. In *Il sistema periodico* he reveals that, during the isolation and uncertainty of his first job in the asbestos quarry, he started writing stories based on his knowledge of the chemical elements. Others were written in the months following his return to Italy, simultaneously with *Se questo è un uomo*. Between 1946 and 1961 he published about a dozen short stories dealing with scientific, technological or biological developments in newspapers and other periodicals, and in 1961 he submitted them to Italo Calvino, then a consultant editor for Einaudi. Calvino's response was one of qualified praise: although he liked their 'intellectual and poetic appeal', he found that the stories lacked the 'rarefied atmosphere' which characterised the work of great writers such as Borges.[15] Five years later, encouraged by the success of *La tregua*, Levi decided to publish these first attempts at fiction, and fifteen pieces collected under the title *Storie naturali* (*Natural Stories*)[16] appeared in September 1966. He hesitated, however, to publish them under his own name; as he explained ten years later, although he fully accepted the role of main Italian witness of the Holocaust, he refused to be frozen into it. He wanted to give literary form to other concerns, which reflected both his work as a chemist and contemporary preoccupations about science:

> I felt uneasy and almost frightened at the thought of coming before my ex-deportee friends in another guise. I felt a little, how shall I put it, as a deserter. When I had previously published so-called science-

fiction stories in newspapers, I had received puzzled, even despondent letters from them. They wanted me to remain duty-bound to themes connected with the camps; they thought I could not write about anything else; they said that they had even felt angry at me, because they (correctly) considered my books as joint efforts, as their books. . . . I told them about the liberating joy of writing, and about the way my work in the laboratory had given me the initial ideas for the stories. . . . I think [the stories] have the right to a life of their own. I refuse to be classified as a concentration camp writer. I came out of the camps, I wrote about them, and possibly, in fact certainly, I have not finished writing about them, but I think I can say something worthwhile about other topics as well (quoted in Poli and Calcagno 1992: 39–40).

The stories were published under the pseudonym Damiano Malabaila. In an interview one month after the book appeared, Levi said that the suggestion had come from Einaudi and that his choice of pseudonym was coincidental: he had spotted the name on a shop sign on his way to work. However, with hindsight he could see a link between the name and the stories. Malabaila is Piedmontese for 'evil nurse', and the stories reflect a contamination of nature:

Malabaila means 'evil nurse'; I now think that from many of my stories emanates a vague smell of milk that has gone off, of nourishment that is no longer that, in short of adulteration, contamination, and evil spells. Poison instead of food: and on this topic I would like to remind you that concentration camps, in their most offensive and unforeseen aspect, had struck all of us survivors as exactly that, a world turned upside down, where *fair is foul and foul is fair*, where professors have to use shovels, murderers are supervisors and hospitals are places where people are killed (quoted in Poli and Calcagno 1992: 37).

The connection with Auschwitz was explicit also in a letter which Levi wrote to Einaudi and which was reprinted on the book cover. It provides not only a transparent clue to the real identity of 'Damiano Malabaila', but also a moral justification for the author writing and publishing what he defines as *'divertissements, moral snares'*:

I tried to give narrative shape . . . to an intuition which is not uncommon today: the perception that in the world we live in there is a discrepancy, a small or large gap, a structural defect which cancels out one aspect or another of our civilisation or our moral universe. . . . I (unexpectedly) entered the world of writing with two books on the concentration camps; it is not up to me to pass judgement on their value, but undoubtedly they were serious books, for serious readers. . . . I would not be publishing [these stories] if I had not realised (not immediately, to tell the truth) that there is continuity, there is a bridge between the camps and this fiction: the camps, to me, were the greatest of the structural defects I mentioned earlier, the most threatening of the monsters begotten by the sleep of reason.

Five years later, in 1971, Levi published a second collection of twenty stories which he linked to the first through its title, *Vizio di forma* (*Structural Defect*). This collection was published under his own name: Levi felt encouraged to be open about his identity because *Storie naturali* had had a fairly good reception and had won the Bagutta Prize in January 1967. Until the end of his life he continued to write scientific-moral fables, whose themes reflect those not only of his earlier writings, but also of his later major works.

Levi's stories have usually been called 'science fiction'. Admittedly they follow the classical science fiction model, where the narrative logic of the text is determined by a scientific or technological innovation which deviates from the author's and implied reader's expectations of reality, yet is consistent with existing scientific knowledge.[17] In Levi's texts, however, this cognitive estrangement is produced not by constructs of different universes or encounters with aliens, but rather through visions of the social and human consequences of the innovation. This leads to critical reflections on the damage produced by science and technology when they are divorced from human and moral concerns, in the tradition of Voltaire's *contes philosophiques* or Aldous Huxley's *Brave New World*. In fact, one story explicitly defines itself as 'a last reverent tribute to Lucian of Samosata, Voltaire, Swedenborg, Rostand, E.A. Poe, Flammarion and H.G. Wells' (III: 219). Levi's stories are also profoundly different from Calvino's *Le cosmicomiche* (*Cosmicomics*, 1965) and *Ti con zero* (*T-zero*, 1967), which appeared at about the same time and with which they have occasionally been linked.[18] In Calvino's texts, the characters are symbols of different scientific models and part of a geometric labyrinth of oppositions between order and chaos, stability and change in the history of the universe; the epigraph of each story is a brief summary of current theories of physics and evolution. The epigraphs of the two collections by Levi[19] anticipate the discourses in the stories. The ironical epigraph of *Storie naturali* is a long quotation from Rabelais' *Gargantua*, which in turn contains a reference to a passage in Pliny's *Natural History* describing 'des enfantements estranges et contre nature' (strange and unnatural childbirths). The epigraph of *Vizio di forma* is Levi's own poem 'Erano cento' (They were a hundred), written in 1959, a mysterious, haunting image of a circle of a hundred ghosts of armed men who wordlessly close in around those who order them in vain to disappear.

Levi's youthful view of nature as 'Mother Matter, our mother and our enemy' (I: 462) in these texts is replaced by an emphasis on what, in the story 'Cladonia rapida' (*Storie naturali*),[20] is defined as 'the convergence taking place between the animate and the inanimate world' (III: 54). At times the convergence takes the form of wild cross-fertilisations: flies and flowers produce butterflies, toads and rocks produce turtles, men and mares produce centaurs ('Quaestio de Centauris', *Storie naturali*).[21] At other times the process is twofold and results in opposite estrangement effects: in some stories, animals or inanimate things progressively acquire human traits which modify their interactions with human beings; in others, human beings come in various ways to lose the traits which make them human.[22]

The stories focusing on non-human beings start from notions which, if obviously far-fetched, do not seem altogether inconsistent with the principles of evolution. Hookworms, through the structures of their epithelial cells, articulate poetic reflections on their existence and their relationship with their hosts ('L'amico dell'uomo' (Man's Friend), *Storie naturali*). An international telephone network begins to act as a nerve centre: it helpfully takes the initiative of connecting pairs or groups of users, gives them advice, and just as helpfully switches itself off once it is told that its behaviour is wrong ('A fin di bene' (For a Good Purpose), *Vizio di forma*). Often what is emphasised are negative consequences of the exploitation by humans of the non-human. Chickens, employed to help with a country's growing need for censorship, gradually take over the administration of censorship completely ('Censura in Bitinia' (Censorship in Bithynia), *Storie naturali*).[23] Trees agree to rebel against human beings, to stop purifying their air and producing fruits for them, and learn to uproot themselves and seek freedom away from them ('Ammutinamento' (Mutiny), *Vizio di forma*). Streams and rivers become viscous, and consequently vegetable, animal and human life becomes more sluggish and eventually ceases ('Ottima è l'acqua' (Excellent is Water), *Vizio di forma*).

The stories where there is a clear continuity with *Se questo è un uomo* – which Levi pointed out in 'Damiano Malabailas', justification – are those which emphasise people's loss of human identity, and which define what is 'human' cumulatively and negatively. Effects of cognitive estrangement result from the ironic representation of situations where moral principles are turned on their heads and where, as Levi pointed out, *fair is foul and foul is fair*. The 'human' traits progressively lost by the characters in these stories are creativity, the wish to keep engaging in social experience, and above all the refusal to surrender one's free will either to material enticements or to scientific curiosity divorced from moral considerations. In 'Le nostre belle specificazioni' (Our Fine Specifications, *Vizio di forma*),[24] a young white-collar worker, while revising the specifications for every item used in the factory where he works, comes across 'Specification No. 366 478. Man', which defines this item's maximum and minimum acceptable height and weight and lays down ways to test its resistance to bending, twisting, heat and cold, its memory, its leadership skills and its emotional stability. Any attempts to oppose the specification fail, and the conclusion of the story ironically states that specifications like this thrive in any system 'where due consideration is paid to normalisation, amalgamation, standardisation, and rationalisation of production' (III: 294). Readers familiar with Levi's later works will probably connect this text with the reflections, in the chapter 'La zona grigia' (The Grey Zone) of *I sommersi e i salvati*, that stress the need to understand mass oppression, whether it occurs in death camps or in big factories (I: 677–8).[25]

Two of the *Storie naturali*, 'Versamina' and 'Angelica farfalla' (Angelic Butterfly), are set amidst the ruins of the Third Reich after the end of the Second World War. In 'Versamina', an Austrian camp survivor who is a chemist hears about a colleague who had become addicted to one of his own discoveries, a compound which converted sensations of pain into pleasure. The title of 'Angelica farfalla' is a bitterly ironic recontextualisation of Dante's admonishment to the souls of the proud in the first storey of Purgatory, about the need for imperfect humankind to strive to become closer to divine perfection:

> *Perceive ye not that we are grubs, each one*
> *Born to produce the angelic butterfly,*
> *Which flies to justice, all its trappings gone?* [26]

The exhortation is followed to the letter by a Nazi scientist, who is based partly on Alfred Rosenberg, the main theoretician of 'racial purity' in Hitler's regime, and partly on Dr Josef Mengele, the SS physician at Auschwitz who experimented on Jewish prisoners. He carries it to a distorted end: convinced that angels are the next evolutionary stage of human beings, he uses Jews as raw material in experiments to accelerate the evolutionary process and transforms them into vulture-like birds which are devoured by starving Berliners in the last days of the war. The full horror of this is discovered gradually in a step-by-step process of detection by Allied officers, whose leader ambiguously comments that 'Leeb, in his way, was a serious scientist: he sought facts, not success' (III: 44).

In a paper he gave at a conference on Jewish literature in 1982, Levi stated that some of his stories 'are linked (perhaps unconsciously) to the midrashic tradition of the parable' (Levi 1984e: 385).[27] He was always, in the words of one of the most perceptive Italian students of his work, aware of 'the possibility, which he probably tended to bury below his consciousness, of interpreting [Nazism and racial persecutions] as the consistent and almost necessary expression of technical development and of the totalitarian vocation of the modern world' (Mengaldo 1989: 93). Some of his 'parables' emphasise the moral tension between the view of science as a constant attempt to expand, through trial and error, the limits of human knowledge, and the awareness that science is inevitably controlled by political and economic forces and is in turn instrumental in bringing about various forms of social control. In these stories the cognitive estrangement effects are obtained through the use of linguistic *pastiche*: the registers used are skilful and humorous parodies of the languages of literary classics, of bureaucracy, of scientific reports and of industrial management.[28]

'Il sesto giorno' (The Sixth Day, *Storie naturali*) is, literally, a morality play. A supernatural Management Committee – where the economic and the moral viewpoints are expressed by two of the gods of Persian mythology, the god of darkness Ahriman and the god of knowledge Ahura Mazda – debate, using stereotypical committee procedures and language, the feasibility and cost-effectiveness of various projects for the creation of Man. They finally decide that the creature-to-be should be a bird, only to discover that a higher authority has already created the new being out of clay and has formed his female from one of his ribs. Two consecutive stories in *Vizio di forma*, set in an unspecified Third World village called Recuenco, describe how it is periodically supplied with a liquid vegetable food. The first story is told from the overawed point of view of the village people, who pass down the legend of a supernatural Nurse 'who brings both repletion and death' (III: 317). The second story is told from the bored and patronising point of view of the international crew of the space rafter which drops tons of food over starving areas without knowing, or worrying, about the concomitant destruction of people, animals and property.

The social consequences of the application of science for profit are explored particularly in a cycle of six 'natural stories' where Levi represents, in Italian contexts and using informal, colloquial Italian, the degeneration of human-ness brought about by technological innovations, a classical theme of traditional science fiction. The machines in the stories, produced by the American company NATCA and marketed in advanced capitalist societies, appropriate some essential natural and human traits: poetic creativity (the 'Versifier'); the ability to copy objects and living beings (the 'Mimer'); evaluation and ranking of human attractiveness (the 'Calometer'); communication with, and consequent control of, gregarious animals; and the ability to experience reality to the full, being aware of one's own sensations and emotions (the 'Torec', or Total Recorder). This last machine is described in 'Trattamento di quiescenza',[29] possibly the most powerful parable in Levi's two collections. It is an anticipation of the multisensor simulations of 'virtual reality', a helmet which transmits sensations and emotions and allows the wearers to relive, as often as they wish, experiences of all kinds previously undergone and recorded by others. The helmet is fascinating and addictive: Simpson, the NATCA salesman who is featured in all the stories, becomes hopelessly enslaved to it and can only find solace in reading *Ecclesiastes* I, 18: 'For in much wisdom there is much vexation; and he that increaseth knowledge increaseth sorrow'.

'The wisdom of Solomon,' the story's narrator concludes, 'had been acquired in pain, over a long life filled with deeds and sins' (III: 183). The notion that knowledge and progress are inseparable from pain, contradictions and confusion is present in nearly all the stories and constitutes the core of a few openly didactic fables. In 'Procacciatori d'affari' (The Hard Sellers, *Vizio di forma*) an as yet unborn being accepts some salespeople's proposal to be born on Earth, with the only proviso that he not be given any intellectual or material advantages but share the struggles, and the necessary anger, of 'defenceless and blind' humankind. In 'Verso occidente' (Westward, *Vizio di forma*) scientists develop a chemical antidote for the self-destruction of lemmings, and offer it to a native South American tribe which accepts and encourages suicide. The antidote turns out to be inadequate to prevent the mass rush of lemmings to their death, and is politely refused by the South Americans who 'prefer freedom to drugs, and death to illusion' (III: 205).

In an interview when *Vizio di forma* was published, Levi stated firmly that he did not see his stories as expressions of despair, because he saw despair as irrational and leading to nothing but death. 'Some of my stories do end in catastrophes', he said, 'but the catastrophes are, at least in my intention, ironic, and, so to speak, conditional: we are going to end up like this if we do not take steps in time, but we have the means, the intelligence and the strength to take steps'.[30] He was even more forthright in a statement on the cover of *Vizio di forma*: 'We have no choice, we cannot go back to Arcadia. Technology, and technology alone, is what can restore order in our planet, and correct any "structural defect".' This moral emphasis on the need to act in an informed manner and to use existing knowledge to bring about changes – a constant in all Levi's works – was condemned as individualistic and reformist rationalism by most Marxist reviewers of the two collections of stories. In the Communist Party journal *Rinascita*, Mario Spinella said that 'Levi appears to believe in technology although he is aware of its dangers, to trust mankind but as a gamble, to reject politics without however replacing it with another way of salvation'.[31] An anonymous reviewer in *Quaderni piacentini* – one of the forums for Marxist intellectuals in the 1960s – dismissed *Storie naturali* as 'awful and utterly meaningless . . . without any original ideas', unlike Levi's 'very good' first two books.[32] This drew an impassioned response from the sharply irreverent literary critic Cesare Cases, who pointed out that some of the stories, where natural relations are turned upside down by capitalist science and technology, are 'a softly-spoken but firm recantation of Levi's own dichotomy between the two spheres of *foul* and *fair*, which was the basis of his first book'.[33]

The connections of these stories with Auschwitz, either as continuity or as rethinking, have been pointed out in nearly every discussion of Levi's fiction.[34] There are also, however, other underlying discourses implicitly connected with Jewish identity. The prevailing tone of most of the stories is, rather than one of bleak pessimism, one of philosophical acceptance of the contradictions of life which, as Levi pointed out in his much-quoted later essay 'Il rito e il riso' (Ritual and Laughter),[35] is also an essential component of Jewish culture and of Jewish humour. Furthermore, a number of stories emphasise – consistently with Jewish tradition and culture – the need to preserve human experience in memory and to learn from memory. In 'Il fabbro di se stesso' (His Own Blacksmith, *Vizio di forma*) – dedicated to Italo Calvino as a tribute to *Le cosmicomiche* – the narrator is a being (coded as male) who has inherited the collective memory of all his ancestors, and who describes his evolution over ten million generations from the aquatic stage to the Neanderthal stage. The estrangement effect here is humorous: the biological adaptation and mutations of living beings over millions of years are described as if they were the result of deliberate choices made by one flexible mind.

Two other stories in *Vizio di forma*, 'Lavoro creativo' (Creative Work) and 'Nel Parco' (In the Park),[36] may have been inspired by Ray Bradbury's dystopia, *Fahrenheit 451*. In Bradbury's novel the classic texts of world literature, philosophy and history, burned by a totalitarian regime, are preserved through being memorised by individual people and passed on from one person to the next. Levi's stories describe a 'National Park' where all the 'vital' characters of literary works continue to live as long as the texts in which they are contained are read and remembered in the 'real world'. The stories are at the same time a tribute to the literary texts which were most meaningful to Levi himself (a notion that he developed ten years later in *La ricerca delle radici*), an amusing speculation on the possible destiny of well-known characters of classical, European and American literature from Ulysses to Alexander Portnoy, and a statement on the role of literature as collective memory and as representation of human experience.

'The sociology of the Park is peculiar', one of the characters explains to a newcomer. 'I don't think you'll find a single baker or accountant; as far as I know, there is only one dairyman, only one naval engineer and only one silk spinner. You'll search in vain for a plumber, an electrician, a welder, a repairman, a chemist, and I really wonder why. Instead, beside doctors . . . you'll find loads of explorers, lovers, cops and robbers, musicians, painters and poets, countesses, prostitutes, warriors, knights, foundlings, murderers and royalty' (III: 300–1). This expression, however lighthearted, of dissatisfaction with literature's partial representation of reality, and particularly of human work, is fully consistent with Levi's conviction that literature has a prevailingly communicative and referential function, as he argues in his much-quoted and much-debated 1976 essay 'Dello scrivere oscuro' (On Obscure Writing).[37] He repeats these comments almost to the letter in 'Argento' (Silver) in *Il sistema periodico*, where the context is his intention to fill one of the gaps by writing a series of stories about experiences connected with chemistry:

> I said . . . that I was looking for events, mine and other people's, which I wanted to set out in a book, to see whether I could convey to laymen the strong and bitter taste of our trade, which after all is a particular instance, a more strenuous version, of the business of living. I said . . . that I did not believe it was fair for the world to know everything about the life of doctors, prostitutes, sailors, murderers, countesses, ancient Romans, conspirators and Polynesians, and nothing about the life of people like us, transformers of matter (I: 620).

To this end, after the publication of *Vizio di forma* he started revising stories he had written in his youth or published in periodicals between 1947 and 1972, to integrate them into a collection which was to be at the same time a partial autobiography and a representation of the life of people who come into direct contact with chemical transformations of matter. He was then still working for SIVA and publishing stories, poems and short essays in periodicals, mainly the *terza pagina*[38] of the

Turin daily paper *La Stampa*, which, although owned by FIAT, was open to contributions by intellectuals of various political allegiances. During those years he also was involved with radio (in 1965) and television (in 1976–8) adaptations of some of his science fiction stories: 'La bella addormentata nel frigo' (Sleeping Beauty in the Fridge, *Storie naturali*), 'Il versificatore', 'Il sesto giorno', and 'Procacciatori d'affari'.

Levi submitted two drafts of this new project to Calvino, who made suggestions about structure and contents.[39] *Il sistema periodico* (*The Periodic Table*) – twenty-one stories, each named after one of the elements of the table drawn up by the Russian chemist Mendeleev in 1869 – appeared in the spring of 1975. It was a turning point in the reception of Levi's works, definitely establishing him, in Italy first and internationally some years later, not only as more than a Holocaust writer but as one of the most important twentieth-century Italian writers. It is a synthesis of the main themes of Levi's writing, and one of the most fascinating texts of post-Second World War Italian and European literature. The discourses of science, history and Jewishness are interconnected and constructed both as never-ending change, which is the nature of life, and as means for questioning and expanding existing knowledge, which is the meaning of human existence.

Mendeleev's table – where the 105 elements are ordered according to their atomic weight and electron configuration – is not used as a structural framework for Levi's text: only twenty-one elements are chosen, and their selection and sequence have no identifiable pattern.[40] This is reflected in the heterogeneous nature of the collection, which includes some entirely fictional pieces (a few vignettes and two stories set in previous centuries) as well as autobiographical narrations which are set, with the exception of the initial and final stories, between 1935 and 1967. The unifying factor is the cognitive effort: every story focuses on what certain individuals learn from the contact with a chemical transformation of matter, with every element represented as a source of knowledge. Chemistry ('lonely chemistry, unarmed and on foot, with a human face', as opposed to 'chemistry on a grand scale, the triumphant chemistry of huge plants and dizzying turnovers', I: 620) is an overall metaphor for life, with its structural defects and failures, which eludes easy global explanations but nevertheless demands a constant search for understanding. The Italian title explicitly posits chemistry as a cognitive model which is predictable (*periodico*) and interconnected (*sistema*),[41] while the epigraph – the Yiddish proverb *Ibergekumene tsores iz gut tsu dertseyln*, (troubles overcome are good to tell) – sums up the way the partial discourses of science, Jewishness and history illuminate one another and are connected both in Levi's autobiographical persona[42] and through the process of narration.

The opening of the book introduces these discourses and alerts the readers to the way they are interwoven. The first paragraph is a factual description of the properties of the gases known as 'noble', 'inert' and 'rare', which however contains a humorous anthropomorphic characterisation: they are represented as 'so inert, so satisfied with their state, that . . . they do not combine with any other element, and for this very reason have gone unnoticed through the centuries' (I: 429). The discourse then shifts, introducing the author's autobiographical persona and establishing a metaphoric relation between science, history, memory and autobiography: 'The little I know about my ancestors relates them to these gases. . . . Noble, inert, and rare: their history is quite modest compared to that of other, famous Jewish communities in Italy and Europe' (I: 429–30).

The first lines of the final story address the reader explicitly, describing the text first in negative terms ('The reader, at this point, will have realised for some time that this is not a treatise on chemistry . . . Nor is it an autobiography, save in the partial and symbolic limits in which every piece of writing, in fact every human work is an autobiography.') and then in positive, but still partial, terms focusing on work: 'a micro-history, the history of a trade and its defeats, victories and woes' (I: 641).

This clearly-stated perspective casts light on Levi's process of autobiographical construction. The process is fully consistent with Levi's view of literature in general, and of his own writings in particular, as having first and foremost a communicative function. The main experiences Levi wants to convey are his deportation and his profession, and the lessons learned from both. He assumes that his readers have some prior knowledge of both, and of at least his first book through references to *Se questo è un uomo* in 'Cerio' (Cerium), 'Cromo' (Chromium), 'Azoto' (Nitrogen), 'Uranio' (Uranium) and 'Vanadio' (Vanadium). The consistent focus of Levi's self-representation is the narrated self as an Italian Jew, as a survivor of Auschwitz and as a chemist: the private self is excluded or marginalised. As in subsequent autobiographical recollections, the feelings and emotions – insecurities, enthusiasms, fears and love – of Levi's persona are revealed only as far as his marriage and the beginnings of his career; from then on his personal and family relationships are kept strictly out of the narrating self's discourse. His wife is never identified by name, and his relatives and friends are identified with fictional names or first names only. The sole emotions to be disclosed, besides the recurring ones of the Auschwitz survivor, are those connected with the discourses of the chemist and the writer.[43]

The elements of Mendeleev's table mediate between the discourses and have different functions within the oppositions inscribed into the text, namely those between matter and spirit, reality and language, fact and fiction, and order and chaos.[44] In some stories they are metaphorically linked, through their properties or traditional associations, to the characters or themes. Levi's ancestors are as 'noble, inert, and rare' as argon, 'the Inactive'; Levi's autobiographical persona is 'the impurity which makes the zinc react' in 1938; the destiny of his generation is as dark and hard as iron.[45] In 'Mercurio' (Mercury) – the first of two fables 'of islands and freedom' which Levi wrote before joining the Resistance, and which are visually differentiated, being printed in italics – the mobility and restlessness of the mercury found on a remote island in the Atlantic by a small motley group of nineteenth-century outcasts symbolises their freedom from social conventions, and its mirroring property symbolises their being able to look at themselves and to choose to act in the way most congenial to each. 'Oro' (Gold) describes a fleeting encounter between the narrated self – recently captured and 'waiting fairly bravely for death' (pp. 555–6) – and a smuggler who is soon to be freed. The precious metal which, according to the smuggler, can be found in secret bends of the river Dora becomes a symbol of the freedom and new experiences which the narrated self believes he is about to lose forever. 'Cromo', set in 1946, implicitly connects the tormented and guilty state of mind of the narrated self, just returned from Auschwitz,[46] with some misshapen cubes of solidified paint, and his process of healing and return to a fully human condition through working, writing and meeting the woman he later married with his own successful attempt to reverse the solidification and return the blocks of paint to a liquid, usable state.

In other stories, the chemical elements are a concrete part of the experiences of Levi's persona or of other characters. Elements and compounds are often characterised anthropomorphically, in order to be made more accessible to the readers, and to be personified as friends or opponents. 'Zinc . . . is a boring metal. It has been known to humanity for two or three centuries, therefore it is not a veteran covered with glory like copper, nor one of those freshly-discovered little elements which are still enveloped in the excitement of their discovery' ('Zinco', I: 458). 'Some metals are friends and others are foes' ('Stagno' (Tin), I: 601). 'Hydrochloric acid . . . is one of those honest enemies who come at you shouting from a distance' ('Stagno', I: 603). In these stories, what is emphasised is the ethical dimension of Levi's view of knowledge. Being open to learning – from other people or from one's own mistakes, from interactions with matter and from personal and cultural differences – is constantly presented as the purpose of human life: 'That is why we are here, to make mistakes and correct them' (I: 498). Consequently, explaining to others the lessons learned is represented as a moral responsibility. In 'Potassio' (Potassium) the narrated self, as a student, sets fire to a laboratory by using potassium instead of sodium, and learns the hard way that

> one must distrust what is almost-the-same . . . what is practically identical, what is approximate, what could do, all surrogates and all patchwork. The differences can be small, but they can lead to radically different consequences, like railroad switch points; the chemist's trade consists largely of being on the alert for these differences, knowing them intimately, and foreseeing their effects. And not just the chemist's trade (I: 484).

In 'Nichel' (Nickel) the narrated self, facing the problems of his first, semi-legal job,[47] reflects on the practical relevance of what he has learned from textbooks and in laboratories: 'To make a mistake was no longer a vaguely comic accident, something that could spoil an examination or lower a grade: to make a mistake was like going on a rock climb, testing oneself, a realisation, a step up, something that makes you more capable and competent' (I: 495). The verbs *misurarsi* and *provarsi*, to test oneself, a notion Levi had probably absorbed from his youthful reading of

Conrad,[48] recur in other stories set in the years before deportation, where learning through trial and error is constructed as an individualistic, Darwinian process: in laboratory practicals, which are compared to hunting in the jungle ('Zinco', I: 456); in mountain climbs, preparing for an iron future ('Ferro', I: 469); and, finally and most poignantly, in forming the first bands of Resistance fighters ('Oro', I: 549).

This Darwinian perspective is consistent with the positivist views of Levi's youthful autobiographical persona. In 'Idrogeno', 'Zinco' and 'Ferro', science is described as a means of conquering 'Mother Matter, our mother and our enemy' (I: 462) and as the only unfailingly objective means of comprehending reality, as opposed to philosophy ('would all the philosophers . . . in the world ever be able to make this gnat? No, nor understand it: this was a disgrace and an abomination', I: 449), literature ('Mendeleev's Periodic Table . . . was poetry, more noble and solemn than all the poems we had swallowed at school', I: 466), and Fascism (see p. 11). Individual struggles against matter are also frequently compared to the adventurous experiences of alchemists. The comparison is couched in negative terms when Levi's young narrated self expects chemistry to provide unfailingly certain answers ('The origins of chemistry were base, or at least shady: the dens of alchemists, their abominable muddle of ideas and language', I: 476). It becomes more positive when the narrating self focuses on the joy of making discoveries. 'Piombo' (Lead), the second fable, is the odyssey of a lead prospector who wanders through the mountains and seas of pre-Christian Europe, encounters different people and customs and exchanges knowledge as well as metals; in 'Oro' the origins of chemistry are represented as '*Scheidekunst*, the art of separating metal from rock' (I: 556).

Darwinian positivism is at the same time reiterated and transcended in 'Cerio' (Cerium), which is set in Auschwitz. Here the *univers concentrationnaire* is explicitly identified as the Darwinian environment *par excellence*, where survival takes priority over abstract moral laws:

> I was a chemist in a chemical plant, in a chemical laboratory . . . and I stole in order to eat. . . . In one moment I had realised . . . that I, the respectable university graduate, was reliving the involution–evolution of a famous respectable dog, a Victorian, Darwinian dog

who is deported, and becomes a thief in order to live in his concentration camp in Klondike, the great Buck of *The Call of the Wild* (I: 559).

At the same time, however, scientific knowledge and its principles and applications are given a joyful moral dimension, emphasised by their contextualisation and gently ironic depiction. Learning by trial and error also applies to what to steal and how to convert it into food:

> I had made . . . various attempts. I had stolen a few hundred grams of fatty acids . . . I had eaten half and it really placated my hunger, but it had such a nasty taste that I gave up the idea of selling the rest. . . . I also tried to ingest and digest glycerin, on the basis of the simplistic reasoning that, since it is a product of the splitting of fats, it must in some way be metabolised and provide calories: and perhaps it did, but at the cost of extremely unpleasant side effects (I: 560).

Learning what to steal, how to steal it, and how to sell it is part of the refusal to give in and thus a way of reaffirming human identity. Once again, as in the Romantic interpretation of Dante's Ulysses and in the episode 'The Canto of Ulysses' in *Se questo è un uomo*, 'virtue' and 'knowledge' are brought together, especially in the representation of the positive discourse of Levi's *alter ego* Alberto:

> Alberto reprimanded me. To him giving up, becoming pessimistic, being despondent, were abominable and wrong: he did not accept the concentration camp universe, he rejected it with his instinct and his reason, he did not let himself be polluted by it. . . . I had stolen the cerium: good, now we needed to find a market for it and launch it (I: 561).

Most of the stories set after the experience of Auschwitz reflect, more or less explicitly, the tension between the positivist view of knowledge and the recognition that knowledge is the necessary but not the sufficient condition to change reality. The positivist perspective is emphasised by the structure of several stories, which coincides with that of the positivist literary genre *par excellence*, the detective story,[49] where an initial sequence of apparently incomprehensible events which disturb order is traced back and explained by human reason, with order being triumphantly restored at the end. This applies particularly to

'Cromo', where the problem of the solidified paints is explicitly defined as 'half chemistry and half police work' (I: 572), to 'Arsenico', where the narrated self discovers that very poison in some sugar given to a shoemaker by a competitor, and to 'Argento', where another chemist traces back, step by step, the chemical source of a serious problem for his firm. The villain of the pieces is always Matter:

> mindless matter reveals a cunning, intent upon evil and obstruction, as if it were rebelling against order which is dear to man; just like those reckless outcasts, craving their enemies' ruin more than their own triumph, who in novels travel from the ends of the earth to thwart the deeds of positive heroes (I: 626–7).

Levi's mature narrated self is aware that some mysteries will remain unsolved, because scientific attempts to classify and categorise matter at times fail against the unpredictability of its changes, especially when human factors are involved. He is also aware that scientific knowledge and applications are inseparable from social relations, and that his own knowledge must satisfy the economic requirements of industrial capitalism. These tensions are represented with constant irony,[50] an irony which recalls other tensions mentioned in 'Argon' which are the basis of Jewish humour: between classical Hebrew and Piedmontese dialect, between the divine calling of Diaspora Jews and the daily misery of their exile, and between spirit and flesh. 'Azoto' describes the narrated self's failed attempt to synthesise a lipstick ingredient from a nitrogen compound found mainly in chicken and snake droppings. The discourse shifts from a learned reference to the origins of chemistry ('the idea of producing a cosmetic from excrement, that is to say *aurum de stercore*, gold from dung, amused me and warmed my heart like a return to our origins, when alchemists extracted phosphorus from urine', I: 598) to a down to earth account of the tasks involved:

> I returned home in the evening, I explained to my very recent wife all about alloxan and uric acid, and announced that on the following day I would leave for a business trip: that is to say, I would get on my bicycle, and go round the farmhouses at the outskirts of Turin (there were still some at that time) in search of chicken manure (I: 588–9).

In 'Stagno', the narrated self and his partner 'Emilio' attempt to make a living transforming tin into stannous chloride by making it react with hydrochloric acid. The irony results from the description of the transformation of matter being juxtaposed with the minimal profits, with the limited resources of the partners' home laboratory ('In the periods when we had many orders, we had to resort to reserve receptacles . . . a soup tureen, an enamelled iron pressure cooker, an Art Nouveau chandelier, and a chamber pot', I: 605), and with the incongruous consequences of the chemical processes ('Acid fumes invaded every room: the wallpaper changed colour, doorknobs and metal fittings became opaque and rough, and every now and then a sinister thump startled us: a nail had corroded, and in some corner of the flat a picture had crashed to the floor', I: 605).

'Argento' is a tale the narrated self hears from a former fellow student at a twenty-fifth anniversary class reunion. The silver of the title is both a material part of the chemical mystery to be solved (the desensitisation of X-ray paper) and a metaphor for the lessons these chemists have learned by the time of their 'silver wedding' with their trade. The discourse of the narrated self is positivistically optimistic: 'we thrash about in the dark for a week or a month, think that it is going to be dark forever, and feel like throwing it all away and changing trade; then we catch a glimmer of light in the darkness, stumble towards it, and the light grows, and finally order follows chaos.' The discourse of the other chemist is diametrically opposite: 'sometimes things did go like that . . . but in general it was really dark all the time, no glimmer of light was to be seen, you kept hitting your head against a roof growing lower and lower, and ended up crawling backwards on all fours out of the cave, a little older than when you went in' (I: 620). The two discourses are allowed to coexist, with the implicit conclusion that, although chaos is only occasionally replaced by order, the only way ahead for chemists – and all human beings – lies in constantly trying to make some sense of it:

> You feel . . . as if you were losing all the battles, one after the other, year after year; and you must be satisfied, to salve your bruised pride, with the few occasions when you glimpse a break in the enemy line, rush into it, and manage just once to hit a target with one swift blow (I: 619).

The recurring battle metaphors are one of the obvious indicators of Levi's gendered model of knowledge. Levi's autobiographical construct is not explicitly gendered: the narrated self's male identity is not, like his identities as a Jew and a scientist, represented as a limited perspective on history and society and thus a partial source of knowledge. Instead, throughout *Il sistema periodico* he explicitly identifies intellectual engagement and learning by trial and error as essentially masculine experiences, from which women are excluded. Levi's discourse assigns women exclusively to the domestic sphere. In 'Idrogeno', young male students' lack of manual skills is contrasted with a list of the typical domestic accomplishments of middle-class women at the turn of the century: 'Our mothers and grandmothers had lively, nimble hands, they could sew and cook, some could also play the piano, paint with water-colours, embroider, braid their hair.' The manual skills men lack, and hope to acquire by becoming chemists, are instead associated with potential acquisition of knowledge: 'Our own hands . . . were unfamiliar with the solemn, balanced weight of hammers, the concentrated power of blades too cautiously forbidden to us, the wise texture of wood, the similar yet different pliability of iron, lead and copper. If man is a craftsman, we were not men' (I: 449–50). Women are assessed in strictly utilitarian terms by both the adventurous pre-Christian prospector in 'Piombo' and the pragmatic soldier-colonist in 'Mercurio': 'We need women to bear us a son, so that our breed may not die out, but we don't take them along. What use would they be? They don't learn how to find the rock' (I: 504). Although in several stories women are shown working in chemical laboratories as students or industrial employees, they are never represented as viewing chemistry as an intellectual adventure and a source of growth. For them, their work as chemists is at best a chance to earn a decent living ('Zinco'), at worst a time-filler before marriage ('Nichel'), and never a source of stories worth telling. The discourse of Levi's mature narrated self summarily wipes women out of the picture of chemical experiences acquired twenty-five years after graduation: 'Eliminate all women first of all: all wives and mothers, all out of active service, none any longer having any "events" to tell' (I: 617).

The last two stories are a dramatic synthesis of the themes of the book. 'Vanadio' (Vanadium) is structured as a double detective story. The narrated self, while trying to ascertain whether his German suppliers are responsible for a faulty shipment of paint, comes across a German chemist who had supervised his own slave labour in Auschwitz,[51] and exchanges a number of letters with him. The way both men articulate their memories of the past is an anticipation of Levi's later reflections in *I sommersi e i salvati*. Müller, the German, attributes Auschwitz to humankind without differentiating between oppressors and oppressed, and hopes to meet Levi face to face so that both may 'overcome [their] terrible past'. Levi's persona is represented as caught in a tangle of contradictory emotions and desires. He longs to confront a representative of his former slave masters ('The encounter I looked forward to so intensely as to dream of it (in German) at night was an encounter with one of them from there', I: 632), and systematically lists the questions he needs to ask Müller, while acknowledging that he is not 'the perfect antagonist'. At the same time he implicitly admits his own survivor's shame, which makes him afraid of a face-to-face meeting ('Fear was the word . . . I did not feel able to represent the dead of Auschwitz', I: 635), and explicitly acknowledges that he can neither forgive nor condemn the other man, who is a typical example of 'the grey zone' of the 'honest and defenceless' Germans who kept their eyes and mouths firmly closed.

Levi's discourses as a chemist, a Jew, and a writer are brought together skilfully. The opening of the story, 'Paint is an unstable substance by definition', symbolically foreshadows the unstable relationship between the two men. Their communication, while it provides the means – the addition of a vanadium compound to some resins – to solve their employers' chemical problem, shows that when it comes to their memories they have no common language. Müller's response to *Se questo è un uomo* is laden with unwittingly ironic Christian clichés ('He perceived in my book a transcending of Judaism, a fulfilling of the Christian precept to love one's enemies', I: 638). Levi incorporates several German expressions into the text to emphasise the otherness of Müller's culture, and glosses each carefully in an attempt to explain the nature of that culture to himself and his readers:

> In his first letter [Müller] had talked of 'overcoming the past', *'Bewältigung der Vergangenheit'*: I later found out that this is a cliché, a euphemism of contemporary German, where it is universally

understood as 'redemption from Nazism'. However, the root *'walt '* contained in it also occurs in words meaning 'domination', 'violence' and 'rape', and I believe that if the phrase were to be translated as 'distortion of the past' or 'violence done to the past' one would not stray very far from its deep meaning (I: 639).

Unlike the chemical mystery, the human mystery does not result in any further knowledge. All communication, and the story, abruptly comes to an end with the unexpected, and unexplained, death of the German.[52]

The final story, 'Carbonio' (Carbon), is a synthesis between a view of all life as a constant transformation of matter, the autobiographical thread, and the text's reflection on itself. Matter is no longer an opponent or a source of lessons: it becomes the protagonist. The evolutionary journey of an atom of carbon, 'the element of life' (I: 642), is traced through the centuries and through a variety of forms, arbitrarily chosen among its myriad transformations by the authority of the narrating voice.

The journey briefly takes on metaphoric significance: released from a limestone oven, the atom goes 'out through the chimney' (I: 643). It also acquires a philosophical significance: as carbon dioxide, the atom is an ever-renewed impurity of air, from which all life and all history derive, as the young narrated self had discovered when working with zinc in his university laboratory. The older self, however, also knows that the opposition between 'matter' and 'spirit' is illusory, as is the opposition between 'order' and 'chaos'. Life is temporary order which, in a constant dialectical movement, is replaced by chaos which is again replaced by temporary order.

Before attempting his final description of the atom's metamorphoses, Levi inserts a caveat, his discourse expressing its awareness of its own limitations: 'I will tell [the last story] with the humility and the restraint of someone who knows from the start that his theme is impossible, his means weak, and the trade of clothing facts with words bound by its very nature to fail' (I: 649). This recalls the solemn conclusion of 'Ferro', where Levi first states that 'it is an impossible task to clothe a man with words' and then acknowledges that now that Sandro Delmastro's life is over, 'nothing is left of him, nothing but just that, words' (I: 473). Language is recognised as inadequate, but it is all that is available to human beings to produce and convey meanings, and to entrust them to memory through writing. Thus the narrating self represents the atom as it enters his own brain, gives his hand an impulse, and leads it to impress the final full stop of the book on paper: 'this full stop, here, this one' (I: 649).

This ending recalls that of Calvino's novel *Il barone rampante* (*Baron in the Trees*), where the narrator comes to coincide with the author as the discourse identifies the only possible harmony with the act of fiction and the graphic image of words:

> this thread of ink, as I let it run over pages and pages . . . and it runs and runs and unravels itself and wraps itself around a final meaningless bunch of words ideas dreams and is over (Calvino 1957: 247).

In Levi's discourse, however, the coincidence between narrating self, narrated self, transformation of matter and the act of writing expresses the tension between the need for narrative closure and the awareness that autobiographical writing is always incomplete.

Il sistema periodico was received enthusiastically. Reviewers defined it as one of the best modern Italian examples of integration between science and literature (see Petrucciani 1978: 91 and Poli and Calcagno 1992: 56–73). They also praised the wit and clarity of Levi's literary style – some in fact compared it favourably to the linguistic experimentations of the avant-garde – and recognised him as one of the most important contemporary writers, without qualifying this in any way (see Cannon 1992: 33). In September a panel of writers and literati awarded the book the Prato Prize.

By then Levi had decided that he wanted to devote all his time to writing. As he repeatedly stated in interviews and essays, he had always believed that working as a chemist had never been incompatible with writing, and in fact had trained him to write.[53] However, as he explained in an interview conducted in English with Philip Roth almost ten years after retiring,

> factory life, and particularly factory managing, involves many other matters, far from chemistry: hiring and firing workers; quarrelling with the boss, customers and suppliers; coping with accidents; being called to the telephone, even at night or when at a party; dealing with bureaucracy; and many more soul-destroying tasks. This whole trade is brutally incompatible with writing (Roth 1986: 41).

Therefore, at approximately the same time as *Il sistema periodico* appeared, Levi retired as general manager of SIVA, although he continued to work for them as an occasional consultant until 1977.

The early period of his retirement was filled not only with working on *La chiave a stella* (*The Wrench*), but with involvement in a variety of social and political issues. He became a more regular contributor, on a contract basis from the end of 1975, to *La Stampa*. He was active on the council of the Liceo D'Azeglio, where his son was a student, and agreed to become its president. He continued his visits to schools throughout Northern Italy, to comment on his first two books and to discuss the social and political lessons of the death camps with the young.

By the end of 1975, reflecting on his meetings with the younger generation over twenty years, he realised that certain specific questions on the Holocaust kept recurring and decided that these needed to be answered in a fuller, readily accessible form. In early 1976 a list of these questions, with Levi's own detailed, straightforward answers, was published in *La Stampa* (Levi 1976a) and then as an afterword to the Einaudi school edition, in a single volume, of *Se questo è un uomo* and *La tregua*. This afterword was subsequently included in the reprinted translations of those books in many languages.

It contains additional reflections on history which Levi developed fully ten years later, in *I sommersi e i salvati*. He states that he always refused to cultivate feelings of hatred, even when faced with the resurgence of Fascism in new, respectable guises. He explains that he 'deliberately adopted the calm, sober language of the witness rather than the plaintive one of the victim or the angry one of the avenger, in order to prepare the ground for the judges', his readers (I: 187). He acknowledges that the German people had very limited knowledge of what was actually occurring in the concentration camps, but says that 'most Germans did not know because they did not want to know, in fact because they wanted not to know', and concludes that section with a clearly and strongly-worded historical judgement:

> To know, and to let others know, was a way . . . of distancing oneself from Nazism. I think that the German people, as a whole, did not choose this way, and of this deliberate omission I believe that they are entirely guilty (I: 191).

He lucidly explains that the differences between the camps established by the Germans and those established by the Russians lay in their aims: '[In the Soviet camps] the death of the prisoners was not expressly sought: it was a very frequent accident, it was tolerated with brutal indifference, but basically it was not planned. In short, it was a byproduct' (I: 198). He endeavours to provide explanations for anti-Semitism, but admits that none seems adequate to account for the magnitude and irrationality of the phenomenon in Nazi Germany. He hesitantly states that 'maybe what happened cannot be comprehended, in fact *must not* be comprehended, because comprehending is almost justifying . . . "comprehending" a human purpose or behaviour means (also etymologically) taking its author in, putting oneself in his place, identifying with him' (I: 208). Yet immediately afterwards he emphasises the imperative need to keep striving to acquire further knowledge about history, because knowledge is the necessary, although not sufficient, condition for human survival. This tension is one of the constant themes of Levi's writings, and not only of those on the Holocaust:

> If to understand is impossible, to know is necessary, because what happened may recur, consciences may once more be seduced and blurred. Ours as well. . . . It is better to renounce revealed truths, even if they excite us with their simplicity and their brilliance . . .. It is better to be content with other, more modest and less exciting, truths, those which are gained by hard work, little by little and with no short cuts, through study, discussion and reasoning, and which can be verified and demonstrated (I: 209–10).

Additional reflections on the death camps, which Levi later incorporated almost verbatim into *I sommersi e i salvati*, can be found in the foreword Levi wrote in 1976 to his translation of a novella by the Dutch writer Jacob Presser, *De nacht der Girondijnen* (*The Night of the Girondists*), an account of the deportation to Auschwitz of the Dutch Jews from the transit camp at Westerbork.[54] Here for the first time he also stated his view of Western European Jewry: 'conditioned by dispersion . . . [and] so interwoven with the culture of the host countries as not to have a language of its own . . . it nevertheless preserved, through all the metamorphoses due to history and geography, some features which characterise it' (1976b: 11–12).

The years 1975–8 were a time of confusion and disaffection in Italian social and political life, as a consequence of the crisis of oppositional politics which led to a spiral of violence and state repression.[55] Against the background of a world-wide crisis of the capitalist economy, the Left was divided between the Communist Party policy of a 'historic compromise' with the other progressive forces within Italian society (including the left wing of the Christian Democrats) and a new mass youth movement, disaffected with traditional politics and torn between attempting to create an alternative culture and waging an armed struggle against the state.

One of the ideological bases of the youth movement was the 'rejection of work', the belief that all work, particularly factory work, was oppressive and alienating, and the consequent refusal to consider it as one of the bases of human identity (see Lumley 1990: 300–1). This conflicted strongly with the work ethic upheld by the trade union leadership, which – informed by the theories of Antonio Gramsci – considered the training and skills of the *operaio professionale*[56] a source of dignity, and work not as alienating but as something to be reclaimed on the workers' own terms. In Turin, where Gramsci's ideological legacy was still particularly strong, the disaffection with dehumanising assembly line work coexisted with a working-class culture which saw industrial work as a craft with individual responsibilities and thus a source of individual pride in *lavoro ben fatto*, work done well.[57]

This ideological crisis inevitably also affected literary production, especially novels, which in the 1970s were widely seen as consumption goods. Many writers chose to articulate their increasingly pessimistic view of politics through metaphorical texts, such as Calvino's self-referential narratives *Le città invisibili* (*Invisible Cities*, 1972), *Il castello dei destini incrociati* (*The Castle of Crossed Destinies*, 1973) and *Se una notte d'inverno un viaggiatore* (*If on a Winter's Night a Traveller*, 1979), and Leonardo Sciascia's satirical political parables *Il contesto* (*The Context*, 1971), *Todo modo* (*One Way or Another*, 1974) and *Candido* (1977).[58] A few writers chose instead to give voice to their commitment to radical political change through surreal, symbolic texts. The most famous are probably *Vogliamo tutto* (*We Want Everything*, 1971), by the avant-garde writer Nanni Balestrini, which moves from the first-person narration of the growing frustration of a

Southern-born FIAT worker to the collective voice of political leaflets and speeches, and *Le ferie di un operaio* (*A Worker's Holidays*, 1974), angrily distorted sketches of factory life by the engineering worker Vincenzo Guerrazzi. In both, work is represented as violence and enslavement, as the total negation of freedom and dignity.

Levi's *La chiave a stella*[59], published in early 1978, is the product of a writer who had extensive first-hand knowledge of industrial work, had spent his entire working life – apart from his period of deportation – in Turin and was deeply rooted in its culture. He was acquainted with the notion of the rejection of work – both his children were involved in movements to the left of the Communist Party – but condemned it outright as 'senseless and masochistic'. He argued, from a reformist perspective close to that of the traditional union leadership, that 'many energies spent in empty protest could be channelled towards the aim of eliminating repetitive and alienating work'.[60] While acknowledging the 'sad and obvious' truth that not all work is pleasant, he also argued that work in the 1970s was less degrading than it had ever been and could be a source of responsibility and occasional happiness.[61] The title he chose for his book is part of this perspective. Spanners and wrenches, widely used in the 1970s as tools to smash factory machinery or as weapons against the police, had become in the discourses of the 'extra-parliamentary' left a symbol for the workers' struggles against the capitalist system. In Levi's discourse, the wrench acquires the epic connotations of a weapon in the workers' struggle for professional achievement and knowledge: 'the skilled worker . . . with his wrench hanging from his belt, because, for us, it's what a sword was for knights in olden times' (III: 74).[62]

La chiave a stella is, however, far more than a simple response to a political view with which Levi disagreed. It is another instance of his constant wish to build bridges of knowledge. Just as *Il sistema periodico* conveys aspects and meanings of the work of a chemist to non-chemists, *La chiave a stella* aims to convey aspects and meanings of technical work to readers unfamiliar with skilled manual labour. Levi's initial motivation had been in fact to bridge the gap between intellectuals and manual workers:

In our culture there's always been a gap between intellectuals and technicians; between those who work with their minds and those who work with their hands. I try to put a plank across this gap. Novels deal with complex existential themes, books are often full of violence and sex. But how great a part do violence, sex, and existential crises play in everyone's life? Eight hours' work a day takes up much more space. I am writing about the problems of these eight hours.[63]

La chiave a stella in many ways stands apart from the rest of Levi's work. It is his first major piece of fiction where the autobiographical component is understated and Auschwitz no more than an occasional faint shadow. Addressing the Turin Jewish community in an interview for its newspaper *Ha Keillah*, he explained that it would be 'a very serious limitation' for him to write exclusively about the concentration camps, and that he was entitled, 'for [his] own benefit and possibly for that of others', to draw on his profession: 'the main focus of [his] life, as it is for everyone in general'.[64] It is the most joyful and the most positive of his books, and the one he wrote most lightheartedly. Significantly, the epigraph is the line from Act I of *King Lear*, where Gloucester, talking about his illegitimate son Edmund, admits that 'though this knave came somewhat saucily into the world . . . there was good sport at his making'. Clearly suggesting a parallel, Levi at the same time warns his readers of the anomalous nature of his latest brainchild and informs them of his own delight in representing his 'other' experiences.

The book consists of fourteen stories, eleven of which are told by the same narrator, a highly skilled industrial master rigger called Tino Faussone. Tino is short for Libertino: a compromise between the wish of his father to call him Libero (free) and the objections of the Fascist bureaucracy. Throughout the text, the notion of 'freedom' occurs in the context of work: 'possibly the most accessible kind of freedom, the most enjoyed subjectively, and the most useful to human society coincides with being good at one's job, and thus enjoying doing it' (II: 146). Throughout Levi's discourse the word *libertinaggio* is used with the meaning 'seeking adventure', and has connotations of intellectual rather than sexual poaching.[65] The surname Faussone, albeit a typical Piedmontese one, recalls the Piedmontese word *faus*, false, *fictum*, and identifies Faussone as Levi's fictional alter ego.[66] As Levi himself readily admitted, the character is a compound of many skilled workers he had known at SIVA, and some FIAT fitters he had met in Togliattigrad, where they worked as instructors and troubleshooters.[67] Without ever being referred to by name, Togliattigrad is in fact the setting of the book. It is represented as a timeless place, in the middle of huge unspoiled landscapes, almost unaffected by the eccentricities of the Soviet bureaucracy. Its people are depicted with the same amused affection as in *La tregua*: they are at the same time disorganised, warm-hearted, rough, subjected to mysterious central powers and resourcefully creative.

Tino Faussone is the sum of Levi's experiences of work and workers, as well as the result of the influence of a number of literary texts from different cultures. At the end of the book, Levi quotes – without comment in the Italian edition, with a few explanatory lines in the English version – Joseph Conrad's statement in the preface to *Typhoon* that Captain MacWhirr is 'the product of twenty years of [Conrad's] own life', and that, although he is fictional, he is 'perfectly authentic'. Like MacWhirr, Faussone is imaginary yet 'authentic'; like Conrad's hero, Levi's is unimaginative, pragmatic and willing to test his competence and courage in difficult feats.

Another literary source, acknowledged in *La ricerca delle radici*, is the novel *Remorques* (*In Tow*), written by Roger Vercel in 1935, whose protagonist is the captain of a tugboat which rescues ships in danger along the French coastline. Consistent with his interest in the professional rather than the personal sphere, Levi was impressed not by the romantic elements of the novel (the captain's marriage and his doomed love affair), but by the representation of the courage and competence of the crew on their missions. In his introduction to two extracts reproduced in his 'anthology', he states that the lesson of *Remorques* is 'that the relationship between man and machine is not necessarily alienating, and can in fact enrich or complement the old relationship between man and nature' (II: 111).

The narrative mode points to a different kind of relationship with other literary texts. As in *Il sistema periodico*, each story is self-sufficient yet contributes to the overall discourse. Unlike the earlier work, however, the stories are not chronologically sequential, and are told by Faussone to an industrial chemist who does not have a name but is an expert on paints, a survivor of Auschwitz and a writer. The fictional listener or 'narratee' is a device used in four other works which Levi collected and acknowledged as his 'roots' in *La ricerca delle radici*. These are the sonnets written in Roman dialect by Giuseppe Gioacchino Belli in the first half of the nineteenth century, Conrad's stories and novels featuring Marlow, the poems 'Desgrazzi de Giovannin Bongee' and 'Olter desgrazzi de Giovannin Bongee' ('Misadventures of Giovannino Bongeri' and 'Further Misadventures of Giovannino Bongeri'), written in Milanese dialect by Carlo Porta at the beginning of the nineteenth century, and the stories about Tevye the Dairyman written in Yiddish at the turn of the century by Sholom Aleichem.[68] In these last two texts the central character, speaking directly to the narratee, introduces his tale, promises that it will be amazing and entertaining and proceeds to tell it. Similarly, nine of the fourteen stories of *La chiave a stella* open as if Faussone and his narratee were in the middle of a conversation, with Faussone's comments and outbursts marked by inverted commas and ellipses:

> . . . because you mustn't believe that certain tricks are played only in our country, and that we're the only ones who are good at cheating and who never get cheated. Besides, I don't know how much you've travelled, but I've travelled a lot, and I've found out that you shouldn't believe that countries are the way they taught us in school. (II: 143).

The influence of Belli, Porta and Sholom Aleichem can be seen in the language as well as the structure of *La chiave a stella*. Belli's narrators – one for each of his two thousand sonnets – are the Roman proletariat, whose experience is expressed in their concrete, forthright dialect. Porta's Giovannino Bongeri, an assistant in a second-hand goods shop, describes his misadventures in a dialect which, in Levi's own words, is 'fluent, native, mimetic'.[69] Tevye the Dairyman, a pious, long-suffering Russian Jew, tells the events of his family and his village in witty, colloquial Yiddish, interspersed with proverbs and Hebrew quotations from the Bible and the Talmud. Like the languages of Giovannino and Tevye, Tino Faussone's language is a metaphor for his culture. It could best be termed *italiano popolare*, the variety of Italian used by people with little formal education.[70] It is the Italian spoken by someone whose first language is Piedmontese dialect and whose reading, after the adventure books by Kipling and Jack London of his adolescence, has consisted almost exclusively of current events magazines and technical manuals. It is a lively blend of technical expressions, vernacular terms, Italian proverbs and clichés, Piedmontese expressions translated into standard Italian, occasional Piedmontese words in their original forms, words from the languages of the countries Faussone visited and a few of Faussone's own lexical creations. Its deliberate colloquial nature is a clear, if understated, political choice. It reveals Levi's awareness that standard Italian, although it is gradually replacing dialects, is not the spoken language of working-class Italians and cannot express the heritage of regional cultures.[71] It is, in Levi's own words, 'a sort of subtle criticism of [himself] and of lofty, elegant, polished writing, which is essentially remote from everyday life'.[72] This language, reflecting as it does specifically Italian working-class culture, is extremely hard to translate; this may partly account for its low-key reception by the public, in spite of positive reviews,[73] in English-speaking countries.

In the texts by Porta and Sholom Aleichem, however, there is no interaction between narrator and narratee. As in Coleridge's *Rime of the Ancient Mariner* – another text which had a lifelong profound influence on Levi – the interlocutors of both Giovannino and Tevye are addressed respectfully, since they belong to a higher social class, but listen passively, without speaking or commenting. The narratee in *La chiave a stella*, on the contrary, is not only an active participant in the conversation, but in fact voices the privileged discourse of the text. He makes a number of comments on Faussone and on the narrative itself:

> 'You never let me tell a thing my own way', and he withdrew into a sulky silence. The reproach seemed (and still seems) totally unfair to me, because I have always let him talk as he wanted and as long as he wanted, and anyway the reader is my witness (II: 98).

He also directly encourages the readers, with the help of another reference to Conrad, to broaden their extra-textual horizons:

> But perhaps the reader . . . is not following me, here and elsewhere, when I talk about mandrels, molecules, ball bearings, and lugs. Well, I'm sorry, but there's nothing I can do about it; there are no synonyms. If, as is likely, in his youth the reader accepted the seafaring novels of the nineteenth century, then he digested bowsprits and fo'c'sles; so he must be resolute, use his imagination,

or consult a dictionary. It may well be of benefit to him, since we live
in a world of molecules and ball bearings (II: 154).

The juxtaposition of 'molecules' and 'ball bearings' indicates
the main feature of the relationship between narrator and
narratee: their exchange of knowledge, experience and culture.
As in *Se questo è un uomo, La tregua* and some stories in *Il sistema
periodico*, a fruitful rapport grows between Levi's autobiographical persona and another man who has different, and
complementary, experiences and attitudes. Levi's alter egos are 'a
sort of psychological splitting of the writer, as a similar,
alternative potential . . . which did not find a way of expressing
itself directly' (Frassica 1991: 1).

Faussone's part in the exchange is to describe tools and
processes of his trade in terms accessible to his listener, and to the
readers. His tales, however, move beyond that role and represent
his work as a relationship with the world. Each new assignment
– assembling pylons in the Alps, cranes in the Middle East,
hanging bridges in India, derricks in the tropics and oil drilling
rigs in Alaska – provides opportunities for contact with different
places, customs and languages. 'Factual' accounts of distant
countries are opposed to the 'romantic' descriptions found in
adventure books. Faussone emphasises above all competence
and incompetence at all levels, and gives humorous thumbnail
sketches of international variations on the theme: an obsessive
Italian head of section, an imaginative Indian civil engineer, a
shady Russian factory inspector.

For Faussone, work is a source of personal growth ('for me a
man who's never failed an inspection is not a man, it's as if he
were still at his first communion', II: 156) and responsibility,
especially when it presents problems ('. . . a trade without screw-
ups is something I can't even imagine. I mean, yes, they do exist,
but they aren't real trades, it's like being cows out to pasture,
who at least give milk, and then get slaughtered anyway', II:
150). In Faussone's discourse, problems at work can in fact be a
source of existential questions on the meaning of life:

> Oh yes, there are days when everything goes wrong . . .. And then
> you even ask yourself questions that don't make any sense, like
> what are we in the world for? And if you think about it, surely you
> can't answer that we're in the world to rig pylons, right? . . . Then
> . . . you begin to think that there's nothing worth doing, and you'd

like to have another job, but at the same time you think that all jobs are the same, and that the world is out of kilter as well (II: 47).

Above all, work is presented as a form of love, both in the initial enthusiasm ('to me, every job I start is like a first love', II: 41) and in its failures ('It was like when you're fond of a girl, and she suddenly dumps you, and you don't know why, and you suffer, because you've lost not only the girl, but your self-confidence', II: 126). This emotional involvement is emphasised – as in *Il sistema periodico* – by recurrent anthropomorphic character-isations of the components and the final results of work:

> It was as if, in that breath of wind, the bridge was waking up as well. Yes, like someone who's heard a noise and wakes up, shakes himself, and gets ready to jump out of bed (II: 123).

> . . . setting up a machine like that, working on it with your hands and your head for days, seeing it grow like this, tall and straight, strong and slim as a tree, and then it does not work, it's depressing. It's like a pregnant woman who gives birth to a crippled or retarded baby, I don't know if you follow me (II: 146).

Levi's autobiographical persona contributes to the exchange by contextualising Faussone's experiences in a wider framework. He often interrupts Faussone's narrations to ask questions which help the other clarify details of his feats, and makes frequent 'frivolous digression[s]' (II: 30) which provide additional historical, etymological and cultural information. Above all, he constantly compares his own work experiences with Faussone's, defining himself as someone who both sews together molecules and sews together stories: 'it may well be that, having spent more than thirty years sewing together long molecules, presumably useful to others, and in the parallel occupation of convincing others that my molecules really were useful to them, I have learned something about how to sew together words and ideas' (II: 149–50). Two of the last three stories are in fact a reversal of the roles of narrator and narratee: Faussone listens and comments as the other man tells of one of his ultimately successful battles against the stubbornness of paints and of industrial administration. As a prelude, however, Levi's persona announces his intention to devote himself exclusively to telling stories: 'My own stories as long as my store lasted, then other people's stories, lifted, stolen, extorted or received as gifts,

Faussone's own for example; or even everybody's and nobody's stories . . . provided they made sense to me, or could give the reader a moment of wonder or laughter' (II: 149).

The entire story 'Tiresia' (Tiresias) is an ironic comparison and evaluation of technical work, chemical work and story-telling. The reference to the mythical man who for seven years had experienced life as a woman is used as a metaphor for the twofold experiences of Levi's persona as a chemist and as a writer. Writing is represented as a process of learning through trials and failures, similar to, if less reliable than, scientific or technological work:

> you may well . . . write messy or useless things . . . and not realise it, or not want to realise it, which is quite possible, because paper is too tolerant a material. . . . In the writer's trade the instruments and the warning signals are rudimentary: there isn't even a reliable equivalent of the T square or the plumbline (II: 48).

The two men end up agreeing that both Faussone's work and the chemist's trade are – as in *Il sistema periodico* – confrontations with matter: 'they teach us to be whole, to think with our whole hands and with our entire body, not to give up when you have a bad day or find a formula you don't understand, because you'll understand as you go; and they teach us to know matter and confront it' (II: 53). All three trades, the fitter's, the chemist's and the writer's, are passionately defined in the conclusion of the story – with the help of a further personification of the fruits of labour – as sources of pride and identity:

> the pleasure of seeing your creature grow, plate upon plate, bolt after bolt, solid, necessary, symmetrical, suited to its purpose, and when it's finished you look at it and think that maybe it will outlive you, and maybe will be useful to someone you don't know and who doesn't know you. Perhaps you'll go back to look at it when you're old; and you find it beautiful, and it doesn't matter very much if you're the only one to think so, and you can say to yourself 'maybe somebody else could not have done it' (II: 53).

In the discourse of the text – explicitly for Faussone, implicitly for Levi's persona – the challenges and creativity of work are constructed as male prerogatives. As in *Il sistema periodico*, women are peripheral mother figures, occasional objects of attraction, or threats to Faussone's self-sufficiency. The few female characters represented as workers are, as in *La tregua*, mainly marginal and sexless. The only exception is the nameless 'bold girl' of the eponymous story ('La ragazza ardita'): a Southern Italian fork-lift driver, an independent, sexually active young woman with whom Faussone is physically and emotionally involved. Although he respects her, he considers her dangerous and unsuitable as a wife: 'Marry her? I can't do that: first because of my job, second because . . . yes, well . . . marrying a girl like that, a fine girl, no two ways about it, but as cunning as a witch, well, know what I mean?' (II: 44).

Men's ambivalence about autonomous women is a theme Levi was to take up again in *Se non ora, quando?*, describing Mendel's conflicting feelings about Line, 'a comrade' but 'not a woman for life'. In the male world of *La chiave a stella*, Faussone's inability to see women as anything but a mysterious 'other' ('all girls are strange, one way or another', II: 133) is, however, implicitly constructed as one of the many limitations of his essentially work-centred identity. He has no personal life; his friends 'last as long as the job: three months, four, six at the most' (II: 28). His rough nature is 'real, ingrained, reinforced by countless duels with an opponent who is hard by definition, the iron of his beams and his bolts' (II: 166).

The only happiness Faussone finds is in his work. In the middle of the central story – a recollection of Faussone's coppersmith father and of his pride in his independent craft – the text suddenly moves away from particular categories of work to a long general authorial statement. In the gnomic present tense of proverbs and scientific statements, work, all work, is represented in terms of individual attitudes to it, as opposed to both the 'cynical' discourse of the ruling class and the 'profoundly stupid' discourse of left-wing fringes:

> loving one's work (which unfortunately is the privilege of a few) is the most concrete approximation to happiness on earth. But this is a truth of which not many are aware. . . .. To praise work, in official ceremonies an insidious rhetoric is resorted to, which is cynically based on the consideration that a commendation or a medal cost much less, and are more profitable, than a pay rise. There is, however, also an opposite rhetoric, which is not cynical but profoundly stupid, which tends to disparage work and depict it as base . . . .. It is sadly true that many kinds of work are not pleasant, but it is harmful to approach work full of preconceived hatred . . . .. We can and we must fight for the fruits of work to remain in the

hands of those who produce them, and for work itself not to be painful, but love or, conversely, hatred for work is an inner, original heritage, which depends greatly on the individual's past, and less than people believe on the productive structures within which work is done (II: 81–2).

Levi's digression is, because of its explicitly didactic nature, the most frequently quoted and discussed passage in the book. Initially most critics tended to overemphasise it and to read the whole text exclusively as an ideological statement against the theories of the rejection of work. This was true both of conservative reviewers (Roberto Vacca expressed the hope that the passage would be 'written not only on walls as it should be, but also in minds and hearts')[74] and of trade unionists and reviewers aligned with the traditional left. Both the writer Corrado Stajano and the trade unionist Luigi Bruschi – although neither explicitly mentioned the bitter irony of *Arbeit macht frei* (work makes free), the slogan above the main entrance to Auschwitz – pointed out that Levi's view of work as individual freedom was consistent with his past experiences as a slave labourer, and stressed that his notion of work as growth contained a commitment to changing both working conditions and the division of profits.[75] Reviewers sympathetic to the ideas of the new workers' and students' movements expressed a number of reservations. They focused mainly on the fact that the individual challenges faced by both Faussone (a highly skilled fitter who is sent all over the world and has a great deal of control over his work) and Levi's persona (a professional chemist and factory manager) were remote from the repetitiveness and alienation of most workers' experience.[76] From this perspective, *La chiave a stella* can be read as an anachronistic text, celebrating the work of the *operaio professionale* rather than that of the *operaio massa*. The text's emphasis on the joy of work, however, can also be interpreted as a highlighting of its human side (personal growth, moments of humour, and contacts and cooperation between workers of many nations); it is significant that many skilled factory workers did identify with it and read it with delight.[77]

More importantly, *La chiave a stella* is also a discourse on the craft of narration, framed by two ironic statements which open and close it. Both are, rather than the privileged discourse of Levi's persona, an outsider's – Faussone's – view. The initial statement represents narration in terms of craft, a shaping of facts akin to the filing and welding of metals:

> Then, if you really want to tell [what happened], you work on it, grind it, hone it, smooth it down, hammer it into shape, and you'll have a story (II: 5).

The final statement recalls the caveat at the end of *Il sistema periodico* and expresses the writer's own awareness of his limitations. It asserts the superiority of technical work to story-telling when it is a matter of learning from experience. Story-telling is consigned to sedentary, reflective late middle age:

> Listen, doing things you can touch with your hands is better: you can make comparisons and see how good you are. You make a mistake, you correct it, and the next time you don't make it again. But you're older than I am, and perhaps you've seen enough things in your life (II: 181).

La chiave a stella was not translated into English until 1986, in the wake of the success of *Il sistema periodico*. Its reviewers, unaware of its complex political and cultural background, did not emphasise the political dimension of Levi's discourse and focused very briefly on the narrative structures.[78] Other reasons for the comparative lack of interest by English-speaking readers may have been the profoundly Italian, in fact Piedmontese, nature of the book, and Levi's name and reputation having by then become inextricably linked with Auschwitz first and foremost, and chemistry second. In Italy the book has recently been analysed not only in the historical and political context of the 1970s, but in the wider contexts of literature dealing with industry and of linguistic experimentation, specifically the attempt to give literary form and dignity to the language spoken by Italian skilled workers.[79]

In July 1979 *La chiave a stella* won the Strega Prize. Levi was delighted by the recognition and stated what many intellectuals and readers believed, that he had been awarded the most prestigious Italian prize not only for his latest book but 'for the sum total of [his] books, which [he] loved equally' (Poli and Calcagno 1992: 165).

With *La chiave a stella* Levi had successfully, in his own favourite phrase, 'tested himself' in conveying the various lessons of his work experiences. Although he sporadically worked on a collection of stories he never completed, which was to have taken up the chemical themes of *Il sistema periodico*, he was never to return to the theme of work in a full-length piece of fiction. Instead, he described his forays into other intellectual fields, explored the constituents of Jewish identity and, never sparing himself in his desire to understand and to communicate, went back to reflecting on the Holocaust.

Notes to Chapter Three

1. Detailed analyses of the political and social changes that took place in Italy in the 1960s can be found in Balestrini and Moroni (1988) chapters 3 and 6, Ginsborg (1990) chapters 7 and 8 and Lumley (1990) chapters 1–3.
2. See Balestrini and Moroni (1988) chapter 6, Tarrow (1989) chapters 6, 7, 9 and 11, Ginsborg (1990) chapter 9 and Lumley (1990) chapters 4–17.
3. See *I sommersi e i salvati* (I: 730–1) and Camon 1987: 46–7.
4. See the interview with Giovanni Pacchioni (1982f).
5. See the interview with Giulio Nascimbeni (1984b).
6. *La Stampa*, 7 June 1967, p. 6. The caption pointed out the Auschwitz number tattooed on Levi's arm.
7. In his interview with Edoardo Fadini (1966) he emphasised that his writing, his reputation as a writer and the new encounters they led to were 'totally separated' from his work and everyday life.
8. For details on the literary trends of the 1960s see Manacorda (1967) and Petronio and Martinelli (1975). See also Calvino's brief, perceptive analysis entitled 'Right and Wrong Political Uses of Literature' (Calvino 1989: 89–100).
9. See Petrucciani (1978: 287–9).
10. 'Philosophy and Literature', first published in *The Times Literary Supplement* of 28 September 1967, and reprinted in Calvino (1989: 45–6).
11. A summary of the Italian critiques of science as an absolute value is found in Ciccotti, Cini, De Maria and Jona-Lasinio (1976).
12. The term is taken from Suvin (1979).
13. Levi's debt to Rabelais has been analysed in depth in Santagostino (1993b).

14. This anthology is discussed in detail in chapter 4.
15. See the letter Calvino wrote to Levi on 22 November 1961, reprinted in Calvino (1991: 382–3).
16. The Italian *storia* corresponds to both 'story' and 'history'. The title of Levi's collection is thus both ironically self-referential and an ironic reference to Pliny's *Natural History*.
17. See Suvin (1979: 66–70).
18. See the reviews by Vittorio Spinazzola, Claudio Marabini, Walter Mauro, and 'C. Qu.'.
19. A selection from *Storie naturali* and *Vizio di forma* was published in English in 1990 under the title *The Sixth Day*. In this book the two original collections are discussed together, because they were written in the same period and are similar in themes and discourses.
20. Not included in *The Sixth Day*.
21. Levi returned to the theme of evolution through cross-fertilisation fifteen years later in the story 'Disfilassi': see chapter 4 and, for a detailed discussion, Santagostino (1993a: 15–17).
22. For detailed discussions see Klein (1990), Grassano (1991), Santagostino (1991a) and Santagostino (1993a).
23. Not included in *The Sixth Day*.
24. Not included in *The Sixth Day*. A sophisticated analysis of this story, particularly its intertextual references, is developed in Santagostino (1993a).
25. See chapter 5.
26. *Purgatory* X, 124–6; the translation is by Geoffrey L. Bickersteth (1972), Oxford: Basil Blackwell.
27. *Midrashim* (plural of *midrash*, 'research' or 'commentary') are non-literal interpretations of the text of the Bible in the form of legends, parables and allegories.
28. A detailed and extremely perceptive analysis of Levi's use of specialised linguistic registers is found in Mengaldo (1990: 54–63).
29. In *The Sixth Day* this title is translated as 'Retirement Fund'. The term is in fact a bureaucratic expression meaning 'involuntary retirement'; one of its contexts was Article 8 of the law of 5 September 1938, which decreed the forced retirement of Jewish public servants. A more accurate translation, which encompasses the moral as well as the economic aspects of the story, might be 'Early Retirement'.

30. See the interview with Luca Lamberti (1971).
31. Review of *Vizio di forma* (1971).
32. *Quaderni piacentini*, 29 January 1967, p. 88.
33. See Cases' 1967 review in *Quaderni piacentini*, p. 100.
34. See especially Paolo Milano's reviews of *Storie naturali* and *Vizio di forma*, Mauro (1979: 6891–2), Grassano (1981: 62–4), Tesio (1987: 286–8), Cases (1987: 30–1) and particularly Santagostino (1991a).
35. Published in 1985 in *L'altrui mestiere*; discussed in chapter 5 of this book.
36. Neither is included in *The Sixth Day*. A very perceptive analysis of both is found in Santagostino (1993b).
37. This essay, reprinted in *L'altrui mestiere*, is discussed more fully in chapter 5.
38. The *terza pagina* (literally 'page three') of most Italian newspapers was, until the late 1980s, dedicated to cultural topics: extended book or film reviews, debates on art or philosophy and occasional short stories by famous writers.
39. See Calvino (1991: 606).
40. See Riatsch and Gorgé (1991: 66).
41. See Girelli-Carasi (1990a: 14–15).
42. See Schehr (1989).
43. See Cicioni (1989).
44. The first two oppositions have been discussed in depth in McRae (1988).
45. See the discussion of the cultural and historical metaphors of these stories in chapter 1.
46. See chapter 2.
47. See chapter 1.
48. In *La ricerca delle radici* Levi refers to 'Conrad's "testing oneself"' (p. 111) and gives the title 'Un'occasione di provarsi' (A Chance to Prove Oneself) to an excerpt from Conrad's *Youth*.
49. For a discussion of *Il sistema periodico* as literary detective fiction, see Cannon (1990: 101–4).
50. For a perceptive and lucid analysis, see Bàrberi Squarotti (1991: 7–10); see also Santagostino (1991a: 140–4).
51. In two later texts, the 1984 essay 'Auschwitz città tranquilla' ('Auschwitz, the Quiet City', reprinted in *Racconti e saggi*, and published in English as 'The Quiet City' in *Moments of Reprieve*) and *I sommersi e i salvati*, Levi refers to separate

exchanges of letters he had with two German chemists who had been on the other side of the Auschwitz barbed wire and whom he had traced through German friends. In 'Vanadio', these two real-life relationships are collapsed into one and given a more conventional narrative shape.

52. A very sensitive analysis of this story can be found in Angress (1988: 322–5).

53. 'My trade has been useful to me also for my way of writing, in which I aim at conciseness and clarity' (4 June 1975, at the launch of *Il sistema periodico*, quoted in Poli and Calcagno 1992: 61). 'Precision and conciseness, which I'm told are my way of writing, have come to me from my trade as a chemist' (Levi and Regge 1984: 49). 'Chemistry is the art of separating, weighing and discriminating between things: three exercises useful also to anyone who attempts to describe events or to give form to his imagination' ('Ex chimico' (Ex Chemist), in *L'altrui mestiere*, III: 597).

54. Levi worked from a German translation of the Dutch original.

55. See especially Balestrini and Moroni (1988). For discussions in English, see Lumley (1990: 306–10) and chapter 10 of Ginsborg (1990).

56. See the beginning of this chapter.

57. For the culture of skilled work in Turin see Bottiglieri and Ceri (1987) and Payone (1991: 359).

58. The only one of these books to have been translated with a different English title is *Il contesto* (*Equal Danger*), 1973.

59. In the United States the English translation appears under the title *The Monkey's Wrench*.

60. See the interview with Giorgio De Rienzo (1979a).

61. Interview with Giorgio De Rienzo and Enzo Gagliano, *Stampa Sera*, 13 May 1975, p. 3.

62. Wilde-Menozzi (1989–90: 156) points out that the original title translates literally as 'star-shaped key' (*chiave a stella*), would suggest both unlocking mysteries and the symbol of Jewishness.

63. Interview with Giorgio De Rienzo (1979a).

64. Interview with Georgina Arian Levi, *Ha Keillah*, February 1979, p. 6.

65. In the essay 'Le parole fossili' (Fossilised Words) published in *L'altrui mestiere* and not included in the English translation,

Levi describes his delight in straying into realms of knowledge other than his own. He says that the main aim of the exercise is 'the attempt in itself, the adventure (*libertinaggi*), the exploration' (III: 789). In the preface to *Racconti e saggi* (published in *The Mirror Maker*) he explains that the diverse nature of the collection is a result of '[his] own dabbling in many fields (*libertinaggio*), partly deliberate, partly due to the journey fate had reserved for [him]' (III: 833).

66. See the review by Francesco Leonetti; see also Frassica (1991).
67. See an interview in *Uomini e libri* (1982l: 40). After the book appeared, Levi admitted that most of the adventures he had described had been lifted from reports he had read in technical journals, or had been related to him by friends and acquaintances (Poli and Calcagno 1992: 117–18).
68. See Porta [1954] 1971. Sholom Aleichem's Tevye stories were first translated into Italian in 1928. See *Tevye's Daughters* (New York: 1949) and *The Best of Sholom Aleichem* (London: 1979) for English translations. Levi openly acknowledged Belli, Porta, Conrad and Sholom Aleichem as structural sources of *La chiave a stella* in a 1979 interview for *Uomini e libri* (see Poli and Calcagno 1992: 161).
69. *La ricerca delle radici*, p. 49.
70. For *italiano popolare*, see Lepschy and Lepschy (1988: 36–7). For detailed analyses of the Italian of *La chiave a stella*, see Grassano (1981: 126–8), Beccaria (1983: x–xi), Bura (1987) and Mengaldo (1990: xlvii–liv). The Marxist critic Asor Rosa, reviewing the book in the Communist Party's daily paper *L'Unità*, stressed that the rhythm of Faussone's speech and its pauses for proverbs and corrections reflect the way the character concentrates on his work (Asor Rosa 1979).
71. In the 1986 essay 'Bella come una fiore' (As Beautiful as a Flower), never translated into English, Levi identifies some specific traits of Piedmontese culture as 'love for work done well, for law and order . . . the rejection of show . . . and of rhetoric . . . Respect for human rights. The harshness of the class struggle.' (III: 970)
72. Interview with Giorgina Arian Levi (see note 64).
73. Many reviewers justly praised the fluent colloquial English of William Weaver's translation. Levi found it 'clean, antiseptic, with a rather too gentlemanly Faussone' (Poli and Calcagno

1992: 328). Alfred Kazin, in *The New York Times Book Review* (12 October 1986), said instead that 'Faussone often sounds like a New York cabbie looking for someone to punch'.
74. See also the review by Fausto Gianfranceschi (*Il Tempo*, 5 January 1979, p. 12).
75. Stajano's review was published in *Il Messaggero*, 11 December 1978, p. 3; Bruschi's in *Battaglie del lavoro*, no. 3 (March 1979), p. 6.
76. See, among many others, the reviews by Enrico Deaglio, Francesco Leonetti (himself a committed left-wing writer and poet), Marco D'Eramo and Giorgio Binni. For the numerous debates on the political stance of *La chiave a stella* which took place in Italy in 1979 see Poli and Calcagno (1992: 136–47).
77. See Levi's comments in his interview with Giovanni Pacchioni (1982f) and Poli and Calcagno (1992: 152–3).
78. Philip Roth, in his important interview with Levi, implicitly identified another possible literary source by referring to Faussone as Levi's 'blue-collar Scheherazade' (Roth 1986: 41). D.J. Enright (1987: 41) wondered briefly 'What stories will the ever-increasing unemployed have to tell?'
79. See Mengaldo (1989: 93), Santagostino (1994) and Varoli Piazza (1994).

4

Roots and Reactions

By the end of the 1970s Levi was an important cultural and public figure. He had completely abandoned chemistry to work intensely at the second of his chosen trades. He wrote stories which were published as *Lilít*, and also contributed frequent short essays to *La Stampa*. The essays, mostly lighthearted observations on various literary and scientific topics, 'raids into other people's trades', were collected in 1985 under that very title, *L'altrui mestiere* (*Other People's Trades*).

Other contributions, however, were not lighthearted and went directly back to what was still seen as Levi's central role, that of Auschwitz witness. In late 1978, a heated historical controversy followed the publication of two articles in France. In the first, an interview published in *L'Express* on 28 October, Louis Darquier de Pellepoix, former General Commissioner for Jewish Affairs in the Vichy government and thus directly responsible for the deportation of 70,000 Jews, denied outright that any mass extermination had taken place. In the second, an essay published in *Le Monde* on 29 December, Robert Faurisson, a lecturer in French literature at the University of Lyon, denied that Hitler had ever ordered anyone to be killed on the grounds of race and religion, and endeavoured to use the evidence collected in the French National Jewish Research Centre to demonstrate that the statistics on the genocide had been exaggerated.[1] It was logical for Levi to speak out publicly against such attempts to deny past history. In a statement in *Corriere della Sera* five days after the publication of Faurisson's essay, his language was strong and angry:

> If you deny the massacre . . . you must explain why the seventeen million Jews of 1939 had been reduced to eleven in 1945. You must deny the evidence from thousands of widows and orphans. You must deny the evidence of each of us survivors. You must come to

argue with each of us, professor; you will find it more difficult than preaching nonsense to your helpless students. Were they all so helpless as to accept your nonsense? Didn't any of them raise a hand in protest? And what did the French education and legal authorities do? Did they tolerate your killing the dead a second time by denying their deaths? (Levi 1979a: 1).

A few days later, he was less emotive and more specific in his refutations, using his own first-hand experience both as a survivor and as a chemist:

[Faurisson asks] how two thousand and more people could fit into the 210 square metres of the Auschwitz gas chambers. They *did* fit, they were brutally forced to, in fact *we* did fit. I never entered the gas chambers (those who entered them did not get out to tell the tale!); however, while waiting for a selection for the gas chambers, I was crowded with 250 other men in a room seven metres by four. . . . [Faurisson also states that the poison used would have killed the Germans carrying out the orders]. He never noticed that the people carrying out orders were not Germans, but other prisoners, about whose safety the Germans cared little; and the poison, which was hydrocyanic acid, was extremely volatile in the conditions under which it was used (it boils at 26 degrees centigrade, and in the chambers, packed with human beings, the temperature was around 37 degrees) (Levi 1979b: 3).

The beginning of 1979 also saw some worrying, if not dangerously widespread, episodes of anti-Semitism in Italy (slogans daubed on walls and offensive chants aimed at a visiting Israeli basketball team). Levi agreed to take part in a national conference organised by the Jewish Youth Organisation and stated, indirectly referring to Romain Rolland's famous formula 'pessimism of the intellect, optimism of the will', that for survivors 'a basic pessimism in outlook can and must coexist with the optimism of daily actions'. For those who survived, the only option was to 'continue to repeat our testimony over decades and generations, as long as we have voice left to do so' (Levi 1979c: 3).

In 1980 the Polish government completed a restructuring of the central camp of Auschwitz, and inside the barracks built memorials for each of the nationalities of the people who had been deported there. Levi was a member of the planning committee for the Italian one. This memorial – on the ground floor of Block 21 – consists of a wooden boardwalk surrounded by a tunnel of unbroken spirals of material, painted with episodes of Italian history from the Fascist takeover to the end of the war.[2] In April Levi wrote the epigraph, which was printed on a white plaque at the entry of the building:

> Visitor, observe the remains of this camp and meditate: from whichever country you come, you are not a stranger. May your journey not have been useless, may our deaths not have been useless. For you and your children, may the ashes of Auschwitz be a warning: may the horrible fruit of hatred, of which you have seen the traces here, not bring forth new seed, tomorrow or ever (Poli and Calcagno 1992: 175–6; also quoted as the epigraph to Devoto and Martini 1981).[3]

During the same year, Levi also embarked on a new autobiographical project. Giulio Bollati, one of the chief editorial managers of Einaudi, had conceived the idea of asking a number of well-known Italian intellectuals to compile their own 'personal anthologies' of texts that had shaped their intellectual and artistic developments. The proposed series never materialised: Levi's collection, which was to have been the first in the series, remained an isolated volume and was published in early 1981 with the title *La ricerca delle radici* (*A Search for Roots*). It is a collection of thirty excerpts from both literary and non-literary texts, each preceded by a short introduction by Levi. The literary texts are mainly variations on the theme of men testing themselves through suffering and adventure: *Youth* by Joseph Conrad ('a good example of how a man can construct himself'), *Joseph and His Brothers* by Thomas Mann ('in my opinion, the highest literary product in this century'), *Moby Dick*, *The Book of Marco Polo*, *Gulliver's Travels*. Homer is represented by a passage from the *Odyssey*, the poem of the 'reasonable hope' for peace after war and exile, rather than the *Iliad*, 'that orgy of battles, woundings and deaths'. The non-literary texts include Lucretius's *On Nature*, Bertrand Russell's *The Conquest of Happiness* and Arthur C. Clarke's *Profiles of the Future* ('Clarke is a living refutation of the cliché that practising science and exercising imagination are mutually exclusive activities'). Levi lucidly acknowledges the limitations of his choices: 'I did not foresee, when I embarked on this task, that among my favourite authors there would not be a single rascal, nor a single woman, nor a single representative of non-European cultures.' His preface points out the autobiographical character of the project, and its function of 'guided tour' to his cumulative self-inscription. Since the aim of the anthology is 'to identify the traces of what [he] read in what [he] wrote' (Levi 1981: vii), the result is a mirror game, where the selected texts on the one hand shape Levi's autobiographical persona by being connected with what the readers already know of it, and on the other hand are invested with new meanings by being read in the light of Levi's own writings. He also acknowledges that the undertaking is at least as self-revealing as his previous writings:

> While making my choices I felt more exposed, more disclosed, than while I was writing my own books. Halfway through I felt naked, and divided between the opposing emotions of an exhibitionist (who is happy when naked) and of a patient on the operating table, waiting for the surgeon to slit his stomach open (Levi 1981: viii).

Levi tried to direct his readers' responses to his anthology by providing, at the beginning, an ellipse-shaped graph suggesting four 'pathways' through a series of chosen authors: 'salvation through laughter', 'man suffering unjustly', 'the stature of man' and 'salvation through understanding'. The upper pole of the graph, and the starting point of all the pathways, is the Book of Job, which opens the anthology. Job, in Levi's formulation, is 'crushed by God's omnipotence', but at the same time becomes the symbol of humankind's eternal questions, 'those questions to which man has not yet found an answer, nor ever will, but to which he will keep seeking one because he needs it to live, to understand himself and the world' (Levi 1981: 6). Readers are thus implicitly encouraged to integrate the Book of Job intertextually into Levi's own writings, re-reading it in the light of Auschwitz (see Wilde-Menozzi: 150) and connecting it with the problematised biblical references in *Se questo è un uomo, La tregua, Il sistema periodico* and *I sommersi e i salvati*.

The lower pole of the graph is labelled 'Black Holes' and refers to a 1975 article by the astrophysicist Kip Thorne, entitled 'The Search for Black Holes'. The positioning of this text, and Levi's introduction to it, are ambivalent: all of Levi's chosen pathways, including 'salvation through understanding', which consists of scientific texts, lead to black holes and the universe is ultimately unknowable ('The sky does not contain Elysian Fields, but rather matter and light distorted, compressed, dilated to an extent which goes far beyond our senses and our language'). Yet, if it was possible for humankind to conceive of black holes, then it may also be possible for it to 'decipher' the sky, and also to 'defeat fear, need and pain' (Levi 1981: 231). The religious dimension explicitly denied in this introduction is, however, present in a number of metaphoric connections between science and religion made in the introductions to the 'salvation through understanding' texts. These connections are consistently based on the notion of order replacing chaos. Shortly after the Book of Job comes a passage from Darwin's *Origin of the Species*, introduced with the words 'from Darwin's work . . . emanates a profound and grave religiosity, the sober joy of man who extracts order from tangles' (Levi 1981: 23). Levi's introduction to Ludwig Gattermann's *Die Praxis des organischen Chemikers* (*A Practical Manual for Organic Chemists*), one of his university textbooks, is also couched in religious terms: 'The words of the Father . . . which awake you from your childhood and declare you an adult under certain conditions' (Levi 1981: 83).[4] Gattermann's textbook, however, appears for the first time in Levi's work in a far less optimistic context: in *Se questo è un uomo*, it sits, as a reminder that there are always links between science and power, on the table of Doktor Pannwitz during Levi's 'chemistry examination' (I: 110). *La ricerca delle radici* is pervaded by this basic ambiguity. Levi calls the optimistic, unproblematic view of science as the key to all the mysteries of the universe naive, in the introductions both to Sir William Bragg's *Concerning the Nature of Things*, the very book which determined Levi's own decision at the age of sixteen to become a chemist (Levi 1981: 31), and to Lucretius' *On Nature*, a book he nevertheless loves.

Another highly ambiguous 'root' is the 'proposed method for checking the resistance of dried adhesive films to attacks by cockroaches', published by the American Society for Testing Materials. This is a totally factual text, which merely specifies the correct equipment and procedure for carrying out the required resistance tests, and in itself is anything but sinister. Yet the cockroaches – inserted into an alien environment, controlled and tested in life and death – indirectly but clearly recall the helpless terror of the protagonist of Kafka's novella *The Metamorphosis*. Their death or survival, scrupulously supervised and recorded by all-powerful overseers, also evokes other obvious, sinister images. Levi, while on the one hand admitting that 'the foundations of our technological civilisation must be consolidated by precise measures and definitions' (Levi 1981: 183), on the other hand – in an implicit connection with his own story 'Le nostre belle specificazioni'[5] – expresses his concern that 'the monstrous network of specifications is destined to grow, since every object mentioned in a specification must in turn be specified'. The apparently neutral American scientific specification, Levi's morality tale and his own testimony on Auschwitz constitute the implicit discursive space of the last but one of Levi's 'roots', the conclusion of *Menschen in Auschwitz* (*Human Beings in Auschwitz*) by the Austrian historian (and camp survivor) Hermann Langbein:

> This is the lesson of Auschwitz: the first step, the first surrender to a social structure which aims at total control over human beings, is the most dangerous (Levi 1981: 227).

Mengaldo's remarks about the death camps being 'the coherent and almost necessary expression of the technical development and the totalitarian vocation of the modern world' (Mengaldo 1989: 93) seem particularly appropriate to this 'pathway'.

Two other texts which are at the same time broken and opened by the implicit recontextualisation into Levi's own work are T.S. Eliot's *Murder in the Cathedral* and Paul Celan's poem 'Todesfuge' (Fugue of Death), one of the best-known poems on the Holocaust. Two of the women's choruses from Eliot's play, one before the murder of Thomas à Becket, ('God is leaving us, God is leaving us') and one after it ('Clear the air! clean the sky! wash the wind! . . . / this is out of time,/ An instant eternity of evil and wrong') are introduced by Levi with the words 'something happened which will never again be cleansed'. These are much the same words he had used to describe the aftermath of the selection for the gas chambers in *Se questo è un uomo* ('What has happened today is an abomination, which no propitiatory prayer, no pardon, no atonement by the guilty, which nothing at all in the power of man can ever clean again', I: 134). The 'partial shelter' that the women of Canterbury built around themselves is referred to again in *I sommersi e i salvati*; there it is glossed as 'the screen of deliberate ignorance' built by most Germans in the Nazi period and denied to the survivors of the camps, who felt submerged by shame and pain for 'the misdeeds others and not they had committed' and which 'could never again be cleansed'

(I: 718). Celan's poem, placed immediately after Eliot's choruses, is introduced by Levi with the words 'I carry it within me like a grafting' (Levi 1981: 211). Its recurring phrase 'we dig a grave in the air it is not crowded there' reappears in *Se non ora, quando?*, first in Mendel's recollection of the massacre of his village ('Half the villagers are scattered through the countryside and the forest, and the other half are in a pit, and it's not crowded there', II: 188), and subsequently in an intertextual reference in the poem written by Levi and placed, as the partisans' song, at the centre of the novel ('Our brothers have gone to heaven/Through the chimneys of Sobibór and Treblinka,/They have dug themselves a grave in the air', II: 336).

The pathway of laughter shares the word 'salvation' – with its religious connotations – with that of scientific understanding: science is the only possible, if remote, source of hope, and laughter is often the only possible reaction against injustice. In this pathway Job is immediately followed by *Gargantua* and *Pantagruel*, in whose universe 'everyone has access to the noble joys of virtue and knowledge, but also to the physical joys, God's gift like the others' of the pleasures of the flesh (Levi 1981: 87). The feature emphasised by Levi is Rabelais' passionate interest in human beings in all their aspects, 'body and soul, *tripes et boyaux*': the same words Levi uses in 'Cromo' to describe his own passionate involvement with both his work and his future wife.[6] Rabelais is followed by two nineteenth-century dialect poets, the Milanese Carlo Porta and the Roman Giuseppe Gioacchino Belli, whose influence is visible in the narrative structures of *La chiave a stella*.[7] They are included because of their pity for Job-like, humiliated, degraded beings (Levi 1981: 49, 165).

Another just man oppressed by injustice is Sholom Aleichem's Tevye the Dairyman, the pious yet questioning Russian village Jew who is a humorous stereotype extremely well-known throughout Eastern European Jewish culture and its reflections in Western – particularly American – Jewish literature. Tevye is however, as Levi puts it in his introduction to the passage he has chosen, a representative of a world destroyed by Hitler's gas chambers and by Stalin's labour camps (Levi 1981: 154). This twofold aspect is emphasised by the positioning of the chosen passage: it is in the pathway of 'salvation through laughter', but it is at the very bottom of it, next to the 'black holes'. Tevye, while describing his struggles against the poverty and oppression of his daily life, is nevertheless scrupulous in drawing 'all due distinction' between human beings and animals, between the synagogue and the forest and between the sacred and the profane.

Traces of Tevye reappear in *Se non ora, quando?*. In the initial episode, Mendel asks another fugitive Jew whether he is infested by lice: 'They're a patient race: they know how to wait. Like us, in other words, making all due distinction between man and louse' (II: 191). The Yiddish saying 'A sick man you ask [if he wants something to eat], a healthy man you give', quoted by Tevye (Levi 1981: 160), is also quoted by a member of the band who rejoins it after having been wounded (II: 320).

In his general introduction Levi identified the connections between Job, Sholom Aleichem, Isaak Babel – two of whose gruesome war stories he included among his 'roots' for their 'shy pity, clothed in irony' (Levi 1981: 145) – and himself as 'a remote Jewish kinship' (Levi 1981: x). His investigation of these connections was one of the components of a general effort on his part to rethink and redefine the question of 'Jewish identity' and to mediate his reflections to his (Italian, mostly Gentile) implied readers. This was his contribution to a widespread interest in *Ostjudentum*, Eastern European Jewish cultural and literary traditions, which was one of the most intriguing aspects of Italian intellectual life in the 1970s and 1980s. The event that led to awareness of, and fascination with, *Ostjudentum* was the publication in 1971 of *Lontano da dove* (*Far from Where*), a monograph by Claudio Magris, who held the chair of German at the University of Trieste – a city which, because of its geographical position and history, had had a diversity of contacts with middle and Eastern European cultures for at least a century. Magris' monograph introduced non-specialist Italian readers to the works of Joseph Roth, Sholom Aleichem, the brothers Israel and Isaac Bashevis Singer, and Elias Canetti, which were translated or re-translated[8] throughout the 1970s and 1980s and often published or re-published with scholarly introductions.[9] So were works with Jewish themes by contemporary American writers such as Bernard Malamud and Saul Bellow (already well-known in Italy since the 1960s) and Chaim Potok (whose novel *The Chosen* had been translated as early as 1964). The interest was further stimulated by the Nobel Prize being awarded to two Jewish writers in consecutive years (Bellow in 1977 and I.B.

Singer in 1978) and to Canetti in 1981.

Magris argues that Western intellectuals' view of *Ostjudentum* was a complex phenomenon. On the one hand they saw that culture essentially as 'other', as a symbol of rigid alien traditions and of resignation to pain and oppression; on the other hand, after the Holocaust they looked at it through the filter of collective guilt, focusing on issues connected with the search for Jewish identity after the destruction of the world of the *shtetlach*[10] (Magris 1989: 107). This argument applied well to Italians, whose reading tended to concentrate on religious observance and the conflicts deriving from the assimilation – or lack of assimilation – of Jews into contemporary society and history. Another source of interest and implicit cultural comparisons for Italians was the view of religion as inseparable from memory, history and narration: 'a God who may be spoken of only by telling stories (hence the great Jewish narrative tradition)' (Gentiloni 1982: 3).[11]

There are many reasons for this interest. In the first place, there is the obvious 'otherness' of the closed communities of *Ostjudentum*, with their inextricable links between religion, history, language, family life, lifestyle and collective identity, to a country like Italy, where 'Jewish culture' had never represented a visible 'other'. This often involved respect and admiration for what one well-known Gentile communist journalist called the 'disinterestedness' of Orthodox Jews, their striving for righteousness as an end in itself rather than something to be rewarded in the afterlife (Melloni 1979). Furthermore, by the end of the 1970s Italian intellectuals, most of whom had shared the hopes for radical political and social change of the movements of the left and second-wave feminism, were experiencing a crisis of disillusionment. Their feelings of loss and uncertainty were partly reflected in Jewish literary works – both European and American – which investigated the sense of loss and exile following the disintegration of the patriarchal culture of the *shtetl*, and the consequent search for new identities (see Freschi 1992). There was also the hope that understanding the culture of a minority would help redefine the prevalent notions of 'majority' and 'minority' in society.

However, the relationship between 'Jewish' and 'Gentile' in Italy was not unproblematic. Beside the danger of the objectification of Jewish culture, there were also elements of political ambiguity: the historian and political scientist Ernesto Galli della Loggia spoke of 'a kitsch pro-Semitism . . . used by the Left and part of its formerly extremist fringes to clean its slate and start again, with Jews used as a means to an end' (Rasy 1992: 110). Further problems were inherent in the way Italian intellectuals reacted to the expansionist policies of the Israeli government, determined by a ruling class which originated mainly from the very same *Ostjudentum* which had been destroyed by the Holocaust and was the object of their fascination.

Levi's own position was simultaneously that of an insider and an outsider. As he readily admitted in several interviews,[12] his main identity was as an Italian: the few brief essays about his family history which he wrote for *La Stampa* in the 1980s contain hardly any specifically Jewish elements, and thus implicitly point out the degree of integration of the Turin Jewish community. He saw modern Italian Jewish culture as a revival culture, attracting interest from Jews and non-Jews not so much because it was living but rather because it was gradually disappearing (Sodi 1988b: 44–5). When he looked at *Ostjudentum*, he was all too aware that its traditions, languages (most significantly Yiddish) and strict religious observance were as unfamiliar and 'other' to him and most Italian Jews as they were to the rest of Italians. The fact that most of that world, as he himself had stated when presenting Tevye the Dairyman, had been wiped out by Hitler and Stalin was particularly and uncomfortably significant to him, who had come into contact with it for the first time in Auschwitz. He needed therefore to return to his memories of the camps in order to analyse the mutual 'otherness' between assimilated and non-assimilated Jews and to convey it to his readers.

Finally, he needed to confront the overall problematisation of 'Jewish identity' arising from his experiences and analyses. Was there one 'Jewish identity' or a plurality of Jewish identities, each to be defined on the basis of geographical and historical factors? What was the role of Yiddish – an essential part of *Ostjudentum* with its legends, stories, songs, jokes and proverbs, but practically unknown to Western European Jews – in the construction of collective identity and in the contacts between Eastern and Western European Jews? What was left of 'Jewish identity' after the destruction of *Ostjudentum*? Did the creation of the State of Israel mean the same thing for the Eastern and

Western European Jews of the generation which had survived the death camps?

In 1980 he found a specific stimulus to focus his interests and questions. Among his files he came across some notes on a story he had heard some ten years previously from his friend Emilio Vita Finzi, an ex-partisan who had been president of the Turin branch of ANPI (National Association of Italian Partisans). In 1945 Finzi had worked in Milan for the Ufficio Assistenza, an organisation which provided aid for Jewish refugees and camp survivors. There he had met a group of Russian Jews who had formed a partisan unit in the Soviet Union, behind the frontline, and had fought their way through Eastern Europe to find temporary refuge in Italy on their way to Palestine: 'men and women whom years of suffering had hardened but not humiliated, survivors of a civilisation (almost unknown in Italy) that Nazism had destroyed to its roots' (afterword to *Se non ora, quando?*, II: 515). For ten years Finzi's story had lain fallow in Levi's mind: in 1980 it became the genesis of his novel *Se non ora, quando?*.

Levi's motivations, as he explained in several interviews,[13] were manifold. In the first place, he wanted to test his own ability to construct an entirely fictional text. He also wished to pay tribute to that destroyed culture and to those Jews who had fought back. The medium of an action novel accessible to a wide public would further give him the opportunity of mediating a discourse on *Ostjudentum* and a problematisation of 'Jewish identity' to Italian readers. The action aspect was foremost in his mind: he frequently defined his novel as 'an adventure story, a Western' and stressed that, being an unsophisticated reader, he had written a book for unsophisticated readers. There was also an indirect autobiographical motivation: since his own experience as a partisan had been brief and unsuccessful, he deliberately set out to create partisans who were both competent and effective.[14] A few years after the publication of the novel, Levi admitted that he had also hoped to reach a wide readership in the English-speaking world, especially in the United States, after the limited success of *Se questo è un uomo* and *La tregua* and some unsuccessful attempts in the late 1970s to interest British and American publishers in a translation of *Il sistema periodico*.[15]

For eight months, until the end of 1980, he immersed himself in Eastern European Jewish culture. He tried to teach himself

Yiddish from grammars, lexicons and popular reference works on Yiddish lore such as Leo Rosten's *The Joys of Yiddish* and S. Landmann's *Jüdische Witze* (Del Buono 1982: 85; Sodi 1988: 44). Although he was obviously aware that his competence in Yiddish was not only passive, but also extremely sketchy, he hoped that his mediation would be adequate for his Italian readers.[16] One of the Yiddish books he practised on was the diary of one of the Jewish partisan bands (Kaganovic 1956), which contained some events Levi reworked and used. With his scientist's rigour, he listed that diary along with the most important historical reference works he had consulted in the afterword to the novel. He worked on *Se non ora, quando?* throughout 1981, and later told Philip Roth that the year he had spent writing it had been a happy one and that it had therefore been 'a liberating book' (Roth 1986: 41).

At the end of 1981 the collection of stories *Lilít* appeared. Levi divided the stories – written between 1975 and 1981, mostly for *La Stampa* – into three groups, corresponding to the three areas of his writings: the concentration camps and their aftermath; science fiction stories, akin to those collected in *Storie naturali* and *Vizio di forma*; and stories set in the contemporary Italy of *Il sistema periodico* and *La chiave a stella*. The three sections are entitled, respectively, 'Passato prossimo', 'Futuro anteriore' and 'Presente indicativo'. These are designations of three verb tenses, corresponding to the English 'present perfect', 'future perfect' and 'present indicative'. The Italian names, however, have connotations which – if considered in the overall context of Levi's writings – introduce elements of sombre reflection. 'Passato prossimo', literally 'close past', emphasises the closeness of the Nazi genocide and the need to keep remembering and to make sense of the memories. 'Futuro anteriore', literally 'future which precedes [another future action]', emphasises the importance of questioning scientific and technological choices in the near future in order to prevent undesirable developments in the long term. 'Presente indicativo' points out that some present phenomena may be indicative of tendencies which might be causes for concern.

In a note printed on the back cover of the original edition, Levi stated categorically: 'There are, to the best of my knowledge, no messages or fundamental prophecies; if the reader finds them, he is too kind.' Yet the different discourses articulated in the stories do lead to authorial reflections which are sometimes implicit and sometimes explicit social or moral comments. Most of the stories in 'Futuro anteriore' are obvious moral fables. Some of them are transparent, pessimistic variations on possible developments of capitalism: in 'I gladiatori' (The Gladiators), society solves at the same time the problems of unemployment, vehicle obsolescence and mass entertainment by recreating circuses where unemployed men and criminals are made to fight automobiles. Others, such as 'I costruttori di ponti' (The Bridge Builders),[17] are reflections on the consequences of humankind's ingenuousness: the intelligent beings who conceive and build bridges also burn forests, mercilessly causing the death of other living species in their quest for progress.

The topic of 'Disfilassi' (Dysphylaxis) vaguely recalls that of John Wyndham's 1964 novel *The Chrysalids*: as a consequence of a rapid increase in the tolerance of alien seed, every living species can and does fertilise others, and new kinds of 'basically human' beings, who are partly plant or animal, multiply. However, Wyndham's novel is basically anthropocentric, and envisages the development of a breed of telepathic, techno-logically advanced men and women as one of the consequences of a nuclear catastrophe. Levi's story returns instead to the theme – already explored in his previous science fiction stories – of the convergence of the animate and inanimate worlds, and views it as a hopeful alternative to nuclear destruction. It is significant that these last two stories are the only ones in the collection told from a female point of view. In both, a gendered discourse on nature is evident: the young protagonists – respectively a giantess and a woman who is one-eighth larch – are constructed as emotional and trusting and are identified with the harmony of nature, only to be destroyed by man's rationality in one case, and to be a passive agent of mutation in the other.

The stories of 'Presente indicativo' are variations on some of the themes of *Storie naturali*, *Vizio di forma* and especially *Il sistema periodico*. The prevailing tone is pessimistic, with an emphasis on the inadequacies, defeats and failures of men in their confrontations with nature. The ironically titled 'Gli stregoni' (The Witch Doctors) is akin to the two 'Recuenco' stories in *Vizio di forma*, in that its central characters are two English ethnographers who come into contact with the Sirionos, primitive inhabitants of the Bolivian jungle.[18] However, the story is much more pessimistic than the two earlier ones. Left without most of their equipment after a fire, the two highly-educated representatives of Western civilisation prove to be unable to reconstruct their tools, and even to manufacture something as deceptively simple as a knife or a match. The theme of the need to be skilled with one's hands, introduced in *La tregua*, expanded in *Il sistema periodico* and fully developed in *La chiave a stella*, is here taken to its extreme logical consequences: Western technological civilisation inevitably causes the loss of skills which in any other context may prove vital.

'La sfida della molecola' (The Molecule's Challenge) deals with the very same problem described in 'Cromo': the unexpected and unwanted solidification of a paint. However, the two stories are each other's perfect opposites. In 'Cromo', the chemical problem is represented as a classic detective story, both in Levi's explicit discourse and in the structure of the story: the casualty, namely the solidified paint, is the starting point, and the chemist doggedly traces all the clues back to the initial mistake, manages to restore order by reversing the process, and comes out of his ordeal a stronger and more confident man. In the later story the chemist first confesses his failure, then relates the relevant procedures step by step and suddenly describes how, with no rational explanation, matter becomes man's opponent, challenges him and wins over him. Levi's final comment is chilling:

> A livering [the solidification of a paint] . . . involves an attitude of mockery: it is a gesture of derision, the sneer of soulless things which ought to obey you and, instead, rise against you, a challenge to your carefulness and caution. The single 'molecule' . . . which is born/dies in your hands is . . . a symbol of the other unerasable and irreparable disfigurements which darken our future, of the prevailing of chaos over order, and of indecent death over life (III: 543).

In this conclusion, which fully contradicts the relatively optimistic statements of 'Cromo' and 'Argento', Levi emphasises the dark side of his trade and represents scientific and technological progress as ultimately doomed. This acknowledgement of defeat, both personal and collective, coexists with what critics have seen as Levi's positivist optimism (Cases 1987: 28) and foreshadows instead the sombre admissions of fear of the victory of chaos in *I sommersi e i salvati*.

A similar acknowledgement of powerlessness, this time historicised, comes at the end of the story 'Decodificazione' (Decoding), where Levi's autobiographical persona encounters a fifteen-year-old boy who vents his frustrations by spraying Fascist graffiti on walls:

> I thought . . . about the thousands of other writings on Italian walls, faded by forty years of rain and sunlight, often riddled with holes by the war they had contributed to unleash, yet still legible, thanks to the obnoxious persistence of paints and corpses, which decay in a short time, but whose final remains last gruesomely for ever: tragically ironic writings, yet perhaps still able to breed errors from their error, and catastrophes from their catastrophe (III: 567–8).

The English translation of *Lilít* was published in 1985 and contains only the stories of the first section ('Passato prossimo') with the addition of three more recollections. Its title, *Moments of Reprieve*, taken from Levi's preface, perceptively sums up its basic theme: the stories show moments in which some Auschwitz prisoners are fleetingly reprieved from total degradation through small acts of self-assertion or human contact. Some prisoners are represented as making one angry, defiant stand, such as the man who shouts to the sky that Hitler did not 'have' him ('Capaneo')[19]; others are shown as retrieving, however briefly, their identity through their former interests, such as the music-loving prisoner who for a few hours acquires and plays a violin ('Il nostro sigillo' (Our Seal)). Other men choose to accept the rules of the reverse education outlined in *Se questo è un uomo*, such as the honest young newcomer who learns to steal in order to survive ('Un discepolo' (A Disciple)); still others internalise the rules of survival but apply them as fairly as conditions allow, such as the Kapo who hits Levi for attempting to smuggle out a letter but does not report him, which would have meant Levi's death ('Il giocoliere' (The Juggler)). Readers are assumed to be familiar with *Se questo è un uomo* and *La tregua*, which are briefly mentioned or alluded to, or simply constitute the immediate intertextual background of some recollections. The initial paragraph of 'Il nostro sigillo' plunges the readers into the middle of a universe taken entirely for granted:

> This is how things go here in the morning: when reveille sounds (and it's still long before dawn) first of all we put on our shoes,

otherwise somebody will steal them, and it is an unspeakable tragedy. Then, in the dust and crush, we try to make our beds according to regulations (III: 396).

Some themes central to Levi's writings are taken up and more or less explicitly problematised. The naive newcomer of 'Un discepolo' is a conscientious worker who firmly adheres to Faussone's ethics of 'work well done'. Levi's narrating self, however, takes pains to teach him that this principle is contingent rather than universal: ethical behaviour in Auschwitz is to work as little, and as badly, as one can get away with (III: 393–4). The story 'Il ritorno di Lorenzo' (Lorenzo's Return) develops what Levi had recorded in *Se questo è un uomo* about Lorenzo Perrone, the civilian worker who brought him and others food for six months, risking his own life, and who reminded him that good still existed and that Levi himself was a man. Yet, after returning to his village, Lorenzo lost his will to live and passively let himself die within a few months. 'He, who was not a survivor, had died of the survivors' disease' (III: 436).

Another basic theme developed in these stories is Levi's encounters with, and reactions to, *Ostjudentum* both in Auschwitz and afterwards. In 'Lilít', the evaluation of Levi's autobiographical persona made by a Polish Jew echoes Levi's own mocking and dismissive self-evaluation in 'Zinco':

> ... everyone knows that western Jews are all Epicureans, *apikorsím*, unbelievers ... of course, you people – they teach you a bit of Hebrew when you reach thirteen, and that's the end of it ... (III: 387)

Levi's respect for *Ostjudentum* is evident from his conveying its legends and traditions, such as the ones connected with Lilith, who according to Jewish oral tradition was the first woman, created before Eve.[20] Yet at the same time he stresses with regret that the culture from which those legends and traditions came is irretrievably lost and remote even to those who, like himself, try to convey some of it to others:

> It is inexplicable that fate has chosen an unbeliever to repeat this pious and impious tale, woven of poetry, ignorance, daring acumen, and the unhealable sadness that grows on the ruins of lost civilisations (III: 390).

An even more careful distancing occurs in the authorial comment which concludes 'Il cantore e il veterano' (The Cantor and the Barracks Chief), the story of the pious Ezra who in Auschwitz refuses food on Yom Kippur, the Day of Atonement – prescribed as a day of fasting – and quotes the Law and the relevant opinions of various commentators:

> [Ezra] was heir to an ancient, sorrowful, and strange tradition, whose core consists in holding evil in opprobrium and in 'erecting a hedge around the law' so that evil may not flood through the gaps in the hedge and submerge the law itself. In the course of the millennia, around this core has become encrusted a gigantic proliferation of comments, deductions, almost obsessively subtle distinctions, and further precepts and proscriptions. And in the course of the millennia many have behaved like Ezra throughout migrations and slaughters without number. That is why the history of the Jewish people is so ancient, sorrowful, and strange (III: 410).

The adjective 'strange' comes after 'ancient' and 'sorrowful' in summing up both religious observance and Jewish history, identifying one with the other. Significantly, Levi quotes without further explanation the well-known Jewish precept to 'erect a hedge around the law', namely to ensure that it is obeyed (*Pirké Avoth*, I: 1).[21] Yet religious observance is defined with the detachment of the unbeliever, as an unqualified 'other', though it preserved the identity of the people of Israel through its history of oppression.

This section of *Lilít* ends with 'Il re dei Giudei' the real story of Chaim Rumkowski, installed by the Nazis as president of the Lodz ghetto, who supervised the exploitation of the ghetto workers, occasionally protected them, and was eventually deported to Auschwitz along with 'his' people.[22] Levi ends the story with some reflections – stated, as in his first two works, in the present tense of all indisputable generalisations – about the ways in which absolute power corrupts its victims:

> It is typical of regimes in which all power rains down from above and no criticism can rise from below, that they weaken and confuse people's capacity for judgement, and create a broad zone of grey consciences that stands between the great men of evil and the absolute victims (III: 443).

The notion of the 'grey consciences' was to be developed later, in the chapter 'La zona grigia' (The Grey Zone) of *I sommersi e i salvati*, at the end of which, significantly, the story of Chaim Rumkowski is repeated. In a bleak final statement, Levi posits Rumkowski with his unquestioning greed for power as a symbol of Western civilisation as a whole:

> Like Rumkowski, we too are so dazzled by power and money as to forget our essential fragility, forget that we are all in the ghetto, that the ghetto is fenced in, that beyond the fence stand the lords of death, and not far away the train is waiting (III: 444).

This conclusion situates the notion of the constant presence of 'evil' in the world in a historical as well as moral perspective. The conclusions of two other stories share this awareness, but from a religious perspective. In 'Lilít', the legend told to Levi attributes the pain and suffering of the world to God's taking Lilith as his lover, and rests all hopes in the coming of the Messiah:

> As long as God continues to sin with Lilith, there will be blood and pain on Earth. But one day a powerful being will come – the one we are all waiting for. He will make Lilith die and put an end to God's lechery, and to our exile (III: 390).

In 'La bestia nel tempio' (The Beast in the Temple) the eponymous character is imprisoned in a dilapidated temple on a small island in Latin America, and seals itself deeper and deeper in with each attempt to escape. Outside the temple a crowd of beggars have been waiting for an immeasurable time for the beast to come out, so that they may kill it and thus heal the world. Their waiting, and their hopes, are in vain and are implicitly represented as equally remote and alien to modern thought as the waiting and the hopes of the Jewish tradition.[23]

By the time of *Lilít*'s publication Levi had completed *Se non ora, quando?*, which appeared in April 1982. The title encourages a reading of the novel as a discourse on Jewish identity. As Levi himself explains in the afterword, it is taken from a saying of Rabbi Hillel (first century AD) found in the collection *Pirké Avoth* (Sayings of the Fathers), where famous rabbis sum up their experience and philosophy. In its entirety,[24] the saying stresses that education is always self-education; that it must progress through self-doubt; and that past and future meet in the present. All three notions are posited in the form of questions: in the Jewish cultural tradition, the subject's quest for identity proceeds through a questioning of identity itself. Like all traditional historical novels, Levi's is a quest for the past in order to make sense of the present, and his characters and events – micro-histories of ordinary women and men caught up in events they can understand only partially – are at the same time situated historically and constructed as metaphors for the author's own times.

Two central motifs of Eastern European Jewish – especially Yiddish – literature (identified and explained in Magris 1989: 27–41) are the measure of time, often symbolised by watches and clocks, and the journey from East to West, from the timelessness and the traditional values of the *shtetl* into the core of European history, often with feelings of loss and exile.[25] Both motifs are clearly presented in the opening and closing scenes. In the first page, Mendel the watchmaker, a former Red Army soldier, starts talking about himself to another Jew whom he meets in the middle of a Russian forest behind the frontline. The first and therefore most relevant feature he reveals is the casual relationship of the *shtetl* where he was born with history, expressed through a transparent metaphor:

> In my village, there weren't many clocks. There was one on the church steeple, but it had stopped years and years ago, maybe during the Revolution (II: 188).

History, however, does catch up with Mendel's *shtetl* and destroys it irreparably, leaving him without the security of his past and lost in a totally uncertain present:

> If you want to know the name of this village, the name is Strelka . . . and I'd cut off a hand if that could make time run backwards and everything could be the way it was (II: 188).

The language of this passage blends biblical parataxis, (with the typical anaphoric 'and'), a biblical reference to the Garden of Eden (before time, before knowledge and before pain), and the chilling refrain from Celan's poem 'Fugue of Death'.

The novel ends with Mendel and the survivors of the Jewish partisan band he has joined finding temporary respite in Milan after fighting their way through the Soviet Union, Poland and Germany, and hoping to make their way to Palestine. Their journey is obviously parallel to the one described in *La tregua*: in both cases Levi provides detailed maps, with the travellers' itineraries clearly marked. Both journeys, however, end with uncertainty about the future rather than the victory of order over chaos. Just as the last page of *La tregua* juxtaposes Levi's homecoming and his dream of ultimate despair, in the last page of *Se non ora, quando?* there is a transparent juxtaposition of contradictory symbols. A son is born to the two most innocent members of the band, a pious Orthodox woman and a teenage boy, representing a new beginning, a total break with the past of the whole group. Immediately afterwards, Mendel sees without understanding it the front page of an Italian newspaper bearing the date 7 August 1945 and announcing the dropping of the first atom bomb on Hiroshima.

The measure of time is always present both literally – the narrative is divided into chapters whose titles are chronological diary headings – and metaphorically: Mendel the watchmaker, from the initial scene onward, constantly refers to watches and clocks whenever he tries to understand himself and the people he meets. He repeatedly thinks about his brooding companion Leonid in terms of a watch which needs to be cleaned (II: 213) and a watch which has been irreparably bashed (II: 374); he compares the empathy between himself and a Polish resistance fighter to two good clocks which mark the same time, even if they are of different makes (II: 423); after encountering the survivors of a small Polish concentration camp, he dreams about many clocks marking each a different time, and feels guilty about the ones that run backwards (II: 395).

Mendel is the character through whose perspective the third person narration progresses, the only character whose thoughts are revealed with each development of the plot. There are, however, recurrent shifts in narrative voice: from the third to the second person to express Mendel's guilt and self-reproaches, and from the third to the first to express his self-questioning, his memories and desires, his drifting present, his uncertain future.

> Where is my house? It is nowhere. It's in the knapsack I carry on my back, it's in the shot-down Heinkel, it's at Novoselki, it's in the camp of Turov and in Edek's camp, it's beyond the sea, in fairy-tale land, where milk and honey flow. A man enters his house and hangs up his clothes and his memories; where do you hang your memories, Mendel, son of Nachman? (II: 439).

Levi posits the question of identity, individual and collective, as central for every member of the band. His didactic intentions are obvious in his creation of the group of fighters. Each member represents first of all one or more specific skills: one is a multilingual actor, one a former ritual butcher whose skill in handling a knife has shifted from religious to profane contexts, one – the leader – is a violinist, two have worked on farms, and five are ex-soldiers. In addition, and more significantly, the members of the band are representatives of diverse facets of *Ostjudentum* and voice a multiplicity of discourses on Jewishness. Three are survivors of destroyed *shtetlach*, and only one of them, the widow of a rabbi, has strong religious beliefs; one, a Georgian, is a Sephardic Jew, one is the son of a man persecuted first by the Tsar as a communist and subsequently by Stalin as a Jew, and one is a socialist Zionist feminist. This character, Line, is a clear instance of Levi's ambivalent representation of women. On the one hand she is chosen to voice all the most progressive Jewish ideologies; on the other hand, her determination and independence are constructed as absence of tenderness and thus as unsuitability as a lover or wife. Mendel's dominant discourse defines her as 'not lighthearted, but confident', someone who 'always knows exactly what must be done' (II: 485), yet not as 'a woman for a lifetime' (II: 513) – significantly, the very same words Levi used in *Il sistema periodico* to describe the woman he married.

One of the soldiers is a Christian, the token Gentile of the group. He has a central function as an outsider in that he is forced to learn 'what it's like to be a Jew; that is to say, what it's like to have a head made in a certain way, and live among people whose heads are made in a different way' (II: 358). In addition, his total ignorance of Judaism and Jewish culture is the pretext for his comrades giving him – that is to say, for Levi giving his implied readers – several lessons about the laws of the Torah, the precepts of the Talmud and numerous examples of Yiddish proverbs and stories. Similarly, a Polish partisan leader, whom the Jewish partisans learn to respect and admire, is at the same time the spokesman for reflections on the continuous experience of oppression in the history of Poland[26] and the ideal audience for the band's utopian hopes for their future in Palestine:

> We want to make fertile the sterile land of Palestine, plant orange trees and olive trees in the desert and make it fruitful . . . It sounds like a dream but it isn't: this world has already been created by our

brothers, more farsighted and courageous than we are, who migrated down there before Europe became a concentration camp (II: 417).

This firm statement of belief in a new collective identity, voiced by Gedaleh, the leader of the band, is one of the recurrent discourses of the novel. It echoes some of the central ideas of a diverse movement usually known as 'left-wing Zionism'.[27] Levi had never been a Zionist, yet he acknowledged and wanted to convey to his readers the historical significance of Zionism for the masses of Eastern European Jews who first had experienced Stalinist anti-Semitism and later had lost not only their families but also their homeland and their national identities.[28] However, Zionism, even in its left-wing variety, is far from being the dominant discourse of *Se non ora, quando?* All characters representing it are constructed positively, as strong, rational and determined; yet in Mendel's prevailing point of view, the Zionist ideology is viewed with wry detachment, as a utopia ('It remains to be seen whether the Zionists of Kiev and Kharkhov were right when they preached that the Jews are well off only in the land of Israel, and they should all leave Italy, Russia, India and China and settle there to grow oranges, learn Hebrew and dance the hora all in a circle', II: 234) and with uncertainty ('From the promised land no call reached him; perhaps there, too, he would have to march and fight. Very well, it's my destiny, I accept it, but it doesn't warm my heart', II: 483). Levi significantly avoids representing the practice, as opposed to the theory, of Zionism by ending the novel in Italy in 1945, before the survivors of the band embark for Palestine. The only collective identity Mendel recognises derives from belonging to a group with a shared past and shared memories.

The main obvious common ground is religion. There are many direct or indirect biblical references, often made by a member of the band and instantly recognised by the others. They create implicit or explicit parallels with the circumstances of the Jewish partisans: Moses and the children of Israel in the desert (Exodus 14 and 32), the rivers of Babylon (Psalm 136), Job and his comforters. Yet these sacred references are consistently problematised at the very same time they are articulated. Thus Levi emphasises the essential role in Jewish identity of the habit of questioning everything, even its own tradition. The notion of remembering and avenging wrongs, central to the Old Testament, is forcefully stated by Gedaleh, who quotes Deuteronomy 25: 17 to Mendel: 'Remember what Amalek did to you on the way, after you had come out of Egypt . . . You will extinguish even the memory of Amalek' (II: 329). But the idea of revenge is condemned by Mendel, at the very time he is helping his comrades to avenge the senseless murder of one of the band, a young woman killed by a sniper after the surrender of Germany: 'Does just revenge exist? It doesn't exist, but you're a man, and vengeance cries out on your blood, and therefore run, and destroy, and kill. Like them, like the Germans' (II: 471–2).

Sometimes, as in *Se questo è un uomo* and *Il sistema periodico*, the words of the Father are at the centre of an irreconcilable conflict between belief and rejection. In his first book Levi states forcefully, in the form of a rhetorical question, that the stories of the Auschwitz prisoners are 'the stories of a new Bible'. Here, one of the partisans, during a discussion on Mosaic laws, declares: 'If Moses was here with us . . . he'd smash the tablets . . . and he'd make new ones. Especially if he had seen the things we have seen' (II: 353). And the parallel between the deliverance of the Jews from Egypt and the plight of European Jews in the 1940s, made only to be uncompromisingly rejected in 'Potassio', is again made and again rejected here: 'Who would divide the waters before the Jews of Novoselki? Who would feed them on quails and manna? No manna descended from the black sky, only merciless snow' (II: 263).

Yet God, even when explicitly denied, is constantly addressed by Mendel in the way typical of the Jewish tradition from Job to Tevye the Dairyman: 'Let the war end, Lord in whom I don't believe' (II: 422); ' "You have chosen us among all nations": why us? Why do the wicked thrive, why are the helpless slaughtered, why are there hunger, mass graves, typhus, SS flamethrowers aimed into the holes crammed with terrified children?' (II: 259).

The religious references are situated in a wider context which includes proverbs, songs, blessings for all occasions, examples and explanations from the Talmud and folk tales. There are also unmistakeable references to the surreal Russian-Jewish images of Marc Chagall: 'and above the ceiling you picture a dark, snowy sky, where perhaps a great silver fish, a bride dressed in white veils, and an upside down green billy-goat are swimming together' (II: 432). Gedaleh's violin – which symbolically shatters just before the band reaches Italy and its uncertain new beginnings – can also be traced back to Chagall's recurrent imagery. Some of these cultural symbols are presented as ambivalently as the biblical references. The edifying folk-tale of the *Yeshiva Bucherim*, Talmudic students recruited in the Tsar's army who, although excellent marksmen, refuse to fire in battle because the enemies are human beings like themselves, is ironically used to this very purpose: Mendel is sarcastically addressed as *'yeshiva bucher'* by a Gentile partisan leader just before he is forced to learn about the practical realities of guerrilla warfare the hard way, by having to kill a wounded enemy in cold blood (II: 284–91).

Traditional stereotypes of Jewishness ('the pale blood of the breed from which he knew he descended, tailors, merchants, innkeepers, village fiddlers, meek and prolific patriarchs, and mystical rabbis', II: 205) are redefined in the descriptions of the partisan band:

> They were tired, poor, and dirty, but not defeated; the children of merchants, tailors, rabbis and cantors, they had armed themselves with weapons taken from the Germans . . . in the frozen steppe, in snow and mud, they had found a new freedom, unknown to their fathers and grandfathers, a contact with men who were friends and enemies, with nature and with action, which went to their heads like the wine of Purim (II: 318–19).

Levi also attempts to expose cultural stereotyping by presenting a neat counterpart to his implied readers' notions of 'Jews': his partisans have an image of Italy distorted by distance and ignorance into extreme clichés ('Italy itself is a fairy tale . . . Vesuvius and gondolas, Pompeii and Fiat, La Scala opera house and the caricatures of Mussolini', II: 234; 'Italy, the land of mild climate and notorious, blatant illegality; the affectionate and *mafioso* land whose double reputation had reached even Norway and the Ukraine and the sealed ghettoes of Eastern Europe; the land of evaded prohibitions and anarchic open-mindedness, where every foreigner is welcomed like a brother', II: 483). When some members of the band actually meet a group of Italians – mostly bourgeois Jews, integrated in their society for generations and not irreparably damaged by the war – all attempts to communicate fail (II: 504–9).

The novel is thus a complex discourse on 'Jewishness' and

identity, as well as a respectful tribute to a remote and largely lost culture. Yet, for all Levi's intellectual and emotional involvement, its overall effect is still one of stereotyping. This is inevitable given the structure of the book, built entirely on a system of oppositions (*shtetlach*/forests and swamps; *shtetlach*/cities; orthodox/secular Jews; Eastern/Western European Jews; Jews/ Gentiles). His characters, constructed as elements of these oppositions, are mostly one-dimensional, and differences or conflicts between them are represented through lengthy exchanges of views more than through action. Yiddish is also presented as opposed to all other European languages, as linguistic evidence of the partisans' common Ashkenazi identity distinct from the national identities of official national languages. Levi's tribute to Yiddish is both loving and painstaking: a number of fairly well-known words and expressions (*Nu, shikse, baleboosteh, meshuge, nebech*,[29] and the sarcastic twisting of words obtained by replacing the initial phoneme or phonemes with *shm*) are carefully transliterated according to Ashkenazi phonology and precisely glossed for their denotations and connotations. This, however, unavoidably emphasises the 'otherness' of Yiddish and inscribes it, rather than as a living language, as a set of cultural labels to be preserved and analysed for their historical significance.[30]

The reception of *Se non ora, quando?* was on the whole enthusiastic in Italy. Most Gentile reviewers described it as epic, picaresque and biblical, and some went as far as to compare it to *War and Peace*; a few (Marabini 1982 and Luperini 1982) however expressed reservations on its traditional 'realist' narrative presentation. Jewish reviewers emphasised instead that the novel shed light on Jewish armed resistance and thus helped to demolish the stereotype of Jews as passive victims. Both Jews and Gentiles saw it as a tribute to secular Jewishness and as an important instance of Italian Jewish culture. In English-speaking countries, particularly in the United States with its many intellectuals, writers and critics with Ashkenazi Jewish backgrounds, reviewers noted both Levi's schematicism and his comparative unfamiliarity with Ashkenazi culture, and either sharply dismissed the novel altogether (Eberstadt 1985) or praised it as a well-meaning if not entirely successful effort at cultural mediation (Hughes 1985; Angress 1988: 326–7).

Yet the novel is important, both as part of the evolution of

Levi's preoccupations and as evidence of the tensions, increasingly political as well as cultural, of the period in which it was written. Whatever the author's stated intentions, it reads above all as a constant problematisation of every aspect of Jewishness. Significantly, the prevailing states of mind of the central character, Mendel, with whom by his own admission Levi partly identifies,[31] are doubt and weariness.

A few weeks after the publication of *Se non ora, quando?* Levi visited Auschwitz for the second time, with a group of approximately a hundred people, mostly secondary school students who had written projects on deportation. On 6 June while he was there, explaining to his companions the dynamics of death and survival, the Israeli army invaded Southern Lebanon and mounted a three-pronged attack on Beirut, aiming to corner and trap the PLO leadership whose headquarters were in West Beirut. By mid-June Beirut was besieged by both the Israeli army and the Lebanon Falangists, a Christian right-wing military organisation, and approximately ten thousand civilians had been slaughtered. The operation, dubbed 'Operation Peace for Galilee' by the Israeli government, had political repercussions and caused sharp conflicts within all nations belonging to the Western bloc, including Italy. The Italian left condemned the Israeli aggression in very strong terms, with some journalists going as far as to draw explicit parallels between the Israeli defence minister Sharon and Nazi military leaders, and to talk in terms of a proposed 'final solution' for the Palestinians.

It was inevitable that Levi – by 1982 one of the best-known Italian Jews, the best-known Italian survivor of the death camps, and the author of a very recent best-selling novel about dispossessed Jews in search of a homeland – would be asked to take an open stand. He was specifically addressed in a direct appeal to Jews printed in the left-wing daily *Il manifesto*:

> Their existence, marked, like everyone else's, by a thousand contradictions, is now burdened by one more terrible contradiction. Yet history calls upon them today to distance themselves [from Israel], more explicitly and bravely than yesterday. . . . Stealing words from Primo Levi, *if not now, when?* (Gentiloni 1982: 3).

Some positive reviews of *Se non ora, quando?* (Gentiloni and Jesurum) were also published in those days: they explicitly compared Levi's 'armed Jews' to the invasion of Lebanon, stressing that the attitude of Levi's characters to war and violence was substantially different from the arrogant approach of Begin's and Sharon's soldiers.

On 16 June Levi and seven other Jewish intellectuals (including the writer and camp survivor Edith Bruck, the historian Ugo Caffaz, the writer Natalia Ginzburg and the writer and psychoanalyst David Meghnagi) published an open letter in the influential daily paper *La Repubblica*, which had condemned the Israeli aggression. The letter – subsequently signed by many other Italian Jewish intellectuals – requested that the Israeli government immediately withdraw its troops from Lebanon, stressing the need for mutual recognition between the Israelis and the Palestinians. Within the Italian Jewish community there were strong reactions of dissent to the appeal, focusing specifically on Levi as the author of *Se questo è un uomo*, as 'the symbol of an idea or a community' and as someone whose rediscovery of Jewish culture had helped readers become aware of the 'complex and troubled Jewish conscience'.[32] Levi was undeterred. On 24 June he published an article entitled 'Chi ha coraggio a Gerusalemme?' (Who Is Brave in Jerusalem?), which appeared on the front page of *La Stampa*. He made explicit connections between his return to Auschwitz and his reactions to Israeli policies:

> I happened to hear the news about the Israeli attack on Lebanon while travelling back to Auschwitz as guide to a group of visitors. The two experiences juxtaposed, causing me agony . . . I feel no shame in admitting that I feel torn apart. My bond with Israel stands, in a way I feel it is my second country, I would like it to be different from all other countries. For this very reason I feel anguish and shame at its actions.

The letter in *La Repubblica* also stated that opposition to Begin's policies was 'a way to fight the potential seeds of a new anti-Semitism, which would be added to the old, never dispelled, anti-Jewish tendencies within society'. This warning was timely and appropriate. Within Italian society, which had always found it difficult to face up to its own latent anti-Semitism, it was all too easy to identify Israeli aggression with the Jewish people rather than Begin's and Sharon's leadership. On 25 June, while half a million workers were demonstrating in Rome against unemployment and the government's economic policies, a small group left the march to go and place a symbolic coffin in front of the Synagogue rather than the Israeli embassy. On 9 October some terrorists attacked Jews coming out of the Rome Synagogue with bombs and submachine-guns, causing several casualties and the death of a two-year-old boy.

In September the Israeli army occupied Beirut and backed the Lebanese Falangists as they razed to the ground the Palestinian refugee camps of Sabra and Shatila in West Beirut and massacred their occupants. Jewish intellectuals, particularly those who like Levi identified with the left, saw themselves being placed in an extremely difficult position. On the one hand, they needed to express their anger and disgust as strongly as possible, and to oppose any attempts to use the uniqueness of the Holocaust to justify not only the existence of Israel, but also all its policies.[33] On the other hand, they resented the immediate requests made on them by the (Gentile) Italian left to dissociate themselves from Israel as Jews, as a political and moral duty irrespective of their specific cultural, emotional and often personal bonds with Israel. A number of Italian Jews, including Levi, demonstrated outside the Israeli embassy in Rome on 25 September. *La Repubblica* asked Levi for an interview, which was published on the front page on 24 September with the outspoken title 'Io, Primo Levi, chiedo le dimissioni di Begin' (I, Primo Levi, ask for Begin's resignation). Levi was once again honest in admitting his own internal conflicts and firm in differentiating between the notions of 'Jew', 'Zionist' and 'expansionist'. He implicitly acknowledged that he was being asked to speak as an Auschwitz survivor as well as an internationally famous writer, and agreed to do so to counteract the ideological use of the Holocaust by the Israeli ruling class as a justification of its attempt to wipe out the Palestinian people:

> I do not care whether my words affect Italian readers, I want them to affect Israel, its rulers, its voters, Israeli journalists . . .. We all need to do two or three things. To become aware. To stifle our impulses of emotional solidarity with Israel so as to reflect dispassionately on the mistakes of the present Israeli ruling class. To overthrow this ruling class. . . . I am torn apart, also because I know very well that Israel was founded by people like me, who were less lucky than I was. Men with the Auschwitz number tattooed on their arms, homeless and countryless . . . who found a home and a country over

there. I know all this. But I also know that this is Begin's favourite argument. And I do not recognise this argument as valid.[34]

After that interview, he refused to take any more public stands on the Middle East crisis. There was a further repercussion: the 1983 national congress of the Union of the Italian Jewish communities, at which he had been asked to be the keynote speaker, was postponed for a year, and another keynote speaker was invited for 1984.

Se non ora, quando? was awarded two literary prizes, the Viareggio in June and the Campiello in September. To what extent the awards reflected the Italian cultural establishment's belief in the novel's intrinsic value in comparison with the other books competing, reflected the power of Einaudi, were personal tributes to Levi, or rewarded his explicit distancing himself from Israeli policies while admitting his own personal conflicts, can only be a matter for speculation. Be that as it may, the prizes contributed to the success of the book which sold over one hundred thousand copies in a few years (Einaudi 1990: 35).

As well as his own writings, Levi had undertaken translations for Einaudi, beginning with two anthropological monographs by Claude Lévi-Strauss, *Le regard éloigné* (*Lo sguardo da lontano*) and *La voie des masques* (*La via delle maschere*). Giulio Einaudi then asked him to participate in a new project, a series of foreign novels re-translated by living Italian writers. The underlying assumptions were that the translators would be enriched by the texts they approached, and that a late twentieth-century perspective would shed additional light on these classics (Dentice 1983: 115). Other writers involved in the project were Italo Calvino and Natalia Ginzburg, who were offered respectively *Lord Jim* and *Madame Bovary*. Levi was asked to translate Kafka's *Der Prozeß* (*The Trial*).

Levi's version – there had been two previous ones – appeared in April 1983, with an afterword in which Levi stated that 'reading *The Trial*, a book full of unhappiness and poetry, leaves us changed: sadder and more aware' and admitted that he 'did not believe Kafka was very akin' to him. He explained his ambivalent response in a brief essay[35] two months later:

> I love and admire Kafka because he writes in a way which is totally impossible for me. In my writing, for better or for worse, knowingly or not, I have always strived to move from darkness to light . . .

Kafka forges his path in the opposite direction . . . . My love [for him] is ambivalent, close to fear and rejection: it is similar to the emotion we feel for someone we love, who is suffering and asks for help we cannot give . . . . You feel like one of his characters, condemned by an abject and inscrutable tribunal that is all-reaching, that invades the city and the world (III: 920–1).

Levi also points out that the 'shame' felt by Josef K., as he, innocent, is being killed matter-of-factly by two meticulous bureaucrats, is something familiar to him: it is 'the shame of being a man', of belonging to the same human race which has devised the all-pervasive court that sentenced him. His words clearly recall the first pages of *La tregua* and the anguish of 'Cromo', and anticipate the painstaking and painful analysis of the survivors' shame in *I sommersi e i salvati*.

The translation, which had a mixed critical reception,[36] affected Levi painfully. He confessed to an interviewer that he had felt himself 'becoming as sick as [Kafka]', and that he had 'emerged from the translation as if from an illness'.[37] In another interview, he described Josef K. as the symbol of the fate of Jews, and of every human being, in extraordinary situations and connected Kafka's pessimism to his own present view of the world, specifically his belief that 'the death camps can give birth only to more death camps' (de Melis 1983: 2).

Levi continued to formulate his own reflections on the death camps in articles and occasional papers, most of which were given definitive shape in *I sommersi e i salvati*. On 28 and 29 October 1983[38] the Piedmont regional government and ANED (the National Association of Ex-Deportees) organised an international conference on the Nazi concentration camps. It was held in Turin and was called 'Il dovere di testimoniare' (The Duty to Bear Witness). Its aims were twofold: to record evidence from witnesses and to assemble rigorous historical evidence against attempts, such as Darquier's and Faurisson's, to challenge or deny the magnitude of the Nazi massacres. This was part of a series of projects focusing on the Second World War, the Resistance and experiences of deportation that had been foreshadowed for the 1980s by a 1976 regional law. This commitment was due partly to the active participation of Piedmont in anti-Fascist movements and the Resistance, and partly to the presence in Turin of well-known historians of Fascism and the Second World War such as Guido Quazza and

Nicola Tranfaglia, as well as younger (mainly oral) historians such as Luisa Passerini, Anna Bravo, Anna Maria Bruzzone and Federico Cereja. Historians and camp survivors from eight nations gave papers on current research projects and various aspects of deportation. The paper given by Levi, 'La memoria dell'offesa' (The Memory of the Offence) basically coincides with the first chapter of *I sommersi e i salvati*. It starts with the warning that 'human memory is a wonderful but faulty instrument', and goes on to describe the motivations and processes of the deformation and suppression of memory by both oppressors and victims. In *I sommersi e i salvati*, however, the discussion of memory ends with a personal statement: while acknowledging that his own memory may be suspect, Levi stresses his belief that his personal recollections are precise and reliable.

The scientist's desire to understand fully the processes of memory and to use this knowledge in order to fight historical distortions was always for Levi in painful tension with the more personal aspects of memory. Two months after the conference, in February 1984, he wrote the poem 'Il superstite' (The Survivor), which he dedicated to 'B.V.', his friend Bruno Vasari, a former *Giustizia e Libertà* partisan, a survivor of Mauthausen and the president of the Piedmont branch of ANED. It is one of Levi's most frequently-quoted poems. Its power is the effect of a cumulative structure: a series of images of dead comrades, which recall the pages of *Se questo è un uomo*, haunt a man identified only as 'the survivor' and referred to in the third person. The images are then sharply addressed in direct speech, in a sequence of strongly emotional negative first-person sentences, each emphasising the opposite presupposition by the very act of denying it:

> Stand back, leave me alone, submerged people,
> Go away. I haven't dispossessed anyone,
> Haven't usurped anyone's bread.
> No one died in my place. No one.
> Go back into your mist.
> It's not my fault if I live and breathe,
> And eat and drink and sleep and put on clothes (II: 581).

The last line recontextualises a line from Canto 33 of Dante's *Inferno*. In the circle of traitors, one of the damned refers to a man whose soul is already in Hell and whose body goes through the motions of everyday life while being occupied by a devil. The recontexting, which adds the notion of betrayal to that of guilt and the notion of being only apparently alive to that of surviving, is chilling in the global context of Levi's writings.

Guilt and pain continued to coexist with the commitment to cultural mediation of all kinds. In early 1984 Edizioni di Comunità, a small Milan publisher, started producing a series of interviews between journalists and well-known representatives of Italian culture who talked about the daily tasks, experiences and challenges of their professions. One of the first to be approached was Tullio Regge, Professor of Relativity in the Department of Theoretical Physics at Turin University and the author of many articles explaining scientific theories to the readers of *La Stampa*. Regge, about ten years younger than Levi and already acquainted with him, asked to have him as an interlocutor. *Dialogo*, the result of two days' tape-recorded conversations, was published in late 1984.

Both men begin by comparing their different experiences (Regge is not Jewish) as learners of Hebrew and readers of the Torah, and then move back in time to their childhoods, associating their love for science with their fathers. As the memories proceed chronologically to university and work, the conversation becomes more one-sided: Regge takes centre stage as the expert explaining the theory of fields and the Big Bang, and Levi takes the supporting role of the curious layman asking questions. The discussion on science is thus not a dialectical encounter but a brilliant and occasionally witty summary of physics research in this century, based on a shared unqualified respect for 'objective knowledge'. The dialogue returns to an equal footing in the third part, where the two men investigate their relationship with non-scientific culture: Levi points out the influence of his chemical training on his writing, in terms of precision, conciseness and relatively new metaphors. The conclusion contains the only elements of uncertainty about the applications of scientific knowledge: Levi declares that physicists are the real masters of the world, with boundless power over energy and thus over humankind, and Regge states that recent discoveries leading to the construction of an anti-missile satellite introduce further elements of instability in a world that definitely does not need them.

These expressions of concern are the only references in this text to the contemporary political situation. Levi, however, was still being asked to express opinions – and to take political stands – about events involving Israel. In September 1984 he was interviewed by the Jewish left-wing journalist Gad Lerner on current Israeli political trends. In the interview (provocatively entitled 'Se questo è uno Stato', 'If This Is a State'), he made a number of forthright general statements, connecting his disapproval of the Israeli right wing with his views on the role of Diaspora Jews:

> I am convinced that the role of Israel as the unifying centre for Jews is now – let me stress *now* – declining. It is therefore necessary for the centre of gravity for Jews to be turned upside down, to be once more outside Israel. It must return to us Diaspora Jews, who have the task of reminding our friends in Israel that within Judaism there is a tradition of tolerance . . . .. The history of the Diaspora has, of course, been a history of persecutions, but it has also been a history of exchanges and inter-ethnic relationships, and therefore a school of tolerance. Especially in Italy.[39]

Levi's argument, although consistent with the rest of his writings, was controversial and was received critically. A variety of representatives of Italian Jewish communities, while expressing respect for him as a writer and in some cases agreement with his disapproval of Israeli policies, maintained that Israel and the Diaspora were not in antithesis, or expressed concern at the growing assimilation and erosion of Diaspora communities.[40] His concept of 'the Jewish tradition of tolerance', however, has not only become identified with him in Italian culture after his death but has also become an identification label for Italian Jews who proudly acknowledge their heritage but view it as historical and secular (see Lerner 1985: 40).

Notes to Chapter Four

1. Faurisson's theses have been comprehensively refuted in a scholarly article by the historian Pierre Vidal-Naquet (1985: 195–255). See also Maier (1988) and Vidal-Naquet (1993).
2. See Zevi (1980) and Belgiojoso (1984: 193).
3. Levi's original text consisted of eight paragraphs, which summed up the history of the various categories of Italian

deportees and connected them to the history of Italian Fascism and anti-Fascism. For technical reasons, only the final words were used as the epigraph. The full text is given in Poli and Calcagno (1992: 174–6).

4. The religious reference is even more explicit in a 1982 interview: 'I perceived [my introduction to Gattermann's book] as the voice of the Father: thou shalt do this, thou shalt not do that; command and prohibition' (Interview with Giovanni Pacchioni, 1982f).

5. See the discussion of this story in chapter 3.

6. See Santagostino (1993b) for a detailed analysis of Levi's debt to Rabelais.

7. See chapter 3.

8. The first Italian translation of *The Story of Tevye the Dairyman* by Shalom Alechem (transliterated as Scialom Alechem) was published in 1928. Isaac Bashevis Singer's works were regularly translated from the early 1960s onward. Canetti's *Auto da fè* was first published in 1967.

9. See Freschi (1992).

10. *Shtetlach* (plural of *shtetl*) were the insular town or village communities where Ashkenazi Jewish culture and values were cherished and preserved.

11. See also P. Valabrega (1982: 305–6), Angress (1988) and Segre (1991).

12. 'If compared with someone who is a hundred per cent Jewish, I am twenty, maybe twenty-five per cent' (Jesurum 1987: 95); 'If I had not experienced the anti-Semitic laws and Auschwitz, I probably would no longer be a Jew, but for my surname: however, these two experiences . . . have stamped me, like a sheet of metal' (Camon 1987: 71–2). See also the interview with Giulio Goria (1982c).

13. See especially Roth (1986: 41), and the interviews with Roberto Vacca (1982d) and Fiona Diwan (1982j).

14. See the interviews with Roberto Vacca (1982d) and Fiona Diwan (1982j).

15. See Jesurum (1987: 98). In the late 1970s several British publishers declared their lack of interest to various would-be translators of *Il sistema periodico*, including the present writer. The American scholar George Jochnowitz approached a number of American publishers with similarly discouraging results.

16. See the interviews with Giovanni Pacchioni (1982f) and Gabriella Monticelli (1982h).
17. Based on an idea in Isak Dinesen's *Seven Gothic Tales*.
18. Levi informs the readers (III: 536–7) that his story is based on authentic data, and that the Sirionos still exist, although they are in danger of extinction.
19. In *Moments of Reprieve* the story has the title 'Rappoport's Testament'. The Italian title makes an implicit comparison between the proud stand of the doomed Auschwitz prisoner and the vain defiance of King Capaneus, struck by a thunderbolt from Zeus on the walls of Thebes, and placed by Dante in the seventh circle of Hell (*Inferno* XIV).
20. Levi's fascination with Lilith and the legends and traditions connected with her is evident also from a poem he wrote in 1965, where she is described as 'a beautiful woman down to her waist;/The rest is will-o'-the-wisp and pale light' (*Ad ora incerta*, II: 547).
21. This precept is also quoted in 'Il rito e il riso' (Ritual and Laughter), one of the most important essays in the collection *L'altrui mestiere* (III: 197).
22. The original, ironical title is 'King of the Jews', which is also the title of a novel by Leslie Epstein, based on Rumkowski's life. In *Moments of Reprieve*, the story has the title 'Story of a Coin'.
23. This story is not included in any of the translated collections. Implicit parallels between it and the Auschwitz experience have been pointed out in Santagostino (1992: 239–40).
24. *Pirké Avoth*, 1: 13: 'If I am not for myself, who will be for me? If I am for myself alone, what am I? If not now, when?'
25. See also P. Valabrega (1982: 304).
26. 1981 was a year in which world opinion was sympathetic to the activities of the Polish free union movement Solidarity, seen mainly as a mass rebellion of ordinary people against an oppressive government. In December 1981, as Levi was finishing his novel, the army led by General Jaruzelski seized power and declared a state of siege after Solidarity had demanded free elections.

    Levi said explicitly in an interview (1982l: 41) that he wanted to give his readers a chance to understand how the Polish crisis of 1981 had been foreshadowed in the events of 1944.

27. The definition refers to various socialist Jewish groups founded in Russia around the turn of the century by young people who migrated to Palestine and established the first *kibbutzim*, which were based on the collectivist model of the farming cooperative *mir*. Left-wing Zionism was politically defeated in the late 1920s after the international economic crisis. For a historical background, see G. Valabrega (1974: 337–99) and Meghnagi (1980: 19–73).
28. See the interviews with Giulio Goria (1982c) and Fiona Diwan (1982j).
29. The approximate English equivalents of these words are, respectively, 'Now then', 'non-Jewish woman', 'good housewife', 'crazy' and 'feckless'.
30. For the role of Yiddish in Levi's writings, with particular reference to *Se non ora, quando?*, see Gilman (1991: 300–16).
31. See the interviews with Gabriella Monticelli (1982h) and Fiona Diwan (1982j).
32. See the June 1982 issue of *Shalom*, the monthly paper of the Union of the Italian Jewish Communities (especially the letters by Alberto Nirenstain and Sion Segre Amar).
33. Tzvetan Todorov's comment of ten years later – that the ethical attitude for anyone taking the side of the victims of the Holocaust consists in not taking any advantage of its uniqueness (Todorov 1992: 115) – appears very relevant in this context.
34. Interview with Giampaolo Pansa (1982i: 3).
35. Levi (1983b). The essay was reprinted in *Racconti e saggi* under the title 'Translating Kafka', and is included in *The Mirror Maker*.
36. Oreste del Buono saw Levi as a 'mediator between Kafka and himself, the survivor of Auschwitz' (1983). The Germanist Sandra Bosco Coletsos, while praising some lexical choices, objected to Levi losing the deliberate ambiguities of the original text in his attempts to clarify it (1985: 249–68). See also Cases (1989: 101).
37. Interview with Luciano Genta (1983) quoted in Poli and Calcagno (1992: 306–7).
38. The date coincided with both the fiftieth anniversary of the coming to power of the National Socialist Party in Germany and the sixty-first anniversary of Mussolini's 'march on Rome'.

39. Interview with Gad Lerner (1984a: 41–50).
40. See the discussion on pp. 16–19 of the October 1984 issue of *Shalom* and De Benedetti (1984).

5

'Do Not Call Us Teachers'

*L*evi's recognition, by the public and the media if not by the critics, was growing internationally as well as in Italy. In response to the increasing interest in his work, he set about collecting his poems, essays and short stories. Throughout the last three years of his life, however, he was troubled both by personal difficulties and by the fear that the bridges of communication he had built with his writings would not withstand the multiple threats to civilisation and the end of the century.

In October 1984 he published his collected poems under the title *Ad ora incerta* (*At an Uncertain Hour*). This consists of the twenty-seven poems of *L'osteria di Brema*, another thirty-four original poems (nearly all previously published in *La Stampa*) and ten translations, mainly from Heinrich Heine. Levi explained his choice of title – taken from Coleridge's *Rime of the Ancient Mariner* – by referring to the unpredictable nature of his poetic production. In his brief, self-deprecating introduction to the collection, he admits 'giving in' to the impulse to write poetry at irregular intervals, 'at an uncertain hour', something which '[his] rational half continues to consider unnatural' (II: 521).[1] However, in an interview coinciding with the appearance of the collection, he took issue with the famous statement by Theodor Adorno that 'to write poetry after Auschwitz is barbaric [and] has become impossible':[2]

> My experience has been the opposite. Then [in the years 1945–46, when he was writing poetry before embarking on *Se questo è unuomo*] it seemed to me that poetry was more suitable than prose to express all the weight inside me . . .. In those years, possibly, I would have reworded Adorno's statement: after Auschwitz it is no longer possible to write poetry except about Auschwitz. [3]

From this perspective, the title emphasises one of the central aspects of Levi's autography, namely the survivor's need, parallel to that of the Ancient Mariner, to 'teach' his tale. Significantly, the stanza from Coleridge's poem that contains the title of Levi's collection is paraphrased at the beginning of 'Il superstite' and, in the original English, is the epigraph of *I sommersi e i salvati*:

Since then, at an uncertain hour,
That agony returns,
And till my ghastly tale is told
This heart within me burns.

Just under one third of the poems in the collection were written between 1943 and 1949, before the deportation and after the return to Turin; another third were written between 1952 and 1979 and the remaining third belong to the period 1980–4. The date of each poem is provided by Levi himself, to emphasise the irregular occurrence of his need to express himself through poetry.

The form and language of the poems are not experimental, because – consistently with Levi's central notion of writing as primarily communication – his poems are above all messages, intellectual, moral and social at the same time. The 'concise and gruesome' poems written after his return contain hardly anything but haunting memories of irreparably lost people and moments, in a language which echoes Dante's *Inferno* and Eliot's *The Waste Land*. '25 febbraio 1944', titled after the day before Levi's train reached Auschwitz, addresses (without naming her) Vanda, the woman who was to be swallowed up soon afterwards. The intertextual references to both Dante and Eliot foreground the despair of a loss not comforted by belief in an afterlife:

I would like to believe in something
Beyond the death that has undone you.
I would like to describe the intensity
With which we, already submerged,
Wished then that we could once more
Walk together beneath the sun in freedom (II: 527).

Memories of persecution and death which return to haunt survivors are a recurrent theme throughout the collection.

'Attesa' (Waiting), written in 1949, warns its female addressee that after experiencing 'friendly streets at night' and 'serene meditations', she and the poet will again be awakened by 'the familiar pounding of hobnailed footsteps/Outside our doors' (II: 540). Further echoes of Eliot[4] can be found in 'Il canto del corvo II' (Song of the Crow II, 1953), where a crow haunts a man whose identity remains unspecified to the end, which comes 'not with a bang but silence', and in 'Fuga' (Flight, 1984), where 'rock and sand and no water' surround a man who, on finding water, poisons it for ever with the blood on his hands.

Many of the poems written from the 1950s on are sombre reflections on contemporary events with heavy use of anaphoras, the figure of speech preferred by Levi to convey warnings.[5] 'Per Adolf Eichmann' (For Adolf Eichmann) is dated 20 July 1960, after Eichmann was kidnapped by Israeli agents in Argentina and taken to Israel and before his trial and death sentence. The war criminal is addressed by a first person plural which simultaneously refers to the Israelis ('The wind runs free across our plains,/The living sea beats for ever at our shores', II: 544) and to all Jews ('O son of death, we do not wish you death./May you live longer than anyone ever lived:/May you live without sleep five million nights', II: 544). In 'Dateci' (Give Us), dated 30 April 1984, the subjects speaking in the first person plural are the disoriented young generation emerging from the years of terrorism:

> Give us something to destroy,
> A flower, a quiet corner,
> A fellow believer, a magistrate,
> A telephone box,
> A journalist, a renegade,
> A supporter of the other team.
> . . . Do not despise us: we are heralds and prophets.
> Give us something that burns, hurts, cuts, smashes, befouls,
> And makes us feel that we exist (II: 584).

Levi's agnosticism and his ambivalent view of science find a powerful expression in the anaphoras and metaphors of the ironically titled 'Nel principio' (In the Beginning)[6], written in 1970 when the Big Bang theory began to be known and debated.

Fellow humans for whom a year is a long time,
. . . Hear, and may this be both comfort and mockery:
Twenty billion years before now,
Brilliant, soaring in space and time,
There was a ball of flame, solitary, eternal,
Our common father and our executioner,
And it exploded, and every change began.
. . . From that one spasm everything was born:
The very abyss that enfolds and challenges us,
The very time that spawns and destroys us,
Everything anyone has ever thought,
The eyes of every woman we have loved,
Suns by the thousands,
And this hand that writes (II: 548).

The masculine metaphors for the beginning and the end of life
('our father', 'our executioner', 'spasm') are challenged, yet
constructed as 'comfort' as well as 'mockery': humankind is an
insignificant detail in the process of evolution of matter, yet it has
acquired the knowledge of this process and the skill to record it
as well as its own beliefs, loves and fears. The author's self-
inscription as a fleeting moment in the lifespan of the universe,
and at the same time as an individual reflecting on the universe
and himself and as a writer engaged in a process of
communication and education, is an anticipation of the better-
known final paragraph of *Il sistema periodico*.

Scientific knowledge is at times a source of profound
pessimism: 'The sky is strewn with horrible dead suns,/Dense
sediments of crushed atoms./ . . . And all of us human seed live
and die for nothing,/And the skies perpetually revolve in vain'
('Le stelle nere' (The Black Stars) II: 550) and a source of joyful
pride: the Greek philosopher Empedocles, speaking in the first
person in 'Autobiografia' (Autobiography), sums himself up as
the temporarily final stage of the evolution of living beings, in a
poetic version of the colloquial register of the story 'Il fabbro di
se stesso'. Empedocles, who has 'endured the whip/And heat
and cold and the desperation of the yoke/ . . . [and] known tears
and laughter and many loves' (II: 563) is also partly a metaphor
of Levi himself, as are Pliny the Elder, unaware of the deadly
consequences of his wish to record the novel phenomena of
Vesuvius and convey them to the world ('Plinio') and Galileo

Galilei, deprived of dignity and oppressed by the banality of evil: 'He who chained me to earth/Did not unleash earthquakes or thunderbolts./His voice was soft and mild,/He had the face of everyman' ('Sidereus nuncius', II: 583).

A recurring feature of the poems written in the 1980s is Levi's use of anthropomorphic animal and plant metaphors. The abrupt interruption in 'Schiera bruna' (Dark Column), a description of a colony of ants, creates an instant effect of estrangement and a shift from the literal to the metaphoric, with images of brown-shirted formations all the more threatening because unspoken:

> They have dug their city inside ours,
> Traced their tracks on top of ours,
> And scurry about there unsuspecting,
> Tireless in their petty affairs
> Paying no heed to
>> I do not want to write it,
>> I do not want to write about this column,
>> I do not want to write about any dark column (II: 562).

Often the anthropomorphic animals and plants are speaking subjects and, to some extent, autobiographical metaphors. 'Pio' (Pious)[7] is an angry response to a poem, well known to most Italians, by the late nineteenth-century poet and academic Giosuè Carducci where the 'pious ox' is praised for his gentle mildness. Asserting its own subjectivity and questioning the claims to authority of the oppressor's discourse which constructs it as harmless, the ox becomes a collective historical metaphor, reinforced by the Yiddish exclamation at the end:

> Pious ox my foot. Pious by force,
> Pious against my wishes, pious against my nature,
> Pious by cliché, pious by euphemism.
> . . . Pious yourself, Professor.
> . . . Had you been present when they made me pious
> You would have lost all desire to write poetry
> And to eat beef at midday.
> Or do you think I cannot see, here on this meadow,
> My whole brother, erect, fierce,
> Who with only a thrust of his loins
> Inseminates my sister the cow?

Oy gevalt! Unheard-of violence,
The violence to make me non-violent (II: 586).

Levi also represents himself as an old mole, surviving pain by withdrawing into itself ('Now I travel sleepless,/Imperceptible under the meadows,/Where I feel neither cold nor heat/Nor wind rain day night snow', II: 571); an elephant enslaved by Indians, Egyptians and Phoenicians, a snail, an agave, and a horse chestnut tree enduring the discomforts of city life through the renewals of time ('Under its bark hang dead chrysalides/That will never be butterflies./Still, in its sluggish wooden heart/It feels, savours the seasons' return', II: 558).

The tension between a view of the universe as hurtling meaninglessly towards its own destruction and a humanist attempt to discover and mediate meanings is evident in the way time is represented throughout the collection. Cosmic time is negative, merciless: 'The very time that spawns us and destroys us' ('Nel principio', II: 548), 'And the skies perpetually revolve in vain' ('Le stelle nere', II: 550). Yet human time is consistently represented positively, as something to be spent in activities useful to oneself and others, from the threat of the end in Auschwitz ('face to face with death,/I shouted no from every fibre,/I had not finished yet;/There was still too much to do' ('11 febbraio 1946', II: 536) to the time of reconstruction after the return ('The time has come to have a home,/Or to remain without a home for a long time./The time has come not to be alone,/Or else we will be alone for a long time' ('Da R.M. Rilke', After R.M. Rilke), II: 533). In 'Pasqua' (Passover), which is interwoven with phrases from the ritual of the Pesach Seder – the traditional dinner where food, prayers and ritual all celebrate the deliverance of the people of Israel from Egypt – time is represented as a cycle of pain and oppression, which may lead to justice if everyone's participation is acknowledged: 'Time reverses its course,/Today flowing back into yesterday,/Like a river blocked at its mouth./Each of us has been a slave in Egypt,/Soaked straw and clay with sweat/And crossed the sea with dry feet:/You too, stranger./This year in fear and shame,/Next year in virtue and justice' (II: 569).

Time is in fact too short for all the tasks which human beings will embark on hopefully and will inevitably leave unfinished. 'Le pratiche inevase' (Unfinished Business) is a list of such tasks, ending with a book 'That would have revealed many secrets,/ Soothed pain and fears,/Dissolved doubts, given many people/ The boon of tears and laughter./ . . . I haven't had time to see it through. Pity,/It would have been a seminal work' (II: 565). In 'Scacchi II' (Chess II) the opponent is death: '. . . You mean that, halfway through,/With the game all but over,/You'd like to change the rules of play?/ . . . Move, your time is running out;/ Don't you hear the clock ticking away?/ . . . You knew right from the start/That I was the stronger player' (II: 587). In 'Carichi pendenti' (Pending Tasks) the first-person speaker tentatively states his preference for a quick, quiet end 'But for the pending tasks,/The previously-incurred debts,/The previous irrevocable commitments' (II: 618). In 'Canto dei morti invano' (Song of Those Who Died in Vain) – written shortly after the beginning of the negotiations between the USA and the USSR on the reduction of nuclear weapons – the 'army of those who died in vain' during and after both world wars urge the negotiators to come to an agreement in words which recall the curses of 'Shema': 'Sit and negotiate/Until your tongues dry up:/If the destruction and shame continue/We will drown you in our rot' (II: 619).

Two poems contain no warnings or fears, and give flashes of insight into Levi's rigorously-guarded privacy. They are addressed to his wife and are titled with the dates of composition: '11 febbraio 1946', which presumably refers to their meeting, and '12 luglio 1980', her sixtieth birthday. The first defines her as the answer to his longings and hopes from the time of his childhood to his return from Auschwitz; it opens: 'I searched for you in the stars/When I questioned them as a child' and ends 'I have come back because you were there' (II: 536). The second poem addresses her as an individual in her own right, 'weary', 'impatient', 'ground down, wasted away, flayed' by her own pains and worries. His expressions of love and need are tentative and self-effacing: 'Accept, please, these fourteen lines,/ They are my rough way of calling you dear,/Of saying that I would not be in this world without you' (II: 561).

In November 1984, nine years after its publication in Italy, the American translator Raymond Rosenthal finally succeeded in having *Il sistema periodico* published. Rosenthal was a friend of Saul Bellow and Emile Capouya, the chief editor at Schocken Books, a reputable New York firm founded by German Jewish refugees, which had made it possible for works by international

Jewish intellectuals to become known in the English-speaking world.[8] The publication coincided with the growing interest in the United States in contemporary Italian writers such as Italo Calvino and Umberto Eco, whose *Il nome della rosa* (The Name of the Rose) had become a best-seller a few months earlier. *The Periodic Table* was reviewed enthusiastically by writers (Saul Bellow called it 'what a book should be', and Cynthia Ozick 'a brilliant entry-wedge into autobiography and an ebullient metaphysical creation'), academics and scientists such as the Nobel prizewinner Salvador Luria, a Piedmontese Jew who had fled to the United States. Reviews appeared in science journals such as *Science, New Scientist, Scientific American* and *Journal of Chemistry Education*.[9] Following its success in the United States, *The Periodic Table* was also published in the United Kingdom, and received glowing reviews in all quality periodicals as well as in *Nature* and *New Scientist*.

This lionisation led to frequent invitations for Levi to travel internationally. In April 1985 he went to the United States for a three-week lecture tour organised by Einaudi, the New York Italian Cultural Institute and a Jewish cultural association, and visited several universities in New York, Los Angeles, Bloomington and Boston. He was uneasy both about his success (Stille 1991a: 208–9) and about having to be, on different occasions, an Italian Jew, an Italian writer and a chemist.[10] He also felt uncomfortable about having to account for the integration of Italian Jews into mainstream Italian society and to justify his views on Israeli policies to audiences consisting mainly of elderly, pro-Israeli Jews (see the interview with Germaine Greer, 1985b: 18–19). The following year he and his wife visited Great Britain for the first time and took part in a Festival of Italian Jewry there. His meeting with the relatives of another prisoner, whose name is mentioned in the story 'Vanadio' of *Il sistema periodico*, is described in 'Un "giallo" del *Lager*' (A *Lager* Mystery, III: 887–90).[11]

Throughout this period of international fame, Levi and his wife continued the gruelling task – begun five years previously – of nursing both their mothers, nonagenarian invalids. The restrictions upon Levi's social life and political involvement were great; this probably contributed to his suffering from depression, from which he gradually recovered with the help of his family and friends. He nevertheless endeavoured to remain involved in

Italian cultural life. In early 1985 he was asked by Giulio Einaudi to write an introduction for the second edition[12] of the memoirs written by Rudolf Höss, the Commandant at Auschwitz, before his hanging in 1947. The introduction anticipates one of the arguments in *I sommersi e i salvati*: Höss is a typical example of 'the people on the other side', who were never at any time monsters and yet, step by step within the Nazi machinery, became some of the worst criminals in human history (Levi 1985a: v). As in *I sommersi e i salvati*, clear connections are made between the past and the present, specifically the attempted denial of history by the French revisionists (against which Höss's memoirs provide irrefutable evidence) and the dangers of blind adherence to ideologies, shared by Nazis like Höss and terrorists, both left- and right-wing, in the Italy of the 1970s. Levi also occasionally commented on social and scientific issues, from the explosion of the American shuttle *Challenger* to the disaster at the Chernobyl nuclear plant and the first successful attempt in Italy to pre-select the sex of children;[13] he was, with Moravia, Ginzburg and the Nobel prizewinner Rita Levi Montalcini, among the signatories of a petition requesting a nation-wide referendum to ban hunting, and he continued to write short pieces for *La Stampa*. He completed a series of interviews with the Catholic journalist and writer Ferdinando Camon, published shortly after his death under the title *Autoritratto* (*Self-Portrait*) (Camon 1987).

In January 1985 a collection of fifty-one short essays, written between 1964 and 1984 for the *terza pagina* of *La Stampa* appeared under the title *L'altrui mestiere* (*Other People's Trades*).[14] As Levi states in his preface, they are forays into areas of knowledge other than his own, poaching expeditions into

> the boundless territories of zoology, astronomy, and linguistics: sciences which I have never studied systematically and which, for just this reason, affect me with the endless fascination of unsatisfied and unrequited loves, and excite my instincts as a voyeur and kibitzer (III: 585).

The collection is evidence of Levi's wide-ranging curiosity, constructed as pleasure ('the uncontaminated delight of the *dilettanti*', III: 789)[15] and nourishment: unsystematic observations of scientific and linguistic phenomena 'are not science, but a stimulus to acquire it' (III: 685). There is also a consistent moral perspective, often emphasised in general statements in the initial or final paragraphs of each essay, which connect the specific topic of the essay to some human skill, need or conflict.

The autobiographical elements in the essays confirm the main features of Levi's cumulative self-construct. Evening classes in German, a language which he had 'learned by ear under conditions of hardship' and which he studied more formally at the age of sixty, are represented as 'self-improvement and growth, and also playing, acting, and a luxury' (III: 611). The chemist's trade, re-examined a few years after retirement, is described as providing not only the chance to learn from one's errors but also useful skills for anyone wanting to write, namely the skills to separate, weigh and distinguish things (III: 597) and to choose, weigh and interconnect words (III: 709). Descriptions of the physiology and behaviour of animals (birds, fleas, spiders, beetles) besides being elegant and witty 'encyclopedia entries', as Calvino described them in a review (Calvino 1985), belong to a secular view of the world where living creatures are respected as fascinating in themselves rather than as God's creation or God's gifts to humanity.

> Some readers will ask what is the use of this research [about the leaps of fleas]: a religious mind might reply that the harmony of creation is mirrored even in a flea; a secular mind prefers to state that the question is not relevant, and that a world where only useful things are studied would be sadder, poorer and possibly more violent than the world which fate has allotted us. Basically, the second reply is not all that different from the first (III: 690).

Levi's interest in linguistics – more precisely, in etymology and comparative lexicology – is evident in pieces on the names of chemical elements in various languages, on the words deriving from their inventors' surnames, on the origins of Italian idioms and on Italian popular etymologies.[16]

Levi's autobiographical construct is confirmed by essays on his positive or negative responses to certain writers, where he reveals intellectual affinities or incompatibilities and makes implicit comparisons with his own themes and style. He explains his lifelong love for Rabelais (who is 'rich in the virtues contemporary man, sad, shackled and weary as he is, lacks') with 'his merrily curious spirit, his good-natured scepticism, his faith in the future and in man' (III: 602) and with his belief that

Rabelais 'knows human misery [and] keeps quiet about it because, a good physician even when he writes, he does not accept it, he wants to heal it' (III: 603). He is drawn at the same time to Lewis Carroll because his books 'do not slip anything in on us, neither lessons in ethics nor didactic efforts' (III: 616) and to the nineteenth-century cookery writer Pellegrino Artusi, who 'passionately loves the art of cookery despised by hypocrites and dyspeptics, sets out to teach it, says as much, does so with the simplicity and clarity of someone who knows his subject well, and spontaneously produces a work of art' (III: 617). He describes himself as 'bewildered, cheered up and a little dizzy' after reading Raymond Queneau's *Petite Cosmogonie portative* (*A Portable Pocket Cosmogony*), a poem on the history of the world which, in a language full of puns and linguistic liberties, 'blends in a homogeneous continuum the over-mentioned "two cultures"' (III: 734).[17]

While expressing his admiration and delight at Queneau's style, Levi begins his essay on *Cosmogonie* by firmly stating his own views on writing:

> I always thought that one must write in a clear and orderly fashion; that writing is conveying a message, and that if the message is not understood it is the author's fault; that, therefore, a courteous writer must make it possible for his writings to be understood by the highest number of readers with the least effort (III: 732).

This uncompromising declaration is a repetition and a summary of 'Dello scrivere oscuro' (On Obscure Writing), an essay which Levi had written in 1976.[18] After emphatically rejecting any notion of prescriptive or proscriptive approaches to writing, Levi maintains that 'writing serves to communicate, to convey information or feelings ... and he who is not understood by anyone does not convey anything, he cries in the desert' (III: 635). He justifies his stand by representing his implied reader as someone with motivations very similar to his own:

> My 'ideal' reader is not a scholar but neither is he an ignoramus. He does not read because he has to, or to kill time, or to appear knowledgeable to others, but because he is curious about many things . . . .. He has chosen my books, and would feel uncomfortable or unhappy if he did not understand, line by line, what I have written, indeed, have written *for him* (III: 635).

From these premises, Levi goes on to express a negative evaluation of the poetry of Ezra Pound and Paul Celan:

> [Celan's language] is not a language, or is at best a dark and fragmented language, just like that of a person who is about to die, and is alone, as we all shall be at the point of death. But since we the living are not alone, we must not write as if we were alone. As long as we live we have a responsibility: we must be answerable for what we write, word by word, and ensure that every word reaches its mark (III: 637).

This essay, criticised by writers and literary scholars,[19] can be connected to 'Gli scacchisti irritabili' (The Irritable Chess Players), where chess players and writers are compared on the basis of their 'total responsibility for their actions' (III: 729) and of their 'laying themselves bare' before their public (III: 730). Levi's identification of writing with 'baring oneself', present also in his introduction to his 'personal anthology' *La ricerca delle radici*, occurs again in 'A un giovane lettore' (To a Young Reader), a page of 'professional advice' to a hypothetical young man wishing to become a writer (III: 818–19).

Three essays written after the publication of *Se non ora, quando?* deal specifically with Jewish culture. They are further reflections on the components of the identity of Diaspora Jews, and give the general public – initially, the readers of a large-circulation national daily paper – insights into the notions of 'identity' and 'difference'. In 'Il rito e il riso' (Ritual and Laughter), Levi discusses the most important code (along with that of Maimonides) of the rules of Judaism, *Shulkhan Arukh* (*The Set Table*) by the sixteenth-century Sephardic rabbi Joseph Caro. Levi is far from identifying with the meticulous prescriptions and proscriptions of the code: he lists some of them, such as those referring to the observance of the Sabbath and of the dietary laws, with the same witty, detached curiosity of his descriptions of the behaviour of insects or the etymology of Italian words. Yet, in the last page, detachment gives way first to admiration for the intellectual challenges of Talmudic debates and then to respect for their acknowledgement of exceptions to the rule of 'order prevailing over Chaos':

> [The authors] formulate hypotheses and solutions that bring to mind the problems worked out by chess players: that is to say, they imagine elegantly improbable, abstract situations, which are

however useful for subtle arguments .... Behind these peculiar pages I perceive an ancient taste for bold debate, an intellectual flexibility that does not fear contradictions, indeed accepts them as an inevitable ingredient of life; and life is rule, it is order prevailing over Chaos, but the rule has crevices, unexplored pockets of exception, license, indulgence and disorder. We must not obliterate them, they may contain the germ of all our tomorrows, because the machine of the universe is subtle, and subtle are the laws which rule it . . . (III: 766).

'La miglior merce' (The Best Merchandise) contains reflections arising out of an international conference on *Ostjudentum*, held in Turin. Levi mourns the destruction of the 'prodigiously fertile and creative' Eastern European Jewish culture, and discusses the importance that education (the 'best merchandise') and Yiddish had in it. He also points out that learning has been a central component of Jewishness always and everywhere, and – referring to assimilated communities such as those of the Weimar Republic and present-day Italy – stresses that, unless a community retains its connections with its cultural traditions, the price for equal legal and political rights is the weakening of its Jewish identity.

Jewish culture is linked to late twentieth-century technology in 'The Scribe', where Levi amusingly compares a recently-acquired personal computer to the legend of the Golem, the clay statue which remained lifeless until a scroll of the Torah was inserted into its mouth. Other aspects of the technology of the 1970s and 1980s, from the operation of deep-sea pipe-laying ships to strategies for preventing electrical fires, are unfailingly represented in the same terms as in *La chiave a stella*, as 'the ancient virtues of competence tried and tested and of work done well' (III: 671). In these essays, however, Levi's belief in competence is expressed in less clear-cut terms than in the earlier work, and situated in the context of a world threatened by natural and technological catastrophes. The original Italian collection ends with 'Eclissi dei profeti' (Eclipse of prophets), a series of reflections on contemporary European unease about the future. Levi states that the nuclear threat and the disappearance of charismatic political leaders have shown that 'the human condition is incompatible with certainty' (III: 829); the only viable course he sees is to acknowledge this uncertainty and to 'build our own future, blindly, gropingly' with knowledge and competence the necessary, but by no means sufficient, conditions.

The same feelings of uncertainty, weariness and hope in human solidarity can be detected in the poem 'Agli amici' (To My Friends), which Levi wrote in the same period and addressed to all those who had, for a moment or a lifetime, been close to him. His friend Bianca Guidetti Serra called it[20] 'almost a farewell'. It is the epigraph to his last collection of prose writings, *Racconti e saggi*.

> . . . I speak for you, fellow-travellers
> In a tangled journey, not free of effort,
> And also for you, who have lost
> Your souls, your spirits, your desire to live.
> Be you no one, or some, or maybe just one, you
> Who are reading me: remember the time
> Before the wax hardened,
> When each of us was like a seal.
> Each of us carries the imprint
> Of the friend met along the way;
> In each are traces of each.
> For better or for worse
> In wisdom or in folly
> Everyone imprinted by everyone.
>
> Now that time is pressing close,
> That tasks are finished,
> To all of you the softly-spoken wish
> That the autumn may be long and mild (II: 629).

At the beginning of 1986 two young historians, Anna Bravo and Daniele Jalla, published one of the most important projects sponsored by the Piedmont regional government, the collective oral history book *La vita offesa: storia e memoria dei lager nazisti nei racconti di duecento sopravvissuti* (*Life Betrayed: History and Memory of the Nazi Camps in the Stories of Two Hundred Survivors*). The memories of 223 Piedmontese women and men, of different ages and education levels, who were deported for different reasons, are arranged thematically, to enable readers to acquire a comprehensive picture of deportation by comparing diverse experiences of arrest, arrival in the camps, women's and men's lives and deaths, solidarity and conflict among prisoners and problems of re-integration into Italian society after returning home. Levi, as the most authoritative witness, wrote the introduction to the book. He reaffirmed the survivors' right and duty to bear witness as necessary and urgent because of what he called the 'foul attempts' by the French revisionists to rewrite history, and concluded:

> We are many (but every year our numbers decrease) . . . If we die here silently as our enemies want . . . the world will not know what man could, what man still can, do: the world will not know itself, it will be more vulnerable than it is now to a return of National Socialist barbarism, or any other equivalent barbarism of any political source (Bravo and Jalla 1986: 9).

His own recollection stresses, once again, the assimilation of Italian Jews ('we are the most assimilated Jews living' (Bravo and Jalla 1986: 99)) and their resulting defencelessness in the multi-ethnic, multilingual universe of Auschwitz ('Italian Jews . . . were really without an armour, as naked as eggs without shells' (Bravo and Jalla 1986: 191)). The central place of communication in Levi's view of human relations is strongly emphasised, as it is in *I sommersi e i salvati*:

> I felt our being in a place where *the word* could not be understood, and where people did not manage to make themselves understood, as a red-hot iron, as a torture . . . . And finding a gap, a hole, a way to get through this linguistic isolation was a factor of survival (Bravo and Jalla 1986: 263).

In the following months a number of intellectuals throughout Europe were engaged in a complex historical debate, which came to be known by the German word for its beginnings, a dispute among historians (*Historikerstreit*). In June 1986 Ernst Nolte, a well-known German historian of Fascist regimes, published an article entitled 'Vergangenheit, die nicht vergehen will' (A Past Which Will not Pass Away), which was followed a month later by a very critical reply by the philosopher and sociologist Jürgen Habermas. The debate quickly involved historians such as Joachim Fest, Hans Mommsen and Andreas Hillgruber, extended to the main German papers, and had wide-ranging international repercussions.

The thesis put forward by Nolte, supported – albeit with many differentiations and qualifications – by Fest and Hillgruber, and opposed by Habermas and Mommsen,[21] was not – unlike the arguments put forward by Darquier de Pellepoix and Faurisson – an outright denial that the extermination of the Jews and other groups had ever been planned, or had been more limited than the official figures suggest. The German revisionists, as they soon came to be known, denied neither the existence nor the evidence of the Nazi death camps, but rather their specificity and uniqueness. They attempted to relativise Nazi genocidal policies by representing them as only one instance in the context of all the mass murders of this century, and by representing the Nazi *Lager* ('race genocide') as a response to the Soviet *gulag* ('class genocide') in a cause and effect relationship: without the *gulag*, the *Lager* would never have been conceived. This redefinition aimed to have an impact on what Habermas, in his reply to Nolte, called 'the public use of history', namely the way the past is read for the purposes of the present. In this case the re-interpretation of the camps had the political purposes of freeing the Germans from 'guilt' and 'inferiority' complexes for the period 1933–45 by presenting extenuating circumstances, and of helping them to have a more positive view of their national identity.

Levi's only direct response to the German revisionists was one of the last articles he wrote, and will be discussed later. He had already pre-empted and answered some of their arguments ten years earlier, in his afterword to *Se questo è un uomo*. His last book, *I sommersi e i salvati* – a collection of eight essays which sum up and critically re-examine historical, artistic and psychological representations of the camp experience – appeared in April, before the debates began. This book, however, provides valuable and militant arguments against any attempted recontextualisation of the Holocaust; it is further a series of deeply disturbing reflections on history, on social relations and on the limits of memory and knowledge. It is also Levi's testament, and has been called his 'suicide note'.[22]

Levi had begun writing these essays in 1975, and had kept working on them for over ten years. His initial motivation had been at the same time personal and historical. By the mid-1970s he had spoken in approximately 140 schools (Colombo 1987: 209), and felt that the students no longer related to what he had to say because they saw the historical events of the Second World War as something long gone, which belonged to the past and could never occur again.[23] His contacts with young people, his participation in the projects on deportation and his own re-elaborations of his memories in stories, articles and interviews made him progressively more conscious of the fact that it was necessary not just to tell *about* Auschwitz, but to show its relevance to the present and the future, to 'sound the alarm' to the younger generation. He makes his point urgently in the conclusion of the book, his exhortation to his fellow survivors emphasised by the repetition of the central notion, 'It happened':

> Young people of the 1980s . . . are besieged by the problems of today . . . the nuclear threat, unemployment, the draining of world resources, the demographic explosion. . . . The generation now on the threshold of adulthood is sceptical, bereft of certainties rather than ideals . . . .. We must be listened to: beyond our individual experiences, we have collectively been witnesses of a fundamental, unexpected event, fundamental precisely because it was unexpected, not foreseen by anyone. It happened against all predictions; it happened in Europe . . . .. It happened, therefore it can happen again: this is the core of what we have to say (I: 818–19).

The biblical anaphora foregrounds the ethical and didactic function of remembering, which is at the very root of Jewish identity and culture: to remember the past is imperative, because it means using it in order to understand the present and to help future generations learn.[24] Levi's didactic purpose is evident from the systematic thoroughness with which he sets out the basic questions to which answers must be sought: what were the power relationships between the victims and their oppressors, and between the victims themselves? Which aspects of the *univers concentrationnaire* belong to the past and which may recur, and in which ways? Can their recurrence be prevented?

Levi discusses all these points systematically, referring directly or indirectly to his previous writings and correcting and integrating them with additional recollections, his own[25] and other survivors', and with facts and data taken from historical works. He also makes frequent biblical and literary references – some acknowledged, some implicit – which, as metaphors and similes, help clarify the historical and ethical questions he raises. The most poignant – used to explain the prisoners' state of constant anguish – is the reference to the 'waste and void' universe of Genesis I: 2, 'crushed'[26] under the infinitely powerful and infinitely remote presence of God (I: 717).

The conclusion of the preface pre-empts the German revisionists' claims by stating plainly that, even when contextualised among the horrors of Hiroshima and Nagasaki, the Soviet *gulags*, the Vietnam war and the Cambodian genocide, 'the Nazi concentration camp system remains a *unicum*, both in its extent and its characteristics' (I: 662). The chapter 'Violenza inutile' (Useless Violence) is a lucid demonstration of this statement. The uniqueness of the Nazi camps was due to a combination of features: mass deportation, the systematic effort to exterminate the 'enemy' and the restoration of an economy based on slave labour. All three were characterised by violence which was 'useless, an end to itself, with the sole aim of creating pain; occasionally having a purpose, yet always redundant, always disproportionate to the purpose itself' (I: 735).

Levi delves again into his own memories and into those of other survivors to show how the victims were robbed of every human trait before being destroyed. He describes the loss of dignity caused by the lack of privacy for bodily functions; the way the prisoners were deliberately left without any eating implements, thousands of which were found unused in the storerooms of the camps; the symbolic tattooing of the prisoners' matriculation numbers, 'so that the innocents might feel their sentence written on their flesh' (I: 748) and so that the Jews, forbidden by Mosaic law to be tattooed, might feel twice humiliated; the experiments carried out on living human beings, and the use of human hair in the German textile industry and of human ashes for SS footpaths. Levi points out the inherent contradiction between the practice of useless violence and the rational plan of exterminating the 'enemy'. The only possible explanation he can find is in the words of Franz Stangl, the former commander of Treblinka, who said that the victims had to be degraded so that the murderers could feel able to destroy them.

Levi speaks with the authority acquired from both his writings and his lifelong role as a spokesman for camp survivors; yet, from the very outset of his reflections, he problematises the limits of memory and of knowledge,[27] including his own role as a witness:

The history of the camps has been written almost exclusively by those who, like myself, did not fathom its full depths. Those who did so, did not return (I: 658–9).

This paradox – central to all Levi wrote about the camps – is at the heart of *I sommersi e i salvati*, and is emphasised by its very title. The Italian word for the first element of the opposition, *i sommersi*, is taken from *Inferno* XX, 3, and metaphorically refers to the mass of the damned, dead spiritually as well as physically. Levi applies it to those who did not, in the words of the Book of Job, 'return to tell about it': 'they are the rule, we are the exception' (I: 716). And he adds a chilling corollary: the 'submerged' were often the best people, and 'the saved', those who survived, did so because they were in a few cases lucky and in most cases 'the fittest' for the inhuman conditions in which they lived, that is to say the worst specimens of humanity (I: 715–17). The reference to Darwin's law, and to the irony of its consistent validity in Auschwitz, serves as an implicit reminder of the moral relativity of science.[28] Levi uncompromisingly returns to the 'uncomfortable fact' (I: 716) of the 'survival of the fittest' several times, in different contexts. Just as uncompromisingly, he repeatedly stresses the need to reject simplifications and stereotypes, and his own reservations about psychoanalytic interpretations of the survivors' trauma, even those made by people who, like Bruno Bettelheim, had experienced the camps;[29] instead he sets out conflicting truths and needs, and leaves his readers to face the resulting moral and intellectual dilemmas and to share his own moral and intellectual anguish.

Every page of the book is pervaded by the tension between Levi's need to convey general conclusions and his acknowledgement that reality is complex and multi-dimensional. Even his basic tenet of 'work done well', central to his life and his representations of learning through doing, is questioned here: identification with one's activity is recognised as not valid always and everywhere and is in fact defined as 'a highly ambiguous virtue', since in Auschwitz it was at the same time a source of dignity for some of the victims and a source of professional pride for the mass murderers (I: 750–1).

The most obvious, and painful, instance of this tension is Levi's attitude towards the Germans. Cynthia Ozick has pointed out that he frequently chooses the general term 'Germans' over 'the polite, because narrower "Nazis" ' (1989: 41). 'The failure to spread the truth about the death camps is one of the major collective crimes of the German people', he maintains outspokenly in the preface (I: 656). He indicts the German companies which had made profits from the slave labour in the camps and from supplying goods (including the ovens and the poison gas) to the SS administration. Yet he never ceases to seek dialogue with the Germans: he quotes several statements to this effect from his preface to the German edition of *Se questo è un uomo*,[30] and provides exhaustive evidence in the chapter 'Lettere di tedeschi' (Letters from Germans), a selection of his correspondence with several German readers of his works. His overall judgement of them is, with one exception, favourable; yet he adds the qualification that the sensitive and aware people who wrote to him admitting their guilt cannot be considered a 'representative sample'.

'It was my responsibility to understand, to understand them', Levi stresses (I: 791). 'To know' and 'to understand' are among the most frequently recurring verbs in the book; yet Levi keeps reminding his readers of the limits of knowledge and understanding. In the afterword to *Se questo è un uomo*, he had warned that 'maybe what happened cannot be comprehended, in fact *must not* be comprehended, because comprehending is almost justifying . . . "comprehending" a human purpose or behaviour means (also etymologically) taking its author in . . . identifying with him' (I: 208). Therefore, when faced with the prospect of contacting an actual representative of his former enemies, he hesitates: just as in 'Vanadio' he openly confesses his fear of meeting 'Dr Müller', so in *I sommersi e i salvati* he admits his reluctance to start corresponding with Albert Speer, the 'court architect' and Minister of War Industry in the Third Reich. The contradiction is left unexplained in both cases. Possibly, as Todorov comments, Levi did not merely want to understand the Germans; he also wanted to transform them, and refused to face the inevitable disappointment (Todorov 1992: 258–60). Or possibly he was reluctant to come face to face with what he clearly saw at a distance, namely the fact that, as he states in the last page, [the guards and the SS] were made of the same cloth as we, they were average human beings, averagely intelligent, averagely wicked: save for the exceptions, they were not monsters, they had our faces, but they had had a bad upbringing (I: 822).

Although Levi does not explicitly refer to Hannah Arendt's notion of the 'banality of evil', his words recall Arendt's concluding remarks in *Eichmann in Jerusalem*:

The trouble with Eichmann was precisely that so many were like him, and that the many were neither perverted nor sadistic, that they were, and still are, terribly and terrifyingly normal. From the viewpoint of our legal institutions and of moral standards of judgment, this normality was much more terrifying than all the atrocities put together . . . (Arendt 1963: 253).

Although to know and to understand may be frightening, there is in Levi's moral universe no alternative but to keep trying. Thus he analyses in depth the various factors operating against knowledge and understanding. In the first chapter, 'La memoria dell'offesa' (The Memory of the Offence), Levi admits that memories can be modified, suppressed by defence mechanisms or crystallised into stereotypes by victims and oppressors alike. At the same time he forcefully and repeatedly points out that, although the oppressor and the victim are caught in the same trap, 'they are not interchangeable, the former is to be punished and execrated (but, if possible, understood), the latter is to be pitied and helped' (I: 665).[31] The denials of evidence by the French revisionists, and the self-justifications of the majority of the German people in terms of 'not knowing what was going on' and of the high officials of the Third Reich in terms of 'obeying orders', are thus refuted and condemned, yet partly explained factually as (re)constructions of 'a convenient past' (I: 656–68).

The central role of 'understanding' in Levi's view of human behaviour is evident in the tension between the fear of not being understood and the need and duty to keep trying to communicate. The early part of the chapter 'Comunicare' (Communicating) uncompromisingly reiterates Levi's previous statements on 'obscure writing': 'One can and must communicate . . . .. To deny that communicating is possible is false: it is always possible. To refuse to communicate is a crime' (I: 721). Light is shed on these statements by the discussion of the prisoners' experiences. Their need for verbal communication was 'the mental equivalent of [their] bodily need for nourishment' (I: 725). The essential survival function of communication is shown by the description of the prisoners' desperate attempts to acquire useful snippets of German and other languages from the medley of unfamiliar sounds surrounding them. The role of language as an essential part of a human being's identity, particularly in the death camps, was especially important for Yiddish; Levi's awareness of this, and of his own cultural position vis-à-vis Yiddish, is summed up as the painful feeling that he 'ought to have understood it' (I: 731). The recognition that language is never neutral, and that it at the same time reflects and conditions existing power relations, is evident in the observations on the *Lagerjargon*, the 'particularly barbarised' situational variant of German used for communication purposes in the camps, especially in the pejorative vocabulary used to refer to the prisoners by the authorities and by the prisoners themselves.

The painful tension deriving from conflicting truths pervades the chapter on the 'grey zone' between the victims and the oppressors. Levi's focus on memory as a source of knowledge for the future is stated at the outset:

> From many signs, it would seem that the time has come to explore the space which separates (not only in Nazi camps!) the victims from the persecutors . . . . Only a schematic rhetoric can claim that this space is empty. It never is: it is studded with foul or pathetic figures (sometimes both at the same time), and it is essential to know them if we want to know humankind, if we want to be able to defend our souls should we ever face a similar ordeal, or even if we only want to understand what goes on in a big industrial plant (I: 677–8).

The connection between Auschwitz and industrial plants is, rather than a direct comparison, part of a general reflection on the collective dimension of all power relations and on the mechanisms of collaboration. Levi carefully distances himself both from the simplified black and white stereotype of powerful oppressors and powerless victims, and from the misleading view of the roles of victim and oppressor as freely chosen because of unconscious motivations. He scathingly rejects this view as exemplified by Liliana Cavani's 1974 film *Il portiere di notte* (*The Night Porter*), whose main characters are a former Nazi guard and a former prisoner, bound together by ties of sado-masochist connivance:

I do not know, and I am not very interested in knowing, whether in my depths there lurks a murderer, but I do know that I was an innocent victim, and not a murderer; I know that the murderers existed, not only in Germany, and that they still exist, whether retired or on active duty, and that to confuse them with their victims is a moral disease or an aesthetic affectation or a sinister sign of complicity; above all, it is a precious service rendered (whether intentionally or not) to those who deny the truth (I: 685).

Against both these misleading representations, Levi shows the complex and problematic nature of the network of relationships in the camps. Some victims were forced, or encouraged, to collaborate with the oppressors through a system of power and privileges which reproduced the hierarchical structure of the totalitarian state. They ranged from prisoners with small camp duties to the Kapos to the *Sonderkommandos*, the 'Special Squads' of (mostly Jewish) prisoners whose souls the SS had destroyed by delegating to them the most gruesome responsibility, that of the ovens, in exchange for a few months' survival. In all these cases Levi suspends judgement: the condition of 'being forced to obey orders', later invoked by their oppressors under trial, fully applied to the prisoners and cannot be questioned by anyone who has not experienced the conditions of the camps. Even those who have, like Levi himself, are paralysed by *impotentia judicandi*, the impossibility of passing judgement (I: 696). Some oppressors who showed fleeting mercy towards their victims are not exempted from judgement, but are also placed at the extreme border of the grey zone.

The discussion ends with the story of Chaim Rumkowski, at the same time victim and oppressor. Levi integrates the text already published in *Lilít* with some additional reflections, which highlight its significance and his view of the grey zone as a metaphor for the uncertainties and ambiguities of all social behaviour. Rumkowski's story 'poses more questions than it answers' and exemplifies 'the almost physical necessity that, from political coercion, gives birth to the indefinite area of ambiguity and compromise' (I: 701). Levi's remarks on Rumkowski bring to mind Hannah Arendt's strong indictment of the Jewish leaders in occupied Europe who cooperated with the Nazis in the destruction of their own people (Arendt 1963: 102–6). Like Arendt, Levi finds this form of collaboration profoundly disturbing; unlike her, however, he concentrates on what happened within the death camps in order to draw attention to the universal mechanisms of the corruption which flourishes whenever few have unlimited power over many. The need to understand these mechanisms as fully as possible is explicitly contextualised in the present and in the future: 'what could be perpetrated yesterday may be attempted again tomorrow, may involve ourselves or our children' (I: 689).

The notion of collective moral responsibility is developed in the chapter 'La vergogna' (Shame). The initial pages of *La tregua*, which Levi had written as early as 1947, about 'the shame which the just man feels before the wrong committed by others', are quoted forty years later and expanded into an extended analysis of the shame and guilt of the survivors. 'Shame' and 'guilt' are initially identified with each other (I: 706),[32] and then differentiated in a detailed examination of their components, often exemplified by references to specific episodes. Guilt is connected to the occasions where a choice of behaviour, however minimal, was possible: the victims felt guilty for not trying to resist, even under those conditions, and for failing to help others although the first rule of survival in the camps was to look after oneself first and foremost. Shame is both individual and universal. Individually, survivors must cope with the suspicion that someone else may have died in their place: the same haunted denials of the poem 'Il superstite' are reiterated here, this time in a second-person direct address, as if each survivor in turn accused and justified himself:

> You did not take anyone's place, you did not beat anyone (but would you have had the strength?), you did not accept positions (but you were not offered any . . .), you did not steal anyone's bread; yet you cannot rule it out (I: 714).

Survivors are also burdened with the universal shame of belonging to the human race: unable to withdraw behind what T.S. Eliot calls the 'partial shelter' of deliberate ignorance,[33] they feel submerged by the growing tide of pain for what human beings have been capable of doing.

In the context of the victims' guilt and shame Levi inserts some reflections on the reasons why some of them took their own lives after, rather than during, their period of imprisonment. Suicide, he says, 'is an act of man and not of the animal. It is a deliberate act, a non-instinctive, unnatural choice' (I: 709). While in the camps, the prisoners had little chance and few energies for choice, or for feelings of guilt; these all came later. It is difficult not to read these remarks in the light of Levi's own death.[34] Levi's own judgement is, however, suspended. As he adds when discussing the suicide of the Austrian-born philosopher Hans Mayer, alias Jean Améry, who survived Auschwitz and took his life in 1978, every suicide 'allows for a nebula of explanations' (I: 762).

Améry is the author of an essay entitled 'The Intellectual in Auschwitz' (1987), which Levi discusses in depth in a chapter by the same title. Like Levi, Améry writes for the younger generation, to warn it against indifference and apathy. His endeavour, like Levi's, is to explore and communicate the lessons of Auschwitz; unlike Levi's, however, his lessons are entirely negative. Améry's essay is a drawn-out and extremely lucid cry of despair: he concludes that survivors, having experienced the total collapse of their moral systems, irreparably lost any faith in the world and any belief that life had some meaning.[35] Referring specifically to the experiences of intellectuals, Améry defines them as people with a literary or philosophical background, and maintains that their condition in the camps was particularly painful because of the humiliation of the unaccustomed physical labour (Améry 1987: 30–42). Levi's comments on Améry's text are at the same time important reflections on the subject and contributions to his own self-construct. He takes issue with Améry on the concept of 'intellectual', defining one – and, indirectly, himself – as 'the person knowledgeable beyond his daily profession; whose culture is alive, in that it tries to renew itself, grow and keep up to date; and who does not react with indifference or irritation to any branch of knowledge' (I: 758). He also maintains that his own training as a chemist gave him the 'naturalistic' habit of never being indifferent to the 'samples' of humanity he came across (I: 766). However, he stresses that there were actual benefits in knowing and being able to remember literary texts. The episode of the Canto of Ulysses in *Se questo è un uomo* is recalled, and integrated in a scientifically factual tone by a list of the objective reasons why the literary reminiscences were valuable:

> They made it possible for me to re-establish a link with the past, rescuing it from oblivion and reinforcing my identity. They

convinced me that my mind, though besieged by everyday necessities, had not ceased to function. They gave me dignity in my own eyes and in those of my interlocutor (I: 765).

Levi and Améry, both rationalist non-believers, agree on another point: any faith, be it religious or political, helped those who had it because it gave a meaning to their suffering and was a code they could use to interpret the violence all around them. Levi's own moral position is stated in stronger and more direct terms than in any of his previous writings. Any religious dimension is firmly rejected. He recalls the selection for the gas chambers which he had described in *Se questo è un uomo* and admits that while it was taking place he had been tempted to pray for help, but immediately afterwards rejects prayer in terms taken from the semantic field of religious practice ('a prayer under those conditions would have been ... blasphemous, obscene, laden with the utmost impiety of which a non-believer could be capable', I: 770–1). He defines as 'monstrous' the notion, put forward by his Catholic friend and former lecturer Dalla Porta, that his having been 'saved' was the work of Providence, so that he might bear witness (I: 714–15). Other explicit judgements coincide with Jewish morality: 'understanding' does not mean 'justifying' or 'forgiving'. Levi calls 'revolting' Dostoyevsky's fable of the evil old woman spared from Hell because of her one good deed, the gift of an onion to a beggar (I: 693)[36] and represents forgiveness as alien to him: 'I am not inclined to forgive, I have never forgiven any of our former enemies, neither do I feel I can forgive their imitators in Algeria, Vietnam, the Soviet Union, Chile, Argentina, Cambodia, South Africa' (I: 762).

The conclusion of the book is pervaded by uncertainty and pessimism. Levi points out that everywhere violence, be it 'useful' or 'useless', is accepted as inevitable and justified by the demonisation of the enemy: 'It is necessary to sharpen our senses, to mistrust prophets, charlatans, those who speak and write "fine words" not supported by sound arguments.' Yet he is all too aware that reason is the necessary, not the sufficient, condition for human beings to survive as human beings in the future. The logic that led to Auschwitz, and the ordinariness of the men who designed and ran it, are visible throughout the world, in the nuclear race, in the Middle East, in military dictatorships: 'It happened, therefore it can happen again . . . .. It can happen, and everywhere' (I: 819).

The reception of I sommersi e i salvati in Italy was very political. Some reviewers[37] emphasised that what happened between 1933 and 1945 was not an isolated aberration, but was the product of contemporary industrial–military society. Many others[38] saw it as a militant answer to French and German revisionism. The chapter on the 'grey zone', although it did not give rise to bitter controversies as had Hannah Arendt's judgements twenty years earlier,[39] became part of the debates in Italy during the Austrian presidential elections of June 1986; the successful candidate, the former United Nations Secretary-General, Kurt Waldheim, justified his participation in the deportation of Greeks, Jugoslavs and Greek Jews to Nazi concentration camps in 1944 as 'carrying out his duty as a soldier in wartime'. Some of those who commented on the 'Waldheim affair' argued that Waldheim belonged to the 'grey zone' and needed therefore to be justified and forgiven (Bocca 1986). Levi contradicted this view, maintaining that in cases such as Waldheim's the notion of 'coercion' did not apply (Morpurgo 1986).[40] In the English-speaking countries, where the book appeared one year after Levi's death, reviewers more or less explicitly attempted to establish a cause and effect relationship between its pessimism and its author's suicide, emphasising either its pent-up anger or its ultimate lack of hope.

In June, Levi added a postscript to his spiritual testament: the poem 'Delega' (Delegating). What he bequeathes to the next generation is no prophetic message, but rather the burden of the contradictions of his time, in the uncertain hope that some benefit may be drawn from past experiences:

Do not be frightened if there is much to be done.
We need you, who are less tired.
. . . Reflect again on our mistakes:
There have been some among us
Who set out blindly in their quest,
As a blindfolded man would trace an outline,
And some who set sail like pirates,
And some who tried with good will.
. . . Do not be appalled at the rubble

And the stench of rubbish tips: we cleared them with bare hands
When we were as old as you are now.
Maintain the pace, as best you can. We have
Combed the hair of comets,
Deciphered the secret of genesis,
Stepped on the sand of the moon,
Built Auschwitz and destroyed Hiroshima.
See, we have not been inactive.
Take up the burden, puzzled as you are:
Do not call us teachers (II: 630).

In November, *La Stampa* published *Racconti e saggi*, a collection of some of Levi's writings which appeared in the paper between 1960 and 1986. A selection of these, together with a few poems and essays published between 1986 and Levi's death, was translated into English in 1990 as *The Mirror Maker*. Levi's brief preface sums up his self-representation: he defines himself as 'a normal man with a good memory who was sucked into a vortex . . . and from then on has always remained somewhat curious about vortices, large and small, metaphorical and actual' (III: 833).

The stories are mainly moral fables in the style of *Storie naturali*, *Vizio di forma* and *Lilít*. Again, there are inventions that affect the way human beings experience themselves and their relationships (a mirror which reproduces the wearers' images as others see them in 'Il fabbricante di specchi' (The Mirror Maker); an injection which speeds up or slows down subjective time in 'Scacco al tempo' (Time Checkmated)), and genetic mutations presented through the point of view of a young female character (in 'La grande mutazione' (The Great Mutation), human beings grow wings and become closer to both birds and nature). In other stories, despite the disclaimer in the preface, the 'messages' are apparent. In 'Le due bandiere' (The Two Flags), a man is killed by his own racial prejudice: all his glands and muscles 'seize up' when he first sees his flag flying beside that of the hated neighbouring country. 'Forza maggiore' (*Force majeure*), written a few months after *I sommersi e i salvati*, is a short, Kafkaesque instance of the 'useless violence' analysed in the book: an unidentified sailor wordlessly forces the protagonist, 'M.', to lie down in the street and literally walks all over him.

Some of the essays recall *L'altrui mestiere*, in that they are evidence of Levi's continuing interest in such diverse topics as entomology, the function of rhyme in poetry and weightlessness in space travel. Others are lightweight occasional pieces: impressions of his trip to the United States, a letter to the poet Horace about the changes that have taken place since his times, computer chess programmes, and a classification of the various types of gossip. All, however, reflect Levi's consistent curiosity for scientific and social phenomena, always given additional depth and sometimes humour by the use of literary and cultural allusions:

> Since we have become ingenious we have invented increasingly ingenious weapons. The most recent, I mention in passing, would have startled Lucretius: if atoms, instead of being left whole, as is in the nature of things, are split or condensed in a certain way, the world can be made to explode and every single man can be killed a hundred times over . . . .. We are trying to disinvent this invention, which comes from the infernal regions (III: 928–9).

Levi's preoccupation with the threat of nuclear war is evident in two essays. 'Le lance diventino scudi' (Spears Become Shields) – first published in 1981 – modifies the well-known exhortation in Isaiah 2: 4 to turn swords into ploughshares: Levi suggests that weapons of offence ('spears') be turned first into weapons of defence ('shields') and subsequently used for peaceful means ('ploughshares'). A more radical attitude is evident in 'Covare il cobra' (Hatching the Cobra), a comment on the stands taken by two physicists. They were the American Peter Hagelstein – who had just resigned from a laboratory funded by the Defence Department to work exclusively on medical applications of laser beams at MIT – and the British Martin Ryle, the 1974 Nobel prizewinner, who in 1984 had founded a movement to 'stop science now' because any discovery, including his own in radio-astronomy, could be used for war research. Levi approves Hagelstein's choice unreservedly, while calling Ryle's endeavour 'at the same time extremist and utopian' (I: 976). His own proposal was that science students be asked to swear something like the Hippocratic oath. Couched in imperatives reminiscent of the 'words of the Father' of Gattermann's chemistry textbook, Levi's appeal once again makes a distinction between science and its uses, and urgently emphasises the necessity for knowledge never to be divorced from moral choices:

Do not fall in love with suspect problems. Within the limits that you will be granted, try to know the end to which your work is directed . . .. You will agree to work on a new drug, you will refuse to produce a nerve gas. . . . If you are given a choice do not let yourself be seduced by material or intellectual interests; choose instead from the field which may make less painful and less dangerous the journey of your contemporaries, and of those who come after you. Don't hide behind the hypocrisy of neutral science: you are sufficiently educated to evaluate whether from the egg you are hatching will issue a dove or a cobra or a chimera or perhaps nothing at all (III: 977).[41]

One of the last essays in *The Mirror Maker*, 'The Dispute among German Historians',[42] is Levi's contribution to the controversies arising from the *Historikerstreit*. It is a direct response to two articles published in *La Stampa* on 21 January 1987 by the journalist Paolo Mieli and the historian Ernesto Galli della Loggia. Mieli sums up Nolte's arguments that Auschwitz was an answer, although 'mediated by interpretation', to the *Gulag* Archipelago. Galli della Loggia argues that the 'uniqueness' of the Holocaust was a deliberate misrepresentation both by the Western powers, who needed to play down their own role in cooperating with Nazi anti-Semitism, and by the Soviet authorities, who needed to play down their own massacres and violence. His judgement is that 'one really cannot maintain that the outcome, in numerical terms, was all that different'. Levi's reply, published on the following day, is lucid and explicit. It does not overlook any of the revisionist arguments, and answers them cogently, reiterating his own arguments of *I sommersi e i salvati* with the passionate eloquence of someone who knows that he will need to bear witness against misinformation and misinterpretation as long as he lives:

That 'the Gulag came before Auschwitz' is true; but we cannot forget that the aims of the two hells were not the same. The former was a massacre among peers; it was not based on racial primacy, it did not divide humanity into supermen and submen. . . . This contempt for the fundamental equality of rights among all human beings can be seen in a host of symbolic details, from the Auschwitz tattoo to the use, in the very gas chambers, of the poison originally produced to disinfest ship holds invaded by rats. . . . Nobody ever showed that in the Gulags there were 'selections' like those, described so often, in the German camps, where with one glance at the front and one at the back the SS physicians (physicians!) decided who could still work and who was to go to the gas chambers. . . . It was not an 'imitation of Asiatic deeds', it was fully European, the gas was produced by well-known German chemical factories, and German factories used the hair of the slaughtered women; and German banks received the gold of the teeth extracted from the corpses. All this is specifically German, and no German should forget it. . . . The moral and judicial difference between those who do it and those who allow it to be done remains immeasurable (Levi 1987b: 2).

By the end of 1986 Levi had fallen ill with depression again. His family situation, with the need to look after his mother and his mother-in-law twenty-four hours a day, was inevitably destined to become worse. Yet he was constantly invited to contribute to a variety of social and cultural initiatives. On 21 and 22 November he took part in another international conference organised by the Piedmont regional government and ANED,[43] 'Storia vissuta' (History as it Was Lived), which focused specifically on the role of oral evidence in teaching the history of the Second World War in schools. He limited himself to distributing copies of the afterword to *Se questo è un uomo* and to stressing once again, in a brief comment, both the need to consider memory as a collective property and the need to keep communicating to the younger generations:

> Ever since my first book, *Se questo è un uomo*, I wanted my works – though they appeared under my name – to be read as collective works. . . . More than that: I wanted them to be an opening, a bridge between us and our readers, especially the young ones. . . . As long as we are alive, it is our task to speak, to others, to those who had not been born then, so that they may know 'the extremes to which one can go' (Levi 1988: 113).

He was both part of and apart from ANED and Italian Jewry. As the witness *par excellence*, more respected and more quoted than any other Italian Jewish or political ex-deportee, he felt compelled to take part in every project connecting the past to the present, whatever the intellectual and emotional toll of the repeated efforts to recall, redefine and re-articulate his memories for what he now feared was going to be a diminishing response. Within Italian Jewry, he was in a somewhat anomalous position, as a firmly non-practising and non-participating member of the community who nevertheless was the best-known Piedmontese

Jew, and one of the best-known Jewish intellectuals, in Italy and abroad.

He was still preoccupied with issues of scientific theories and applications. He offered his proposal for a Hippocratic oath for scientists twice more, first in a television interview on the risks and potential of scientific and technological changes[44] and then in an interview on the possible contributions of scientists to a 'culture of peace' (Levi 1987c). The last article he wrote for *La Stampa* was 'Argilla di Adamo' (Adam's Clay), a discussion of a monograph hypothesising the presence of embryo life in silicon clay (Levi 1987d).[45] He was offered, and regretfully turned down, both the honorary post of president of Einaudi (which was recovering from a financial crisis) and membership of a committee investigating the massacre of 2,000 Italian soldiers rounded up and shot by the German Army in Lvov (Ukraine) in 1943. He was, albeit with difficulty and without enthusiasm, working on a book with the provisional title *Il doppio legame* (*The Double Bond*). It was to have been a companion piece to *Il sistema periodico*: a collection of imaginary letters in the manner of eighteenth-century Enlightenment literature, sent by a scientist to a society lady to explain various chemical phenomena.

He admitted his profound weariness in his last published interview: 'Every now and then I have the feeling that I have run out of things to say ... I go through long periods of confusion, possibly connected with my concentration camp experience. I face difficulties rather badly. And I have never written about this ... I am not a strong man. Not at all' (1987: 31, 33).

In March he underwent two prostate operations, and the subsequent physical frailty deepened his depression. He felt unable to work and unable to accept the temporary weakness caused by both illnesses.[46] He grew increasingly isolated and unhappy, in spite of the concerned efforts of friends to keep in touch and draw him out.

On the morning of Saturday 11 April 1987 Italian television announced that Primo Levi had fallen to his death down the stairwell from the third-floor landing of his home. It was four days before the beginning of Passover, the Jewish holiday centred on the need to remember past slavery and to encourage the young to learn about it in order to be free.[47] No notes or messages were found, and the autopsy did not reveal any traces of violence. He was buried two days later in the Turin Jewish cemetery. The funeral was attended by many Italian intellectuals, by ex-deportees and by nearly all the Turin Jewish community. His grave, a plain slab of black marble, is engraved with just his name, the number 174517, and the years of his birth and death.

Italians and those outside Italy who knew and admired Levi's works were devastated: the man who had spent his life 'striving to answer questions' (I: 572) had withheld the answer to the final question about himself. Since Levi's death, friends, acquaintances and strangers have attempted, more or less informedly, more or less sensitively, more or less respectfully, to formulate hypotheses. The easiest, if the most painful, is that Auschwitz had claimed another victim forty years later; this was fostered by the prevailing identification of Levi with Holocaust testimony.[48] Many commentators quoted the last page of *La tregua*, with its recurring nightmare of apparent security followed by disintegration. 'Primo Levi died at Auschwitz forty years later', said Elie Wiesel.[49] 'The memory of the death camps can lead one to despair', said Natalia Ginzburg.[50] And four years later Maurice Goldstein, the president of the Auschwitz international committee, began a paper on Levi with the words 'Auschwitz reclaimed him' (1991: 83). Others connected Levi's death to the deaths of other intellectuals who took their lives years after returning from the camps – Paul Celan, Peter Szondi, Jean Améry – and attributed those suicides to the shame and guilt of the survivors. Bruno Bettelheim, who was to die by his own hand in 1990 after surviving Dachau and Buchenwald, spoke about Levi in his own last interview:

> It is true that those who survived the camps probably were never saved. That is the reason why such remarkable people as Primo Levi ended up taking their lives. ... Within them the terror of the concentration camps was ever present. ... For those who were in the camps it is as if they always lived on the barbed wire (Bettelheim 1990).

Significantly, the only outright denial of any connection between Levi's death and the camps came from a German source: an article in *Die Welt* claiming that after the end of the Holocaust he was 'of course' once more 'a normal Italian like any other' and therefore his death could not be a consequence of the Nazi persecution.[51]

Politically committed intellectuals who had known Levi

suggested that one of the possible factors of his death could have been despair at the attitude of apathy towards history and politics prevailing in the 1980s, which meant that testimony such as Levi's was honoured in words and disregarded in practice, and thus robbed of any meaning. 'If [Levi] was experiencing the triumph of the fatal obliteration of memory ... was this not a renewed loss of existence, a renewed annihilation?' asked the journalist and writer Rossana Rossanda (1987). 'He may not have been able to bear the personal success of his work of memory and testimony, absolutely parallel to the loss of meaning of memory and testimony', wrote the social critic Francesco Ciafaloni (1991: 34). Levi's weariness was also specifically linked to the resurgence of historical revisionism. The writer Mario Rigoni Stern, one of Levi's closest friends, said that 'these sophisticated arguments on the horror [of the genocide] could happen because of people's indifference and because of the resigned, or something yet worse, silence of a world which only wants to forget . . .. Perhaps this final disappointment was the last straw for an already tired man'.[52] Cesare Cases lucidly summed up these complex connections two years after Levi's death:

> He was condemned to talk about Auschwitz, to be the guardian of its memory, and he was forced to acknowledge that this memory was waning. He was disturbed first by the revisionism of Faurisson, and later by that of right-wing German historians. The excellent article he wrote about them in *La Stampa* showed some weariness, that of someone who always needs to repeat the same things. His private world was shrinking, the outside world was expanding enormously, and the spirit of the times was quite different from what he had hoped. He must have been crushed by these contradictions (1989: 100–1).

Some, like Rita Levi Montalcini, steadfastly rejected the notion that Levi had taken his life, and hypothesised a temporary loss of lucidity or a sudden dizzy spell.[53] The American writer William Styron instead maintained that, if his depression had had proper medical treatment, he would have been 'rescued from the abyss' (1988). These interpretations may have been preferred because the choice of taking one's life is an act of final despair, which some saw as a denial of the message of courage and lucidity of Levi's writings. An article in *The New Yorker* went as far as to intimate that 'the efficacy of all his words had somehow been cancelled by his death – that his hope, or faith, was no longer usable by the rest of us'.[54] In English-speaking countries, where *The Drowned and the Saved* appeared posthumously, some reviewers emphasised its anger and pessimism, and concluded that Levi's death was his final act of lucidity, his final warning that 'gratuitous violence . . . serves no purpose, and refuses to be forgotten' (James 1988: 92).[55]

These speculations are inevitable and understandable. They are, however, far less relevant than Levi's legacy to his readers: whatever the despair that may have led him to his final act, his body of writings is anything but despairing. He will probably remain best known, and most admired, as the man who made his Holocaust testimony, begun with his first book and developed in stories, poems, essays and lectures until the end of his life, a lesson of memory and commitment for the future. This lesson, however, goes beyond Auschwitz: the constant in all Levi's works is the moral dimension of all knowledge. He consistently – often earnestly, at times humorously, always lucidly – stresses the need for us to be 'curious about many things', to keep learning from and about history, science, technology, and culture, to apply this knowledge to our daily experiences and to communicate what we have learned. This is our responsibility if we want to at least try to avoid some of the mistakes of the past, both individual and collective. We must keep learning in spite of – possibly because of – the awareness that reality is full of insoluble contradictions and ambiguities, and in spite of – possibly because of – our doubts, contradictions and fears: this is the overall message of the man who warned his readers not to look for messages in his words.

Notes to Chapter Five

1. The notion of the unpredictability of Levi's own poetic production takes a lighthearted form in the story 'La fuggitiva' (The Fugitive), which is part of *Lilìt* (III: 495–9) but has not been translated into English. A poem, the best its author ever wrote, keeps escaping from wherever he puts it and finally disappears altogether. The self-reference is apparent from the fact that the elusive poem is entitled 'Annunciazione' (Annunciation), also the title of one of Levi's own poems,

which appeared in *La Stampa* two weeks before the story (see Tesio 1991a: 198–9).

2. Adorno (1967: 34). The full quotation reads: 'To write poetry after Auschwitz is barbaric. And this corrodes even the knowledge of why it has become impossible to write poetry today.'

3. Interview with Giulio Nascimbeni (1984b).

4. Levi's sources (Dante, Eliot and occasionally other poets such as François Villon, Rainer Maria Rilke and Siegfried Sassoon) were scrupulously acknowledged in notes to each poem, to emphasise the continuity of themes in different times and contexts.

5. See Segre (1988: xxiii–iv), and the 1985 review by Rosato.

6. The irony is emphasised by a footnote which explains that the Hebrew word for 'In the beginning', *Bereshid*, is the very first word of the Bible.

7. This poem was not included in the English *Collected Poems*.

8. See Levi's interview with Germaine Greer (1985b) and Stille (1991a: 205).

9. See, for instance, the reviews by Salvador Luria (*Science*, 5 April 1985) and Philip Morrison (*Scientific American*, February 1985).

10. See a television interview with Giorgio Bocca (quoted in Poli and Calcagno 1992: 325–6) and an interview with Risa Sodi (1987: 360).

11. This story appears in *The Mirror Maker* ('A Mystery in the *Lager*': 66–70).

12. The first edition had been published in 1960.

13. See Levi (1986b) and (1986c).

14. The English translation, *Other People's Trades* (1989), contains forty-four essays, including four which were published in the later collection *Racconti e saggi*.

15. From 'Le parole fossili' (Fossilised Words), not translated into English.

16. These pieces do not appear in the English translation, because of their specific references to the Italian language.

17. This essay was not included in the English translation.

Levi in fact helped Italo Calvino revise Sergio Solmi's translation of Queneau's poem (particularly the 'tangles' of the part entitled 'Song on Chemistry') and provided advice on chemical terms for Calvino's translation of Queneau's

Chanson du polystyrène (Scalia 1987: 6).

18. It was published on p. 3 of *La Stampa* on 11 December 1976.
19. The writer and poet Giorgio Manganelli called Levi's statements 'terrorist' and objected to Levi's identification of 'clarity' with 'rationality' (Manganelli 1977). So, in a public debate organised in 1979 by the then Italian Communist Party, did the writer Paolo Volponi (Poli and Calcagno 1992: 109–10). The Marxist scholar Cesare Cases, in an article written shortly after Levi's death, while strongly disagreeing with Levi's views, stressed that they are essential to the understanding of the origins and nature of his art (Cases 1987: 25, 31). See also the perceptive comments in Rudolf (1990: 43–4).
20. In an unpublished talk given at a commemoration one month after Levi's death.
21. The main contributions to the debate have been collected and analysed in Rusconi (1987). For English-language analyses, see Maier (1988) and Evans (1989). An extremely lucid discussion of the significance of the *Historikerstreit* for historiography and for collective memory is found in Friedlander (1993, particularly pp. 22–41).
22. See the review by Ozick (1989).
23. See Levi's interview with Mario Baldoli (1986b).
24. See P. Valabrega (1982: 305–6) and Todorov (1992: 246–50). The imperative *Zakhor* (remember) is the title of a collection of essays on the role of memory in Jewish history (Yerushalmi 1982).
25. For a detailed analysis of *I sommersi e i salvati* as an amplification of Levi's previous moral discourses see Biasin (1990b).
26. The notion of humankind 'crushed' by God is also found in Levi's comments on the Book of Job: see *La ricerca delle radici* (6).
27. For an extended discussion see Lollini (1990).
28. Darwin and Auschwitz are also connected in two references to Jack London's *The Call of the Wild*. The first is the story 'Cerio' of *Il sistema periodico* (see chapter 3). This comparison is expanded in 'Buck dei lupi' (Jack London's Buck), one of Levi's last articles (1987a); it is included in *The Mirror Maker* (149–53). It is an autobiographical re-reading of London's novel, with the emphasis on what Buck, the 'respectable' dog

from a middle-class household, learns from his 'deportation' to a place where 'he must adjust, learn new and terrible things', and where 'it is no longer civil law that counts, but, rather, the law of the cudgel and the fang'.

29. Some bibliographical information on the vast psychiatric literature on the 'concentration camp syndrome' can be found in Devoto and Martini (1981), Santagostino (1991a) and in Todorov (1992).

30. This preface was originally a letter to Heinz Riedt, Levi's first German translator. See *I sommersi e i salvati* (I: 794–7).

31. The essay in *I sommersi e i salvati* contains a number of warnings not included in the previous version read at the 1983 conference: 'it is essential to be clear' (I: 664); 'We do not want any confusions, cheap Freudianisms, morbidities, leniencies' (I: 665).

32. A detailed discussion of Levi's analysis of 'shame' and 'guilt', which connects the notions of 'shame' and 'guilt' to different cultural backgrounds, is found in White (1991).

33. See a discussion of the reference to Eliot in chapter 4.

34. See, among many others, the interpretations of Cases (1987), James (1988), Ozick (1989) and Todorov (1992: 252).

35. For an extended discussion of the similarities and contrasts between the positions of Levi and Améry, see Molino Signorini (1991).

36. In the version of the fable in *The Brothers Karamazov*, the woman *was about to* be spared, but was in fact sent back into Hell for her refusal to share the onion with other souls.

37. See especially the reviews by Padovani, Gibelli, and Cases; see also Cases (1987: 30).

38. See especially Cases (1986), Raboni (1986) and Sessi (1987).

39. For analyses of the responses to *Eichmann in Jerusalem*, see chapter 6 of Barnouw (1990) and chapter 5 of Watson (1992).

40. Levi expanded his views on Waldheim in his interview with Risa Sodi: 'He was just one of 100,000 others like him . . . He's a grey zoner! He's a man with a very real responsibility, but one that dwells within the greater responsibility of the Nazi machine' (Sodi 1987: 365).

41. Levi restated the main ideas of this essay in early 1987, in a discussion on the possible contributions of individual disciplines to a 'culture of peace' promoted by the periodical *Uomini e libri* (Levi 1987c).

42. The Italian text is entitled 'Buco nero di Auschwitz' (The Black Hole of Auschwitz), and appeared too late to be included in *Racconti e saggi*.
43. See chapter 4.
44. The interview was broadcast on 22 December 1986. See Poli and Calcagno (1992: 341–5).
45. This essay is in *The Mirror Maker* (154–7).
46. Bianca Guidetti Serra and Silvio Ortona, personal communications.
47. See the perceptive comments of Fiorentino (1987).
48. This automatic identification is revealed by the titles chosen by some Italian newspapers to report his death: 'Primo Levi, who wrote about the death camps, kills himself' (*L'Unità*); 'The writer Primo Levi, the Holocaust witness, has killed himself' (*Il Giorno*); 'The memory of the Jewish Holocaust in his books' (*La Nazione*); 'Memory as condemnation and hope' (*Il Giornale*); 'Crushed by the ghost of the camps' (*Corriere della Sera*).
49. *La Stampa*, 14 April 1987, p. 3. See also Wiesel's commemoration of Levi five years later (Wiesel 1992).
50. *La Repubblica*, 12–13 April 1987, p. 4.
51. 'Sprung in die grosse Atempause' (A Leap into the Long Rest), *Die Welt*, 13 April 1987, p. 19.
52. *Il Resto del Carlino*, 12 April 1987, p. 3. See also Galante Garrone (1989: 133).
53. See Levi Montalcini (1987), Sodi (1988b) and Mendel (1994).
54. Anonymous comment in *The New Yorker*, 11 May 1987, p. 32. See also Leon Wieseltier's comment in *The New Republic*, 11 May 1987, p. 42: 'He spoke for the bet that there is no blow from which the soul may not recover. When he smashed his body, he smashed his bet.'
55. See also the review by Ozick (1989).

Bibliography

Primary Sources

Books by Primo Levi

(1947) *Se questo è un uomo*, Turin: De Silva (also (1958) Turin: Einaudi).

(1963) *La tregua*, Turin: Einaudi.

(1966) *Se questo è un uomo*, Theatre adaptation (with Pieralberto Marché), Turin: Einaudi.

(1966) *Storie naturali* (under the pseudonym Damiano Malabaila) Turin: Einaudi (reprinted under the author's own name in 1979).

(1971) *Vizio di forma*, Turin: Einaudi.

(1975) *Il sistema periodico*, Turin: Einaudi.

(1975) *L'osteria di Brema* (Poems), Milan: Scheiwiller.

(1978) *La chiave a stella*, Turin: Einaudi.

(1981) *La ricerca delle radici*, Turin: Einaudi.

(1981) *Lilít e altri racconti*, Turin: Einaudi.

(1982) *Se non ora, quando?* Turin: Einaudi.

(1984) *Ad ora incerta* (Collected poems), Milan: Garzanti.

(1984) *Dialogo* (with Tullio Regge), Milan: Edizioni di Comunità (reprinted (1987) Turin: Einaudi).

(1985) *L'altrui mestiere*, Turin: Einaudi.

(1986) *I sommersi e i salvati,* Turin: Einaudi.

(1986) *Racconti e saggi*, Turin: Editrice La Stampa.

Opere. (Collected Works) Turin: Einaudi.

    Vol. I (1987): *Se questo è un uomo; La tregua; Il sistema periodico; I sommersi e i salvati.*

    Vol. II (1988): *La chiave a stella; Se non ora, quando?; Ad ora incerta.*

    Vol. III (1990): *Storie naturali; Vizio di forma; Lilít e altri racconti; L'altrui mestiere; Racconti e saggi.*

English Translations of Levi's Works

(1960) *Se questo è un uomo*, trans. Stuart Woolf as *If this is a man* (American title: *Survival in Auschwitz*), London: Orion Press.

(1965) *La tregua*, trans. Stuart Woolf as *The Truce* (American title: *The Reawakening*), London: The Bodley Head.

(1984) *Il sistema periodico*, trans. Raymond Rosenthal as *The Periodic Table*, New York: Schocken Books.

(1985) *Se non ora, quando?*, trans. William Weaver as *If not now, when?* New York: Simon and Schuster.

(1986) *La chiave a stella*, trans. William Weaver as *The Wrench* (American title: *The Monkey's Wrench*), New York: Summit Books.

(1986) *Lilít e altri racconti*, trans. Ruth Feldman as *Moments of Reprieve*, New York: Summit Books. (This book also contains three stories not published in *Lilít e altri racconti*.)

(1988) *Ad ora incerta* (selection from), trans. Ruth Feldman and Brian Swann as *Collected Poems*, London: Faber and Faber.

(1988) *I sommersi e i salvati*, trans. Raymond Rosenthal as *The Drowned and the Saved*, New York: Simon and Schuster.

(1989) *L'altrui mestiere*, trans. Raymond Rosenthal as *Other People's Trades*, New York: Summit Books.

(1989) A selection from *Racconti e saggi*, trans. Raymond Rosenthal as *The Mirror Maker – Stories and Essays*, New York: Schocken Books.

(1989) *Dialogo* (by Primo Levi and Tullio Regge) trans. Raymond Rosenthal as *Conversations*, New York: Summit Books.

(1990) *Storie naturali* and *Vizio di forma* (selection from), trans. Raymond Rosenthal as *The Sixth Day*, New York: Summit Books.

Other Essays and Articles by Primo Levi

(1946) With Leonardo De Benedetti, 'Rapporto sulla organizzazione igienico-sanitaria del campo di concentramento per ebrei di Monowitz, Auschwitz, Alta Slesia', *Minerva Medica* 37: 535–44. Reprinted in A. Cavaglion 1993a: 223–40.

(1955) 'Deportati – Anniversario', *Torino* 31: 53–4.

(1966) *La resistenza nei Lager*, Rome: Quaderno del Centro studi sulla deportazione e l'internamento, no. 3.

(1968) Foreword to Léon Poliakof, *Auschwitz*, Rome: Veutro.

(1973) Foreword to Joel Konig, *Sfuggito alle reti nel nazismo*, Milan: Mursia.

(1974) 'Un passato che credevamo non dovesse tornare più', *Corriere della Sera*, 8 May: 5.

(1976a) 'Ma perché Auschwitz?' (answers to questions asked by school students), *Tuttolibri*, 28 February: 4–5. Reprinted as an afterword to *Se questo è un uomo*.

(1976b) Foreword to his translation of Jacob Presser, *La notte dei Girondini*, Milan: Adelphi.

(1977a) Foreword to Itzhak Katzenelson, *Il canto del popolo ebreo massacrato*, Milan: Centro di documentazione ebraica contemporanea.

(1977b) 'I tedeschi e Kappler', *Ha Keillah*, October: 1.

(1979a) 'Ma noi c'eravamo', *Corriere della Sera*, 3 January: 1–2.

(1979b) 'Un lager alle porte d'Italia', *La Stampa*, 19 January: 3.

(1979c) 'Chi vuole l'odio antisemita?' *La Stampa*, 13 March: 3.

(1979d) Introduction to the mini-series *Olocausto*, Special issue of *Radiocorriere TV*, Turin: ERI (Edizioni RAI): 1–5.

(1979e) Foreword to Luciano Caglioti, *I due volti della chimica*, Milan: Mondadori.

(1979f) Foreword to Liana Millu, *Il fumo di Birkenau*, 3rd edn, Florence: La Giuntina.

(1979g) 'L'intolleranza razziale', second in a series of lectures on 'The Nature of Prejudice', given in Turin, November 1979. Reprinted (1988) Turin: Regione Piemonte.

(1982a) 'Chi ha coraggio a Gerusalemme?' *La Stampa*, 24 June: 1.

(1982b) 'È stato un rinascere', *Il Gazzettino*, 25 July: 3.

(1982c) 'Il difficile cammino della verità', *La Rassegna mensile di Israel*, July–December: 17–23. Reprinted as an appendix to Lopez (1987).

(1983a) 'I temerari del Ghetto', *La Stampa*, 17 April: 3.

(1983b) 'Kafka col coltello nel cuore', *La Stampa*, 5 June: 3.

(1983c) 'I collezionisti di tormenti', *La Stampa*, 28 December: 3.

(1984a) Foreword to Hermann Langbein, *Uomini ad Auschwitz*, Milan: Mursia.

(1984b) Foreword to Marco Herman, *Diario di un ragazzo ebreo*, Cuneo: L'Arciere.

(1984c) Foreword to *Ebrei a Torino*, Turin: Umberto Allemandi.

(1984d) 'L'ultimo Natale di guerra', printed privately in Lugano by Levi's friend Sergio Grandini, translated and reprinted in *Moments of Reprieve*.

(1984e) 'Itinerario d'uno scrittore ebreo'. *La Rassegna Mensile di Israel* 5–8, May–August: 376–90. Translated as 'Beyond Survival', *Prooftexts* 4, 1984: 9–21.

(1985a) Foreword to Rudolph Höss, *Comandante ad Auschwitz*, 2nd edn, Turin: Einaudi (German edition (1958) Stuttgart: Deutsche Verlag-Anstalt).

(1985b) 'Con la chiave della scienza', *La Stampa*, 20 September: 3.

(1986a) 'Alla nostra generazione . . .' in *Storia vissuta*, Milan: Franco Angeli: 113–33.

(1986b) 'La peste non ha frontiere', *La Stampa*, 3 May: 1–2.

(1986c) 'Io lo proibirei', *La Stampa*, 2 December: 1.

(1986d) 'Fra Diavolo sul Po', *La Stampa*, 14 December: 3.

(1987a) 'Buck dei lupi', *La Stampa*, 11 January: 3.

(1987b) 'Buco nero di Auschwitz', *La Stampa*, 22 January: 1–2.

(1987c) 'Il sinistro potere della scienza', *Uomini e libri*, January–February: 13.

(1987d) 'Argilla di Adamo', *La Stampa*, 15 February: 5.

Interviews

(1966) Interview with Edoardo Fadini, *L'Unità*, 4 January: 3.

(1971) 'L'inquietante futuro' (with Luca Lamberti), *La Provincia*, 12 January: 3.

(1975) 'In un alambicco quanta poesia' (with Giorgio De Rienzo), *Famiglia Cristiana* 29, 20 July: 40–3.

(1978a) '*La tregua* alla radio' (with Georgina Arian Levi), *Ha Keillah*, April: 9.

(1978b) 'Elogio del libero lavoro' (with Giorgio Manzini), *Paese Sera*, 11 December: 3.

(1979a) 'Lavorare piace' (with Giorgio De Rienzo), *Famiglia Cristiana*, 21 January: 78.

(1979b) 'L'antieroe di Primo Levi' (with Georgina Arian Levi), *Ha Keillah*, February: 6.

(1979c) 'L'opera prima di un ex-chimico' (with Carlo Conti), *Gazzetta del Sud*, 6 March: 3.

(1981) 'Primo Levi – le sue radici', *Nuova Società*, 11 July: 47–8.

(1982a) 'Credo che il mio destino profondo sia la spaccatura' (with Giovanni Tesio), *La Società*, 16 January.

(1982b) 'Mendel, il consolatore' (with Rosellina Balbi), *La Repubblica*, 14 April: 20–1.

(1982c) 'Sono diventato ebreo quasi per forza' (with Giulio

Goria), *Paese Sera*, 3 May: 3. Reprinted under the title 'Ecco perchè sono ebreo', *L'Ora*, 7 May 1982: 3.

(1982d) 'Un western dalla Russia a Milano' (with Roberto Vacca), *Il Giorno*, 18 May: 3.

(1982e) 'La Terra Promessa dei miei ebrei non è una potenza militare' (with Giorgio Calcagno), *Tuttolibri*, 12 June: 3.

(1982f) 'Segrete avventure di eroi involontari' (with Giovanni Pacchioni), *Il Globo*, 13 June: 3.

(1982g) 'Questo ebreo me lo sono inventato' (with Oreste Del Buono), *L'Europeo*, 5 July: 81–5.

(1982h) 'Dove è finita la terra promessa?' (with Gabriella Monticelli), *Epoca*, 17 September: 108–14.

(1982i) 'Io, Primo Levi, chiedo le dimissioni di Begin' (with Giampaolo Pansa), *La Repubblica*, 24 September: 1,3.

(1982j) 'Sono un ebreo ma non sono mai stato sionista' (with Fiona Diwan), *Corriere Medico*, 3–4 September: 15.

(1982k) Interview with Walter Mauro, *L'Arena*, 30 September: 3.

(1982l) 'Un romanzo storico costruito secondo i modelli classici . . .', *Uomini e libri*, November–December: 40–1.

(1983a) 'Un'aggressione di nome Franz Kafka' (with Federico De Melis), *Il manifesto*, 5 May: 1–2.

(1983b) 'Primo Levi: cosí ho rivissuto il *Processo* di Kafka' (with Luciano Genta), *Tuttolibri*, 9 April: 3.

(1984a) 'Se questo è uno Stato' (with Gad Lerner), *L'Espresso*, 30 September: 39–45. Partly reprinted as 'L'accento sulla Diaspora. Un'intervista del 1984', *Linea d'ombra* 28, June 1988: 16–17.

(1984b) 'Levi: l'ora incerta della poesia' (with Giulio Nascimbeni), *Corriere della Sera*, 28 October: 3.

(1985a) 'Come ho pubblicato il mio primo libro' (with Nico Orengo), *Tuttolibri*, 1 June: 1.

(1985b) Interview with Germaine Greer, *The Literary Review*, November: 15–19.

(1986a) 'Quel referendum della nostra giovinezza' (with Neliana Tersigni), *Paese Sera*, 2 June: 5.

(1986b) 'I fantasmi di Auschwitz' (with Mario Baldoli), *Brescia oggi*, 26 July: 3.

(1986c) 'Primo Levi: la mia America e i miei anni in fabbrica' (with Andrea Liberatore), *L'Unità*, 25 September: 10.

(1986d) 'Primo Levi in London' (with Anthony Rudolf), *London Magazine* 7, October: 28–37.

(1986e) (1992) 'Giovani, rifiutate tutti i profeti' (with Milara Spadi), for a West German radio station, September. Reprinted in *L'Unità*, 7 November 1992: 2.

(1987) 'Il necessario e il superfluo – Primo Levi e l'economia nella narrazione' (with Roberto di Caro), *Piemonte vivo*, 1 January: 53–7. Reprinted in a slightly abridged form as 'La fatica di scrivere', *L'Espresso*, 26 April: 30–3.

Secondary Sources

Books and Articles

Accornero, Aris (1988) 'Lavoro e impresa a vent'anni dal 1968: riflettendo sull'industria e su Torino', in Paolo Ceri (ed.), *Impresa e lavoro in trasformazione – Italia-Europa*, Bologna: Il Mulino: 185–245.

Adorni, Daniela (1991) 'Modi e luoghi della persecuzione (1938–1943)', in F. Levi (ed.), *L'ebreo in oggetto*: 39–117.

Adorno, Theodor (1967) *Prisms*, London: Neville Spearman.

Allegra, Luciano (1984) 'La comunità ebraica di Torino attraverso gli archivi di famiglia', in *Ebrei a Torino*: 31–6.

Améry, Jean (1987) *Intellettuale a Auschwitz*, Turin: Bollati Boringhieri. (Trans. of *Jenseits von Schuld und Sühne – Bewältigungsversuche eines Überwältigten*, 1966; English trans. *At the Mind's Limits: Contemplations by a Survivor on Auschwitz and Its Realities*, New York: Schocken Books, 1986.)

ANED (Associazione Nazionale Ex-Deportati Politici) (1982) *Bibliografia della deportazione*, Milan: ANED-Mondadori.

Amsallem, Daniela (1992) 'Images littéraires et figures mythiques dans l'oeuvre de Primo Levi, ou l'expérience sublimée par l'écriture', *Chroniques Italiennes* 31–32: 7–26.

Antelme, Robert (1954) *La specie umana*, Turin: Einaudi. (Trans. of *L'espèce humaine*, 1947.)

Arendt, Hannah (1963) *Eichmann in Jerusalem: A Report on the Banality of Evil*, London: Faber and Faber.

Bailey, Paul (1971) 'Saving the Scaffolding', *New Statesman*, 20 August: 245–6.

Balestrini, Nanni (1971) *Vogliamo tutto*, Milan: Feltrinelli.

Balestrini, Nanni and Moroni, Primo (1988) *L'orda d'oro. 1968–1977: La grande ondata rivoluzionaria e creativa, politica ed esistenziale*, Milan: SugarCo Edizioni.

Barberi Squarotti, Giorgio (1991) 'Il sistema della scrittura', proceedings of conference *Primo Levi: Memoria e invenzione*, San Salvatore Monferrato, 26–28 September.

Barnouw, Dagmar (1990) *Visible Spaces – Hannah Arendt and the German-Jewish Experience*, Baltimore and London: Johns Hopkins University Press.

Bassani, Giorgio (1958) *Gli occhiali d'oro*, Turin: Einaudi.

—— (1962) *Il giardino dei Finzi-Contini*, Turin: Einaudi.

Battaglia, Roberto (1964) *Storia della Resistenza italiana – 8 settembre 1943–25 aprile 1945*, Turin: Einaudi.

Beccaria, Gian Luigi (1983) Introduction to the school edition of *La chiave a stella*, Turin: Einaudi.

—— (1991) 'L'altrui mestiere di Primo Levi', in A. Cavaglion (ed.), *Primo Levi*: 130–36.

Belgiojoso, Lodovico B. di (1984) 'Testimoniare con l'architettura', in *Il dovere di testimoniare*: 187–200.

Benedetto, Pier Paolo (1987) 'Un libro in ogni casa', *La Stampa*, 3 December: 18.

Bernstein, Jeremy (1985) 'The Merely Personal', *The American Scholar* 54: 295–302.

Bettelheim, Bruno (1990) 'Colpa e vergogna: il Lager ti segna cos'. Per sempre', Cultural Supplement of *Corriere della Sera*, 20 May: 3.

Bianucci, Piero (1985) 'Il romanziere in camice bianco', *Tuttolibri*, 26 October: 1.

Biasin, Gian Paolo (1990a) 'Our Daily Bread-pane-Brot-Broit-chleb-pain-lechem-kenyér', in P. Frassica (ed.), *Primo Levi as Witness*: 1–20.

—— (1990b) 'Till My Ghastly Tale Is Told: Levi's Moral Discourse from *Se questo è un uomo* to *I sommersi e i salvati*', in S. Tarrow *Reason and Light – Essays on Primo Levi*: 127–41.

Blandi, Alberto (1966) 'L'inferno del Lager di Auschwitz in *Se questo è un uomo* di Primo Levi', *La Stampa*, 20 November: 7.

Bocca, Giorgio (1966) *Storia dell'Italia partigiana (settembre 1943 – maggio 1945)*, Bari: Laterza.

—— (1986) 'La via del perdono passa per Vienna', *La Repubblica*, 12 June: 12.

Bosco Coletsos, Sandra (1985) 'La traduzione di *Der Prozeß* di Franz Kafka', *Studi Tedeschi (Annali dell'Istituto Universitario Orientale)* 1–3: 229–68.

Bottiglieri, Bruno and Ceri, Paolo (eds) (1987) *Le culture del lavoro*

– *L'esperienza di Torino nel quadro europeo,* Bologna: Il Mulino.

Bravo, Anna (1986) 'Raccontare e ascoltare: la memoria dei sopravvissuti', in F. Cereja and B. Mantelli (eds), *La deportazione nei Campi*: 69–81.

Bravo, Anna and Jalla, Daniele (1986) *La vita offesa. Storia e memoria dei Lager nazisti nei racconti di duecento sopravvissuti,* Milan: Franco Angeli.

—— (1990) *La memorialistica della deportazione in Italia,* Turin: Centro Stampa del Consiglio Regionale.

—— (1991) 'Primo Levi: un uomo normale di buona memoria', in A. Cavaglion (ed.), *Primo Levi*: 67–78.

—— (1994) *Una misura onesta. Gli scritti di memoria della deportazione dall'Italia 1944–1993,* Milan: Franco Angeli.

Bura, Claudio (1987) 'Primo Levi, *La chiave a stella*'. *Gli Annali – Università per Stranieri,* no. 8. Florence: Le Monnier: 111–80.

Caffaz, Ugo (1975) *L'antisemitismo italiano sotto il fascismo,* Florence: La Nuova Italia.

—— (ed.) (1988) *Discriminazione e persecuzione degli ebrei nell'Italia fascista,* Florence: Consiglio Regionale della Toscana.

Calcagno, Giorgio (1987) 'Primo Levi e i tedeschi: un carteggio sconosciuto', *Tuttolibri,* 18 April: 1.

Caleffi, Piero (1955) *Si fa presto a dire fame,* Milan and Rome: Edizioni Avanti!

Calvino, Italo (1957) *Il barone rampante,* Turin: Einaudi.

—— [1987] (1989) *The Literature Machine,* London: Picador.

—— (1991) *I libri degli altri,* Turin: Einaudi.

Camon, Ferdinando (1987) *Autoritratto di Primo Levi,* Padua: Edizioni Nord-Est.

Canarutto, Anna (1988) 'La legislazione razziale del fascismo', in A. Cavaglion and G. Romagnani (eds), *Le interdizioni del Duce*: 69–76.

Canepa, Andrew (1989) 'Christian-Jewish Relations in Italy from Unification to Fascism', in I. Herzer (ed.), *The Italian Refuge*: 13–33.

Cannon, Jo Ann (1990) 'Chemistry and Writing in *The Periodic Table*', in S. Tarrow (ed.), *Reason and Light – Essays on Primo Levi*: 99–111.

—— (1992) 'Canon-Formation and Reception in Contemporary Italy: the Case of Primo Levi', *Italica* 69: 30–44.

Capriolo, Ettore (1966) 'Per non dimenticare – nazismo alla ribalta', review of the stage adaptation of *Se questo è un uomo,*

Vie Nuove, 1 December: 48.

Carbines, Louise (1988) 'Painting Humanity's Horror', *The Age (Saturday Extra)*, 15 October: 13.

Cases, Cesare (1987) 'L'ordine delle cose e l'ordine delle parole', *L'Indice*, 10: 25–31. Reprinted in a slightly abridged version as the introduction to vol. I of Levi's *Opere*: Turin: Einaudi: ix–xxxi.

—— (1989) 'Ricordo di Primo Levi', in Gianfranco Folena (ed.), *Tre narratori – Calvino, Primo Levi, Parise*, Padua: Liviana Editrice: 99–103.

Cavaglion, Alberto (1986) 'La deportazione degli ebrei piemontesi: appunti per una storia', In F. Cereja and B. Mantelli (eds), *La deportazione nei campi*: 107–25.

—— (1989a) 'The Legacy of the *Risorgimento*: Jewish Participation in Anti-Fascism and the Resistance', in I. Herzer (ed.), *The Italian Refuge*: 73–92.

—— (1989b) 'Argon e la cultura ebraica piemontese (con l'abbozzo del racconto)', *Belfagor* 43: 541–62.

—— (1991) 'Il termitaio. Primo Levi e *Se questo è un uomo*', *L'asino d'oro* 4: 117–28.

—— (ed.) (1991) *Primo Levi – Il presente del passato*, proceedings of the Turin conference, 28–29 March 1988, Milan: Franco Angeli.

—— (1992) 'Alle radici di un libro. Un contributo a quattro mani su "Minerva Medica"', *Millelibri* 52, April: 53–7.

—— (1993a) 'Il "ritorno" di Primo Levi e il memoriale per la *Minerva Medica*', in A. Cavaglion (ed.), *Il ritorno dai Lager*, proceedings of the international conference, 23 November 1991, Milan: Franco Angeli: 221–40.

—— (1993b) *Primo Levi e 'Se questo è un uomo'*, Turin: Loescher.

Cavaglion, Alberto, and Romagnani, Gian Paolo (eds) (1988) *Le interdizioni del Duce. A cinquant'anni dalle leggi razziali in Italia (1938–1988)*, Turin: Albert Meynier.

Cereja, Federico (1986) 'La deportazione italiana nei campi di sterminio: lettura storiografica e prospettive di ricerca'. in F. Cereja and B. Mantelli (eds), *La deportazione nei campi*: 17–37.

Cereja, Federico, and Mantelli, Brunello (eds) (1986) *La deportazione nei campi di sterminio nazisti. Studi e testimonianze*, Milan: Franco Angeli.

Cesari, Severino (1991) *Colloquio con Giulio Einaudi*, Rome-Naples: Theoria.

Ciafaloni, Francesco (1991) *Kant e i pastori, ovvero: il mondo e il paese,* Milan: Linea d'ombra Edizioni.

Ciccotti, Giovanni, Cini, Marcello, De Maria, Michelangelo and Jona-Lasinio, Giovanni (1976) *L'ape e l'architetto. Paradigmi scientifici e materialismo storico,* Milan: Feltrinelli.

Cicioni, Mirna (1989) ' "Different Springs and Different Airs": Primo Levi's Multiple Autography', *Menorah* 2: 20–31.

Collotti, Enzo (1989) 'Leggendo il revisionismo in Primo Levi', *Belfagor* 44: 98–102.

—— (1991) 'Primo Levi e il revisionismo storiografico', in A. Cavaglion (ed.), *Primo Levi*: 112–18.

Colombo, Arturo (1987) 'Primo Levi: a Acqui, quella sera', *Nuova Antologia* 558: 207–11.

Colombo, Furio (1990) 'Primo Levi: chi parla, chi ascolta', in F. Colombo, *Il destino del libro e altri destini,* Turin: Bollati Boringhieri.

Czech, Danuta (1990) *Auschwitz Chronicle 1939–1945,* New York: Henry Holt & Co.

D'Angelo, Giovanna (1994) *'La chiave a stella* di Primo Levi: una sfida al labirinto', unpublished paper given at the conference *Letteratura e industria,* Turin, May 1994.

Davico Bonino, Guido (1991) 'Primo Levi come per caso, a teatro', in A. Cavaglion (ed.), *Primo Levi*: 141–6.

Dawidowicz, Lucy S. (1975) *The War Against the Jews 1933–1945,* New York: Holt, Rinehart and Winston.

—— (1976) *A Holocaust Reader,* New York: Behrman House.

De Benedetti, Israel (1984) 'Primo Levi, Israele e la Diaspora', *Ha Keillah* 2: 10.

De Felice, Renzo (1977) *Storia degli ebrei italiani sotto il fascismo,* Milan: Mondadori (1st edn (1961) Turin: Einaudi).

De Luna, Giovanni (1982) *Storia del Partito d'Azione. La rivoluzione democratica. (1942–1947),* Milan: Feltrinelli.

—— (1985) introduction to De Luna *et al., Le Formazioni GL nella Resistenza*: 17–31.

De Luna, Giovanni, Camilla, Piero, Cappelli, Danilo and Vitali, Stefano (1985) *Le formazioni GL nella Resistenza – Documenti,* Milan: Franco Angeli.

Del Buono, Oreste (1983) 'Il nuovo processo', *La Stampa,* 28 August: 3.

Dentice, Fabrizio (1983) 'Mi travesto da Kafka', *L'Espresso,* 24 April: 15–20.

Devoto, Andrea and Martini, Massimo (1981) *La violenza nei*

Lager. Analisi psicologica di uno strumento politico, Milan: Franco Angeli.

Di Castro, Carlo (1992) 'Una riflessione sul rapporto tra scienza ed ebraismo', in Ministero per i beni culturali e ambientali: 157–62.

Diena, Paola (1984) 'Il giudeo piemontese. Tracce attuali e testimonianze sociolinguistiche', in *Ebrei a Torino*: 231–44.

Dini, Massimo and Jesurum, Stefano (1992) *Primo Levi – Le opere e i giorni*, Milan: Rizzoli.

Eberstadt, Fernanda (1985) 'Reading Primo Levi', *Commentary*, October: 41–7.

Ebrei a Torino. Ricerche per il centenario della sinagoga 1884–1984 (1984), with a foreword by Primo Levi, Turin: Umberto Allemandi.

Einaudi, Giulio (1990) 'Primo Levi e la casa editrice Einaudi', in P. Frassica (ed.), *Primo Levi as Witness*: 31–42.

Epstein, Adam (1987) 'Primo Levi and the language of atrocity', *Bulletin of the Society for Italian Studies* 20: 31–8.

Evans, Richard J. (1989) *In Hitler's shadow. West German Historians and the Attempt to Escape from the Nazi Past*, London: I. B. Tauris.

Ezrahi, Sidra De Koven (1980) *By Words Alone – The Holocaust in Literature*, Chicago and London: University of Chicago Press.

Fargion, Liliana Picciotto (1989) 'The Jews During the German Occupation and the Italian Social Republic', in I. Herzer (ed.), *The Italian Refuge*: 109–38.

—— (1991) *Il libro della memoria. Gli ebrei deportati dall'Italia (1943–1945)*, Milan: Mursia.

Feinstein, Wiley (1990) 'Primo Levi and Jewish Identity: the Question of Jewish Languages', in A. Mancini, P. Giordano and A. Tamburri (eds), *Italiana 1988*: 189–202.

Ferrero, Ernesto (1987) 'Cronologia', in vol. I of Primo Levi's *Opere*, Turin: Einaudi: xxxiii–lxiii.

Fiorentino, Luca (1987) 'Primo Levi: Il muro, vergogna necessaria', *Il manifesto*, 16 April: 11.

Folena, Gianfranco (ed.) (1989) *Tre narratori: Calvino, Primo Levi, Parise*, Padua: Liviana.

Fortini, Franco (1987) 'I suoi libri sono nostri', *L'Espresso*, 26 April: 32–3.

Frassica, Pietro (ed.) (1990) *Primo Levi as Witness*, proceedings of a symposium held at Princeton University, 30 April–2 May 1989, Fiesole: Casalini Libri.

—— (1991) 'Primo Levi: Eroe, antieroe o *alter ego?*' proceedings of conference *Primo Levi: memoria e invenzione*, San Salvatore Monferrato, 26–28 September.

Freschi, Marino (1992) *La fortuna italiana della letteratura ebraica-orientale (1960–1991)*, Rome: Ministero per i beni culturali e ambientali: 105–13.

Friedlander, Saul (1993) *Memory, History and the Extermination of the Jews of Europe*, Bloomington and Indianapolis: Indiana University Press.

Garrone, Alessandro Galante [1987] (1989) 'Il grido di Primo Levi', *Nuova Antologia*, 558: 212–24. Reprinted in Garrone 1989: 159–73.

—— (1989) *Amalek – Il dovere della memoria*, Milan: Rizzoli.

Galli De' Paratesi, Nora (1992) *Il giudeo italiano e i dialetti giudeo-italiani*, Rome: Ministero per i beni culturali e ambientali: 131–45.

Galli Della Loggia, Ernesto (1987) 'I due compromessi sull'olocausto ebraico', *La Stampa*, 21 January: 3.

Gandus, Valeria and Rossetti, Gian Paolo (1987) 'Finalmente fuori dal lager', *Panorama*, 26 April: 58–61.

Genovese, Giuseppe (1991) 'Profilo quantitativo del gruppo ebraico torinese nel 1938', in F. Levi (ed.), *L'ebreo in oggetto*: 119–44.

Gentiloni, Filippo (1982) 'Palestina, se non ora quando?' *Il manifesto*, 12 June: 1,3.

Getzler, Dvorah (1986) 'Branded in memory', *The Australian Jewish Times – The Jerusalem Post International Edition*, 27 November: xvii.

Gilliland, Gail (1992) 'Self and Other: Christa Wolf's *Patterns of Childhood* and Primo Levi's *Se questo è un uomo* as Dialogic Texts', *Comparative Literature Studies* 2: 183–209.

Gilman, Sander L. (1989) (1990) 'Primo Levi: the Special Language of the Camps and After', *Midstream*, October: 22–30. Reprinted in S. Tarrow (ed.), *Reason and Light – Essays on Primo Levi*: 60–81.

Ginsborg, Paul (1990) *A History of Contemporary Italy – Society and Politics 1943–1988*, London: Penguin Books.

Ginzburg, Natalia (1963) *Lessico famigliare*, Turin: Einaudi.

Girelli-Carasi, Fabio (1990a) 'The Anti-Linguistic Nature of the Lager in the Language of Primo Levi's *Se questo è un uomo*', revised version of the paper 'Literature and the Reality of the

Holocaust', in S. Tarrow (ed.), *Reason and Light – Essays on Primo Levi*: 40–59.

—— (1990b) 'Strategie narrative del macro-testo autobiografico di Primo Levi', in A. Mancini, P. Giordano and A. Tamburri (eds), *Italiana 1988*: 203–23.

Giuntella, Vittorio E. (1979) *Il nazismo e i Lager*, Rome: Edizioni Studium.

Goldstein, Maurice (1991) 'La réalité d'Auschwitz dans l'oeuvre de Primo Levi', in A. Cavaglion (ed.), *Primo Levi*: 83–94.

Grassano, Giuseppe (1981) *Primo Levi*, Florence: La Nuova Italia.

—— (1991) 'La *Musa stupefatta* di Levi. Note sui racconti fantascientifici', proceedings of conference *Primo Levi: memoria e invenzione*, San Salvatore Monferrato, 26–28 September.

Guadagni, Annamaria (1993) 'Primo Levi', *L'Unità*, 21 February: 18.

Guerrazzi, Vincenzo (1974) *Le ferie di un operaio*, Rome: Savelli.

Guidetti Serra, Bianca (1991) 'Minima personalia', *Belfagor* 46: 449–56.

Gunzberg, Lynn M. (1986) 'Down Among the Dead Men: Levi and Dante in Hell', *Modern Language Studies* 16: 10–28.

—— (1990) 'Nuotando altrimenti che nel Serchio: Dante as Vademecum for Primo Levi', in S. Tarrow (ed.), *Reason and Light – Essays on Primo Levi*: 82–98.

—— (1992) *Strangers at Home – Jews in the Italian Literary Imagination*, Berkeley, CA: University of California Press.

Haft, Cynthia (1973) *The Theme of Nazi Concentration Camps in French Literature*, The Hague and Paris: Mouton.

Hartman, Geoffrey H. (1994) *Holocaust Remembrance: the Shapes of Memory*, Oxford: Basil Blackwell.

Herman, Marco (1984) *Diario di un ragazzo ebreo*, Cuneo: L'arciere.

Herzer, Ivo (ed.) (1989) *The Italian Refuge – Rescue of Jews During the Holocaust*, Washington, DC: The Catholic University of America Press.

Hilberg, Raul (1985) *The Destruction of European Jews*, New York: Holmes and Meier.

Howe, Irving (1985) 'How to Write About the Holocaust', *The New York Review of Books*, 28 March: 14–17.

Hughes, Henry Stuart (1983) *Prisoners of Hope – The Silver Age of the Italian Jews (1924–1974)*, Cambridge, MLA: Harvard University Press.

Il dovere di testimoniare (1984), proceedings of the conference *Il dovere di testimoniare*, Turin, 28–29 October 1983, Turin: Consiglio Regionale del Piemonte.

Jemolo, Arturo Carlo (1969) *Anni di prova*, Vicenza: Neri Pozza.

Jesurum, Stefano (1987) *Essere ebrei in Italia*, Milan: Longanesi.

Kaganovic, M. (1956) *Di Milkhomeh fun di jiddische Partisaner in Mizrach-Europe* (The War of the Jewish Partisans in Eastern Europe), Buenos Aires: Union Central Israelita Polaca.

Katz, Jacob (1976) *Out of the Ghetto: the Social Background of Jewish Emancipation, 1770–1870*, New York: Schocken Books.

Klein, Ilona (1990) ' "Official science often lacks humility": Humour, Science and Technology in Levi's *Storie naturali*', in S. Tarrow (ed.), *Reason and Light – Essays on Primo Levi*.

Lagorio, Gina (1990) 'La memoria perenne e la poesia *Ad ora incerta*', in P. Frassica (ed), *Primo Levi as Witness*: 63–75.

Langer, Lawrence L. (1975) *The Holocaust and the Literary Imagination*, New Haven and London: Yale University Press.

Lepschy, Anna Laura and Lepschy, Giulio (1988) *The Italian Language Today*, 2nd edn, London: Hutchinson.

Lerner, Gad (1985) 'Essere ebrei oggi', *Linea d'ombra* 10: 39–41.

Levi, Fabio (ed.) (1991a) *L'ebreo in oggetto*, Turin: Zamorani.

—— (1991b) 'Il censimento antiebraico del 22 agosto 1938', in F. Levi (ed.), *L'ebreo in oggetto*: 13–38.

Levi Della Torre, Stefano (1988) 'Oblio e memoria dello sterminio', *Studi Fatti Ricerche* 44: 3–9. Revised and reprinted in (1994) *Mosaico – attualità e inattualità degli ebrei*, Turin: Rosenberg & Sellier.

—— (ed.) (1990a) *Scritti in memoria di Primo Levi*. Special issue of *La rassegna mensile di Israel*, 56, Rome: Unione delle comunità israelitiche italiane.

—— (1990b) 'Eredità di Primo Levi', in Levi Della Torre (ed.), *Scritti in memoria*.

—— (1990c) 'Primo Levi, la memoria preveggente', unrevised version of a paper given at the round table *L'universo concentrazionario di Primo Levi*, Cologno Monzese, 14 December 1990, Cologno Monzese: Biblioteca Civica of Cologno Monzese.

Levi Montalcini, Rita (1987) 'Non si è suicidato', interview with Lucia Borgia, *Panorama*, 3 May: 62–3.

Limentani, Giacoma (1988) 'Primo Levi e il rifiuto dell'urlo', *Linea d'ombra* 23: 11–13.

Lollini, Massimo (1990) 'La storia come "olocausto": la

testimonianza di Primo Levi', *Romance Languages Annual* 2: 243–9.

Lopez, Guido (1987) *Se non lui, chi?* Rome: Centro di cultura ebraica della comunità israelitica di Roma.

—— (1990) 'Primo Levi: l'opera, gli avvertimenti, l'umanità', in S. Levi della Torre (ed.): 215–28.

Lumley, Robert (1990) *States of Emergency. Cultures of Revolt in Italy from 1968 to 1978*, London and New York: Verso.

McRae, Murdo William (1988) 'Opposition and Reversal in Primo Levi's *The Periodic Table*', *Publications of the Mississippi Philological Association*: 115–24.

Magris, Claudio (1989) *Lontano da dove – Joseph Roth e la tradizione ebraico-orientale*, Turin: Einaudi.

Maier, Charles S. (1988) *The Unmasterable Past: History, Holocaust, and German National Identity*, Cambridge, MA: Harvard University Press.

Manacorda, Giuliano (1967) *Storia della letteratura italiana contemporanea 1940–1965*, 2nd edn, Rome: Editori Riuniti.

—— (1987) *Letteratura italiana d'oggi 1965–1985*, Rome: Editori Riuniti.

Mancini, Albert, Giordano, Paolo A. and Tamburri, Anthony J. (eds) (1990) *Italiana 1988*, conference of the American Association of Teachers of Italian, 18–20 November 1988, River Forest, IL: Rosary College.

Manganelli, Giorgio (1977) 'Elogio dello scrivere oscuro', *Corriere della Sera*, 3 January: 3.

Mantelli, Brunello (1988) 'Al magazzino della storia. Riflessioni sull'Historikerstreit e sui suoi echi italiani', *Quaderno di storia contemporanea* 4: 11–19.

Marrus, M. (1987) *The Holocaust in History*, Hanover NH: University Press of New England.

Maruffi, Ferruccio (1991) interview on Primo Levi with Federico Cereja, in A. Cavaglion (ed.), *Primo Levi*: 213–33.

Mauro, Walter (1979) 'Primo Levi', in G. Grana (ed.), *Letteratura italiana. Novecento. I contemporanei*, vol. VII, Milan: Marzorati: 6885–98.

Mayda, Giuseppe (1984) 'La deportazione degli ebrei italiani', in *Il dovere di testimoniare*: 38–50.

Meghnagi, David (1980) *La sinistra in Israele*, Milan: Feltrinelli.

—— (1987) 'Primo Levi e la scrittura', *Letteratura internazionale* 20: 18–20. Reprinted as 'La vicenda ebraica. Primo Levi e la scrittura', in A. Cavaglion (ed.), *Primo Levi*: 152–61.

Melloni, Mario (1979) 'Fascino della spiritualità ebraica', *Ha Keillah*, February: 8.

Melodia, Giovanni (1971) *La quarantena – Gli italiani nel Lager di Dachau*, Milan: Mursia.

Mendel, David (1991) 'Requiem for a Quiet Man of Courage', *The Sunday Telegraph*, 8 September: viii. Translated and reprinted as 'Un incontro con Primo Levi' in (1994) *L' Indice*, May: 53–4.

Mengaldo, Pier Vincenzo (1989) 'Ciò che dobbiamo a Primo Levi', in Gianfranco Folena (ed.), *Tre narratori: Calvino, Primo Levi, Parise*, Padua: Liviana Editrice: 89–98.

—— (1990) 'Lingua e scrittura in Levi', introduction to vol. III of Levi's *Opere*, Turin: Einaudi: vii–lxxxiii.

Michaelis, Meir (1978) *Mussolini and the Jews: German-Italian Relations and the Jewish Question in Italy*, London: Institute of Jewish Affairs.

Milano, Attilio (1992) *Storia degli ebrei in Italia*, Turin: Einaudi.

Ministero Per I Beni Culturali e Ambientali (1992) *La cultura ebraica nell'editoria italiana (1955–1990)*, Rome: Istituto Poligrafico e Zecca dello Stato.

Morelli, Valeria (1965) *I deportati nei campi di sterminio*, Milan: Tipografia Artigianelli.

Morpurgo, Marina (1986) 'Primo Levi, la memoria senza tregua', *L'Unità*, 14 June: 3.

Motola, Gabriel (1987) 'Primo Levi: the Auschwitz Experience', *Southwest Review* 72: 258–69.

—— (1991) 'Primo Levi: the Language of the Scientist', *Literary Review* 34, 2: 203–10.

Nicco, Roberto (1990) *La Resistenza in Valle d'Aosta*, Aosta: Musumeci.

Nirenstain, Alberto (1982) 'Il censimento delle coscienze', *Shalom* 6: 4–5.

Orengo, Nico (1987) 'Natalia Ginzburg: nessuno censurò Primo Levi', *La Stampa*, 12 June: 3.

Pappalettera, Vincenzo (1965) *Tu passerai per il camino*, Milan: Mursia.

Pavone, Claudio (1991) *Una guerra civile. Saggio storico sulla moralità nella Resistenza*, Turin: Bollati Boringhieri.

Petronio, Giuseppe and Martinelli, Luciana (1975) *Il Novecento letterario in Italia*, vol. 3: *I contemporanei*, Palermo: Palumbo.

Petrucciani, Mario (1978) 'Tra algebra e metafora: la scienza nella cultura letteraria italiana 1945–1975', in V. Branca, P. Mazzamuto, G. Petronio, M. Sacco Messineo, G. Santangelo, A. Sole, C. Spalanca and N. Tedesco (eds), *Letteratura e scienza nella storia della cultura italiana*, atti del IX Congresso dell'Associazione Internazionale per gli Studi di Lingua e Letteratura Italiana, Palermo: Manfredi: 273–330.

Piattelli Palmarini, M. (1985) 'L'occhio del fisico e i sogni del poeta', *Corriere della Sera*, 22 April: 3.

Pirqê Abôth, (1977) trans. Yoseph Colombo, Assisi and Rome: Carucci.

Pivano, Fernanda (1987) 'Il mio compagno Levi e io rimandati a settembre', *Corriere della Sera*, 18 April: 3.

Poli, Gabriella and Calcagno, Giorgio (1992) *Echi di una voce perduta: incontri, interviste e conversazioni con Primo Levi*, Milan: Mursia.

Porta, Carlo (1971) *Poesie*, 3rd edn, Turin: Unione Tipografica Torinese.

Quazza, Guido (1966) *La Resistenza italiana. Appunti e documenti*, Turin: Giappichelli.

—— (1976) *Resistenza e storia d'Italia. Problemi e ipotesi di ricerca*, Milan: Feltrinelli.

Rasy, Elisabetta (1992) 'Mai dire che sei ebreo', *Panorama*, 20 December: 108–10.

Riatsch, C. and Gorgé, V. (1991) 'Né sistema, né periodico: appunti per la lettura di *Il sistema periodico* di Primo Levi', *Esperienze letterarie* 4: 65–81.

Risk, Mirna Cicioni (1979) 'Razionalità e coscienza etica di Primo Levi', *Italian Studies* 34: 122–31.

Rolfi, Lidia (1991) Interview on Primo Levi with Federico Cereja, in A. Cavaglion (ed.), *Primo Levi*: 223–30.

Rosato, Italo (1989) 'Primo Levi: sondaggi intertestuali', *Autografo* 6: 31–43.

Rosenfeld, Alvin H. (1980) *A Double Dying – Reflections on Holocaust Literature*, Bloomington, IN: Indiana University Press.

Rosenthal, Raymond (1990) 'Translating Primo Levi', in P. Frassica (ed.), *Primo Levi as Witness*: 76–85.

Rossanda, Rossana (1987) 'L'impossibilità di essere anacronistico', *Il manifesto*, 16 April: 11.

Roth, Philip (1986) 'A Man Saved by his Skills', interview with Primo Levi, *The New York Times Book Review*, 12 October: 1, 40–1.

Rousset, David (1947) *The Other Kingdom,* trans. of *L'univers concentrationnaire,* New York: Reynal and Hitchcock.

Rudolf, Anthony (1990) *At an Uncertain Hour: Primo Levi's War Against Oblivion,* London: The Menard Press.

Rusconi, Gian Enrico (ed.) (1987) *Un passato che non passa. I crimini nazisti e l'identità tedesca,* Turin: Einaudi.

Sacerdote, Franca, Fubini, Guido and others (1982) 'Discutiamo *Se non ora, quando?*' *Ha Keillah* 37: 10–11.

Salvarani, Brunetto (1987) 'Primo Levi: una testimonianza laica', *Studi Fatti Ricerche* 38: 12–14.

Salvatorelli, Luigi and Mira, Giovanni (1969) *Storia d'Italia nel periodo fascista,* 2 vols., Milan: Mondadori. 1st edn (1964) Turin: Einaudi.

Santagostino, Giuseppina (1991a) 'Destituzione e ossessione biologica nell'immaginario di Primo Levi', *Letteratura Italiana Contemporanea,* XII, 32: 127–45.

—— [1991b] 'Primo Levi e la facce nascoste del tempo', proceedings of conference *Primo Levi: memoria e invenzione,* San Salvatore Monferrato, 26–28 September.

—— (1992) 'Dalle metafore vive alla poetica di Primo Levi', *Letteratura Italiana Contemporanea* XIII, 35: 237–53.

—— (1993a) 'Nuove prospettive nell'interpretazione della narrativa fantascientifica di Primo Levi', in Marie-Hélène Caspar (ed.), *Narrativa 3* Nanterre: CRIX: 7–30.

—— (1993b) 'L'immagine della cultura francese nell'opera di Primo Levi', *Franco-italica* 4: 55–82.

—— (1994) 'Tecnologia e rappresentazione in Primo Levi', unpublished paper given at the conference *Letteratura e industria,* Turin, May 1994.

Scalia, Gianni (1979) 'Calvino, Queneau e le scienze', *Montedison. Progetto cultura* anno 2, no. 5: 6–7.

Schehr, Lawrence, R. (1989) 'Primo Levi's Strenuous Clarity', *Italica* 66: 429–43.

Scurani, Alessandro (1983) 'Le tre anime di Primo Levi', *Letture* 38, 5: 395–412.

Segre, Augusto (1979) *Memorie di vita ebraica,* Rome: Bonacci.

Segre, Cesare (1984) *Teatro e romanzo,* Turin: Einaudi.

—— (1988) Introduction to vol. II of Levi's *Opere,* Turin: Einaudi: vii–xxxv.

—— (1990) 'Primo Levi nella Torre di Babele', in P. Frassica (ed.) *Primo Levi as Witness:* 86–97.

—— (1991) 'Primo Levi: ebreo scrittore o scrittore ebreo?' proceedings of conference *Primo Levi: memoria e invenzione,* San Salvatore Monferrato, 26–28 September.

Segrè, Claudio G. (1990a) 'Italian Jews and the Resistance: the Case of Primo Levi', in S. Tarrow (ed.), *Reason and Light – Essays on Primo Levi*: 14–25.

—— (1990b) 'Primo Levi: A Man for All Seasons', *Midstream*, October – November: 33–5.

—— (1993) 'Primo Levi, Witness of the Holocaust', in John Milfull (ed.), *Why Germany? National Socialist Antisemitism and the European Context*, Providence and Oxford: Berg.

Segre, Renata (1986) *The Jews in Piedmont*, 3 vols, Jerusalem: Israel Academy of Sciences and Humanities and Tel Aviv University.

Segre, Vittorio (1985) *Storia di un ebreo fortunato*, Milan: Bompiani.

Servadio, Gaia (1988) *Un'infanzia diversa*, Milan: Rizzoli.

Shimoni, Gideon (1991) *The Holocaust in University Teaching*, Oxford: Pergamon Press.

Signorini, Franca Molino (1991) '"Uomini fummo . . ." Riflessioni su Primo Levi e Jean Améry', *La rassegna Mensile di Israel* 57: 463–77.

Snow, C.P. (1959) *The Two Cultures and the Scientific Revolution*, Cambridge: Cambridge University Press.

Sodi, Risa (1987) 'An Interview with Primo Levi', *Partisan Review* 3: 355–66.

—— (1988a) 'The Memory of Justice: Primo Levi and Auschwitz', in pre-prints of the conference *Remembering for the Future*, Oxford, July 1988 May – June: 1393–403.

—— (1988b) 'Primo Levi: A Last Talk', *Present Tense* 15: 40–5.

—— (1990) *A Dante of Our Time: Primo Levi and Auschwitz*, New York: Peter Lang.

Stille, Alexander (1991a) 'Primo Levi negli Stati Uniti', in A. Cavaglion (ed.), *Primo Levi*: 203–11.

—— (1991b) *Uno su mille. Cinque famiglie ebraiche durante il fascismo*, Milan: Mondadori.

Storia vissuta, (1988) proceedings of the conference *Storia Vissuta,* 21–22 November 1986, Milan: Franco Angeli.

Styron, William (1988) 'Why Primo Levi Need not Have Died', *New York Times*, 19 December: A 17.

Suvin, Darko (1979) *Metamorphoses of Science – Fiction. On the Poetics and History of a Literary Genre*, New Haven, CN: Yale University Press.

Tarrow, Sidney (1989) *Democracy and Disorder. Protest and Politics in Italy 1965–1975*, Oxford: Clarendon Press.

Tarrow, Susan R. (ed.) (1990) *Reason and Light – Essays on Primo Levi*, Ithaca, New York: Center for International Studies, Cornell University.

Tedeschi, Giuliana (1946) *Questo povero corpo*, Milan: Edit.

Tesio, Giovanni (1977) 'Su alcune giunte e varianti di *Se questo è un uomo'. Studi piemontesi* 6: 270–8.

—— (1983) 'La città inventata, schede di romanzi torinesi', *Studi piemontesi* 12: 39–47.

—— (1985) 'Premesse su Primo Levi poeta', *Studi piemontesi* 14: 12–23. Reprinted in (1991) *Piemonte letterario dell'otto-novecento. Da Giovanni Faldella a Primo Levi*, Rome: Bulzoni: 197–223.

—— (1987) 'Primo Levi tra ordine e caos', *Studi piemontesi* 16: 281–92. Reprinted in (1991) *Piemonte letterario dell'otto-novecento. Da Giovanni Faldella a Primo Levi*, Rome: Bulzoni.

Todorov, Tzvetan (1992) *Di fronte all'estremo*, trans. of *Face à l'extrême*, Milan: Garzanti.

Tomasi di Lampedusa, Giuseppe (1958) *Il gattopardo*, Milan: Feltrinelli.

Toscani , Claudio (1990) *Come leggere 'Se questo è un uomo' di Primo Levi*, Milan: Mursia.

Traverso, Enzo (1991) 'Auschwitz, la storia e gli storici', *Ventesimo Secolo* I: 87–126.

Vacca, Roberto (1971) *Il Medioevo prossimo venturo. La degradazione dei grandi sistemi*, Milan: Mondadori.

Valabrega, Guido (1974) *Ebrei, fascismo, sionismo*, Urbino: Argalia.

Valabrega, Paola (1982) 'Primo Levi e la tradizione ebraico-orientale', *Studi piemontesi* 11: 296–310.

Varoli Piazza, Isolina Dovara (1994) 'Scienze, tecnica e industria nella vita di Primo Levi', unpublished paper given at the conference *Letteratura e industria*, Turin, May 1994.

Vasari, Bruno (1991) *Mauthausen bivacco della morte*, Florence: Giuntina. 1st edn (1945) Milan: La Fiaccola.

Vercors (pseud. of Jean Bruller) (1953) *Les armes de la nuit*, Paris: Albin Michel.

Vidal-Naquet, Pierre (1985) *Gli ebrei la memoria e il presente*, trans. of *Les Juifs, la memoire et le présent*, Rome: Editori Riuniti.

—— (1993) *Assassins of Memory: Essays on the Denial of the Holocaust*, trans. of *Les assassins de la mémoire*, New York: Columbia University Press.

Watson, David (1992) *Arendt,* London: Fontana Press.

White, Naomi Rosh (1991) 'Primo Levi and the Concept of Shame', *Generation* 2: 46–50.

Wiesel, Elie (1981) *Night,* trans of *La Nuit,* Harmondsworth: Penguin Books.

—— (1992) 'Io e Primo Levi', commemorative speech given on 26 March 1992 in Genoa, when he was awarded the Primo Levi Prize, *Nuova Antologia* 127: 204–8.

Wilde-Menozzi, Wallis (1989–90) 'A Piece You've Touched is a Piece Moved – On Primo Levi', *Tel Aviv Review* 2: 149–65.

Woolf, Stuart J. (1991) 'Primo Levi e il mondo anglosassone', in A. Cavaglion (ed.), *Primo Levi*: 197–202.

Yerushalmi, Yosef Hayim (1982) *Zakhor – Jewish History and Jewish Memory,* Seattle: University of Washington Press.

Zevi, Bruno (1980) 'Memorial per Auschwitz', *L'Espresso,* 27 July: 89.

Zuccotti, Susan (1987) *The Italians and the Holocaust – Persecution, Rescue and Survival,* London: Peter Halban.

Selected Reviews

Se questo è un uomo (If This Is a Man)

Beckmann, Heinz, 'Eine komplizierte Unterwelt – Primo Levis Bericht aus Auschwitz', *Rheinischer Merkur,* 1 December 1962.

Calvino, Italo, *L'Unità,* 6 May 1948.

Soriani, David, 'Bisogno di ragione', *Ha Keillah,* (June 1959).

La tregua (The Truce)

Ferretti, Gian Carlo, 'Il ritorno dall'inferno del lager', *Il calendario del popolo,* October – November 1963.

Storie naturali

'C. Qu.', *Roma,* 10 December 1966.

Cases, Cesare, 'Difesa di "un" cretino', *Quaderni Piacentini* 30, 1967.

Marabini, Claudio, *Il Resto del Carlino,* 16 November 1966.

Mauro, Walter, *Momento sera,* 1 December 1966.

Milano, Paolo, 'Lettera aperta a Damiano Malabaila', *L'Espresso,* 9 October 1966.

Spinazzola, Vittorio, *Vie Nuove,* 20 October 1966.

Vizio di forma
Milano, Paolo, 'Il vizio di forma e l'errore di sostanza', *L'Espresso*, 25 April 1971.
Spinella, Mario, *Rinascita*, 4 June 1971.

Il sistema periodico (The Periodic Table)
Bellow, Saul, *Sunday Times Review*, 9 December 1984.
Luria, Salvador, *Science* 4695, April 1985.
Morrison, Philip, *Scientific American* 2, February 1985.

La chiave a stella (The [Monkey's] Wrench)
Asor Rosa, Alberto, *L'Unità*, 24 June 1979.
Bini, Giorgio, *Riforma della scuola*, May 1979.
Bruschi, Luigi, 'Come è bello lavorare! Ma un dubbio rimane', *Battaglie del lavoro*, May 1979.
Deaglio, Enrico, *Lotta Continua*, 31 December 1978.
D'Eramo, Marco, *Rocca-Cittadella Cristiana*, 15 (1979).
Enright, D. J., 'Bridges and Boundaries', *The New York Review of Books*, 15 January 1987.
Gianfranceschi, Fausto, 'Un romanzo "metallico"', *Il Tempo*, 5 January 1979.
Kazin, Alfred, 'Life and Steel: A Rigger's Tale', *New York Times Book Review*, 12 October 1986.
Leonetti, Francesco, 'Un viaggiatore (forse) del Rinascimento raccontato da Levi', *Il manifesto*, 13 January 1979.
Manzini Giorgio, 'Elogio del libero lavoro', *Paese Sera*, 11 December 1978.
Pappalardo, Ferdinando, 'L'apologo dell'operaio Faussone', *Rapporti* 16–17, 1980.
Stajano, Corrado, 'Il lavoro e la sua qualità', *Il Messaggero*, 11 December 1978.
Vacca, Roberto, *Tuttolibri*, 10 February 1979.

L'altrui mestiere (Other People's Trades)
Calvino, Italo, 'I due mestieri di Primo Levi', *La Repubblica*, 6 March 1985.

Se non ora, quando? (If not Now, when?)
Gentiloni, Filippo, 'Quando la stella di David era la bandiera dei perseguitati', *Il manifesto*, 29 June 1982.
Hughes, Henry Stuart, 'A Remnant in Arms', *The New York*

Review of Books 21, April 1985.

Jesurum, Stefano, 'Combattendo per tre righe sui libri di storia', *Shalom* 6, June 1982.

Luperini, Romano, 'La lunga traversia non ha fine', *Gazzetta del Mezzogiorno*, 27 May 1982.

Magris, Claudio, 'Epica e romanzo in Primo Levi', *Corriere della Sera*, 13 June 1982.

Marabini, Claudio, *Nuova Antologia*, 550, July–September 1982.

Mauro, Walter, 'L'epopea della diaspora ebraica', *L'Ordine*, 9 September 1982.

Ad ora incerta (Collected Poems)
Rosato, Italo, *Autografo* 2, 1985.

I sommersi e i salvati (The Drowned and the Saved)
Cameron, J.M., 'The Lie in the Soul', *The New York Review of Books*, 17 March 1988.

Cases, Cesare, 'Levi ripensa l'assurdo', *L'Indice*, 7, 1986.

Gibelli, Antonio, 'Nel nostro lager quotidiano', *Il Secolo XIX*, 8 July 1986.

Howe, Irving, 'The Utter Sadness of the Survivor', *The New York Times Book Review*, 10 January 1988.

James, Clive, 'Last Will and Testament', *The New Yorker*, 23 May 1988.

Jenkins, Jolyon, 'Strong Will and Testament', *New Statesman*, 15 April 1988.

Mengaldo, Pier Vincenzo, 'Ricordando con lucidità gli orrori dei Lager', *Il Mattino di Padova*, 12 June 1986.

Ozick, Cynthia, 'The Suicide Note', *The New Republic*, 21 March 1988. Reprinted as 'Primo Levi's Suicide Note' in (1989) *Metaphor and Memory*, New York: Alfred A. Knopf.

Pachet, Pierre, 'Primo Levi, son dernier livre', *Esprit* 151, June 1989.

Padovani, Paolo, 'Non fu soltanto Hitler a volere lo sterminio', *Paese Sera*, 18 September 1986.

Quinzio, Sergio, 'Non si salvi chi può!' *L'Espresso*, 7 September 1986.

Raboni, Giovanni, 'Quanto è scomodo il buon senso', *L'Unità*, 3 September 1986.

Robertson, Edwin, 'A Survivor Who Could not Find Forgiveness', *The Tablet*, 30 April 1988.

Sessi, Frediano, 'La violenza rivissuta', *Alfabeta*, May 1987.

The Mirror Maker
Denman, Hugh, 'Versatile Invitations', *Times Literary Supplement*,
    9–15 March 1990.

Opere, Vol. I
Rosato, Italo, 'Memoria e stile', *Corriere del Ticino*, 2 April 1988.

Index

Titles are those of works by Primo Levi unless otherwise indicated by the inclusion of the author's name within parentheses following the title. In cases in which there are two or more sub-headings under the name of an author, the author's works are listed first in one alphabetical sequence with subject sub-headings following in a second alphabetical sequence. Entries for works by Primo Levi are listed directly under title but are not listed under his name.

In cases where, in the text, the title of an English translation of a work is given, as well as its Italian title, both are included in the index. Where a translation is given of an Italian title which has not been published in English, or where the translation is different from the English title, the translation is included within parentheses after the Italian title, but the translation does not appear as an entry point in the index.